THE LUSHEI KUKI CLANS

THE LUSHEI KUKI CLANS

LT. - COLONEL J. SHAKESPEAR

GYAN

Published by

Gyan Publishing House
5, Ansari Road
Daryaganj, New Delhi-110002
Phone: 011-47034999, 9811692060
E-mail: books@gyanbooks.com

Distribution Network
gyanbooks.com
India, USA, Canada, UK, Australia

ISBN: 978-93-6433-028-2 (HB)
First Published, 1912

2nd Impression 2024

Printed at: Gyan Press, Delhi.

THE LUSHEI KUKI CLANS
Author: LT. - COLONEL J. SHAKESPEAR

THE LUSHEI KUKI CLANS

THE LUSHEI KUKI CLANS

BY

Lt.-COLONEL J. SHAKESPEAR

Published under the orders of the Government of Eastern Bengal and Assam

WITH ILLUSTRATIONS AND MAP

MACMILLAN AND CO., LIMITED
ST. MARTIN'S STREET, LONDON
1912

I DEDICATE THIS BOOK

TO

"THĀNGLIANA"

LIEUT.-COLONEL T. H. LEWIN

THE FRUITS OF WHOSE LABOURS I WAS PRIVILEGED TO REAP, AND WHO, AFTER AN ABSENCE OF NEARLY FORTY YEARS, IS STILL AFFECTIONATELY REMEMBERED BY THE LUSHAIS.

TABLE OF CONTENTS

PART I

THE LUSHEI CLANS

CHAPTER I

CHAPTER II

CHAPTER III

CHAPTER IV

CHAPTER V

CHAPTER VI.

APPENDIX

PART II

THE NON-LUSHEI CLANS

INTRODUCTORY

CHAPTER I

CHAPTER II

CHAPTER III

CHAPTER IV

CHAPTER V

CHAPTER VI

LIST OF ILLUSTRATIONS

INTRODUCTION

THIS monograph was originally intended to deal only with the inhabitants of the Lushai Hills, but on my transfer to Manipur, I found so many clans living in the hill tracts of that curious little state that I suggested that the scope of the monograph might be enlarged to include all clans of the Kuki race as well.

This term Kuki, like Naga, Chin, Shendu, and many others, is not recognised by the people to whom we apply it, and I will not attempt to give its derivation, but it has come to have a fairly definite meaning, and we now understand by it certain closely allied clans, with well marked characteristics, belonging to the Tibeto-Burman stock. On the Chittagong border the term is loosely applied to most of the inhabitants of the interior hills beyond the Chittagong Hill tracts; in Cachar it generally means some family of the Thado or Khawtlang clan, locally distinguished as New and Old Kukis. In the Lushai Hills nowadays the term is hardly ever employed, having been superseded by Lushai. In the Chin Hills and generally on the Burma border all these clans are called Chins.

The term Lushai, as we now understand it, covers a great many clans; it is the result of incorrect transliteration of the word Lushei, which is the name of the clan, which, under various chiefs of the Thangur family, came into prominence in the eighteenth century and was responsible for the eruption into Cachar of Old Kukis at the end of that century and of the New Kukis half a century later.

The Lusheis, however, did not eject all the clans they came in contact with, many of them they absorbed, and these now form the bulk of the subjects of the Thangur chiefs. In this monograph Lushai is used in this wider sense, Lushei being used only for the clan of that name. Among the people themselves the Lusheis are sometimes spoken of as Dulian, at the derivation of which I will hazard no guess, and the general population of the hills is spoken of as Mi-zo. Among inhabitants of the Lushai Hills are found a very considerable number of immigrants, or descendants of immigrants from the Chin Hills, who are found living among the Lushais under the Thangur Chiefs or in villages under their own chiefs. I have made no attempt to deal with these, as their proper place is the Chin Hills monograph, and Messrs. Carey and Tuck have already described them very fully in their Chin Hills Gazetteer.

I am conscious that there are many omissions in this book; the subject is a very wide one and the difficulty of getting at the facts from so many different clans, each speaking a different dialect and scattered over an area of about 25,000 square miles is extremely great. I trust therefore that my readers will excuse all shortcomings.

I have purposely avoided enunciating any theories and making deductions, considering it wiser to limit myself to as accurate a description as possible of the people, their habits, customs and beliefs. Regarding the affinities between the clans dealt with in this monograph and those described in the other books of the series, I venture to express a hope that the subject may be dealt with by some competent authority when the whole series has been published; until this is done no finality will be reached. It would be easy to fill several pages with points of resemblance between the different clans. Major Playfair, in his account of the Garos, has pointed out many ways in which the subjects of his monograph resemble the inhabitants of the Naga Hills, but reading his book I find many more in which they are like the clans I am dealing with. Sir Charles Lyall has drawn attention to the evident connection between the Mikirs and the Kuki-Chin group; I venture to think that a study of the following pages will confirm his theory. I may mention here that the main incidents of the "Tale of a Frog" given by Sir Charles are found not only in the folk-lore of the Aimol, as he has pointed out, but also among the Lushais, a very similar story having been recorded by Colonel Lewin in Demagri, 250 miles in an air line from the Mikir hills, and published in his Progressive Colloquial exercises in the Lushai dialect in 1874.

My best thanks are due to Lt.-Colonel Cole, Major Playfair, and Mr. Little, P.W.D., for many of the photographs, and especially to my wife, my companion for many years in these hills, for the four coloured illustrations.

I am also indebted to Rev. W. K. Firminger for correcting the second proofs and making the index. I must also acknowledge the assistance I received from many Lushais and others, notably Hrāngzora Chuprasie of Aigal and Pāthong, interpreter of Manipur.

J. SHAKESPEAR.

Imphal, Manipur State.

September 12*th*, 1910.

BIBLIOGRAPHY

McCulloch, Major W. "Account of the Valley of Manipore and the Hill tribes; with a comparative vocabulary of the Manipore and other languages." Calcutta, 1859. Selections from the Records of the Government of India (For. Dept.) XXVII.

This is a most valuable book, full of useful information as regards all the Hill tribes of Manipur. I have made use of it freely in Part II., but space did not allow of my extracting all that I should have liked to reproduce. It would be well worth while to reprint this book, with notes bringing it up to date.

Stewart, Lieutenant R. "Notes on Northern Cachar. Journal of the Asiatic Society of Bengal," Vol. XXIV, 1855.

Another most valuable book, as regard Thados and Old Kukis, which would well repay reprinting. Both these books contain comparative vocabularies.

Lewin, Captain Thomas Herbert. "Progressive Colloquial Exercises in the Lushai Dialect of the 'Dzo' or Kuki Language, with vocabularies and popular tales. (Notated.) Calcutta, 1874.

One of these tales is reproduced in Part II. The tales are well translated, but the Lushai is transliterated in a manner now out of date. The notes are as excellent as one would expect from a writer who certainly knew more of the Lushai than anyone else at that time, and who was more admired by them than any other white man has ever been.

By the same Author. "The Hill Tracts of Chittagong and the Dwellers therein." Calcutta, 1869.

A most fascinating book, full of information, expressed in good English. Pages 98 to 118 deal with Lushais and Shendus, *i.e.* Lakhers.

By the same Author. "A fly on the wheel: or how I helped to govern India."

The portion concerning the Author's life among the Lushais is full of interest, and his word pictures of the scenery and life among the people, for "Thangliana" as he was called really did live among the people, sharing their food even, are accurate and graphic. To few Europeans is the power given to mix thus with such savages and yet retain their respect. I once heard a Lushai's comment on a young officer who with the best of intentions tried to imitate the great "Thangliana." A friend asked him what he thought of So-and-So, the reply being: "I don't know what sort of man he is, all I know is, that he cannot be a sahib to live as he does."

Carey, Bertram S. and H. N. Tuck. "The Chin hills: A History of the People, their Customs and Manners, and our Dealings with them, and a Gazetteer of their Country." Rangoon, 1896.

A model of what such a book should be. The illustrations are particularly good. The Lushais and Thados are only touched. Much of the matter referring to the Haka and Klang-Klang Chins is applicable to the Lakhers.

Lorrain, Herbert J., and Fred W. Savidge. "Grammar and Dictionary of the Lushai Language." Shillong, 1898.

A very complete and accurate work. Unfortunately the standard system of transliteration has not been entirely adhered to.

Soppitt, C. A. "A short account of the Kuki-Lushai tribes on the North-East Frontier Districts: Cachar, Sylhet, Naga Hills, &c., and the North Cachar Hills. Shillong, 1887.

I believe this is a useful accurate work, but have not been able to obtain it.

Sneyd-Hutchinson, R. "Gazetteer of the Chittagong Hill Tracts."

As regards Lushais there is not much of value, as they are beyond the scope of the work, but few being found in the Hill Tracts.

Besides the above there are notes in the Census Reports of 1891 and 1901, various military publications and gazetteers by Mr. A. W. Davis, I.C.S., and Mr. B. C. Allen, I.C.S., all of which contain a certain amount of useful information, but do not pretend to be more than notes giving succinctly the knowledge then obtained of what was then practically new ground. Colonel Woodthorpe's account of the Silchar columns' march to Champhai, though not professing to be an account of the people, is interesting reading. Round Champhai I met several men who had been there when the column arrived, and they all remember the little sahib who drew pictures; and would sit long looking at the pictures in his book and chatting to each other of the good old days.

[Note.—On p. 6 of the present work the Author refers to a passage in Lewin's *Hill Tracts of Chittagong and the Dwellers therein*, in which is cited an account of "the Cucis or inhabitants of the Tipperah Mountains written by J. Rennel, Chief Engineer of Bengal in 1800." In reading through the proofs of the present work, it occurred to me that it would be important to discover whether the "J. Rennel" referred to by Lewin was or was not the famous Major James Rennell, Surveyer-General of Bengal, who is so often described as "the Father of Modern Geography." Major Rennell with his wife (*née* Jane Thackeray—a great aunt of the novelist W. M. Thackeray) left Bengal in March, 1777, and reached England in February 1778. He died on March 29, 1830. It seemed to me possible that the great Rennell might have obtained the information about the Kukis during his period of service in East Bengal, and that he might have published a memoir on the subject in 1800. Mr. W. Foster of the Record Department of the India Office very kindly informed me that no such a memoir could be traced at Whitehall, and drew my attention to Lewin's heading of the memoir, "From the French of M. Bouchesiche, who translated the original from the English of J. Rennel, Chief Engineer of Bengal . . . . Published at Leipsic in 1800." Mr. Edward Heawood, Librarian of the Royal Geographical Society, to whom I am indebted for much trouble taken in satisfying my curiosity, informed me that Bouchesiche gave what purported to be an extract, translated into French, from Rennell's well-known work on India, and that the Frenchman's book was printed in Paris in 1800, although there may perhaps have been a Leipzig issue also. The account of the Kukis given in Bouchesiche's work, however, is not taken from any known work by James Rennell. Dalton in his *Ethnology of Bengal* refers to what has been supposed to be the earliest account of the Kukis—a memoir by Surgeon McCrea, which appeared in 1799 in Volume vii of *Asiatic Researches*. Mr. Heawood most kindly hunted up McCrea's memoir, and found in it a reference to a memoir which appeared in Volume ii of *Asiatic Researches*, 1790. The title of the memoir of 1790 runs "On the Manners, Religion, and Laws of the Cucis, or Mountaineers of Tipra . . . . Communicated in Persian by John Rawlins, Esq." On investigation, Mr. Heawood found that the Memoir of 1790 is undoubtedly the original from which Bouchesiche drew his account in French, and of this the account, attributed to "J. Rennel" by Colonel Lewin, is a rough paraphrase. *Note by the Rev. Walter K. Firminger.*]

GLOSSARY

Only the terms which occur often are given.

Ai. - A ceremony performed to propitiate the spirit of an animal killed in the chase, or of a human being killed in war. The performer's spirit will own the spirit of person or animal killed in the next world. The term is also used for a ceremony performed to celebrate a particularly good crop—Buh-Ai, or Buh-za-ai.

Boi.—Persons who have taken refuge in the chief's house.

Dai-bawl.—A series of sacrifices to the demons of the hills, &c.

Hlam-zuih.—Lushai. A first-born child that dies within a year of its birth and is buried without any ceremony.

Hrilh.—A period during which no work must be done, after a sacrifice, closely resembling the Naga genna.

Huai.—Lushai. Demons who cause sickness.

Jhum.—A piece of land on which the jungle has been felled and burnt for cultivation.

Kawhring.—A person whose spirit takes possession of another's body, the spirit of such a person.

Khāl.—A series of sacrifices to the demons of the village site, only performed by Lushais.

Khuavang.—Lushai. A powerful spirit, sometimes used for "luck."

Kum-ai.—Children's sleeping platform.

Kum-pui.—Parent's sleeping platform.

Kut.—Lushai. Festivals connected with the crops.

Lal.—Lushai. Chief.

Lashi. —Lushai. Mythical beings who control wild animals. Known also to Aimol and Vaiphei.

Mi-thi-khua.—"Dead men's village." Expression used by all clans for the place of departed souls.

Mi-thi-rawp-lam.—A feast in honour of the dead.

Palal.—A man who receives part of the bride-price, and acts as trustee to the bride.

Pathian.—Lushai. The Creator. Very similar names are used by all the clans dealt with.

Pial-ral.—Lushai. The land beyond the Pial river, in the abode of the dead, to which the spirits of those who have acquired merit pass.

Pu.—A word used in most dialects, meaning grandfather, maternal uncle, and other relations on mother's or wife's side. It is also used for a person specially chosen as a protector or guardian.

Pui-thiam.—Lushai. Sorcerer, priest and medicine man.

Rāmhual.—Lushai. Chief's adviser as to distribution of jhums.

Rem-Ar.—The cock killed on occasion of a marriage.

Rotchem.—Mouth organ made of a gourd and reeds.

Sakhua.—Lushai. The guardian spirit of the household and the sacrifice performed to him.

Sawn-man.—Compensation payable to a father for seduction of an unmarried girl.

Sherh.—Lushai. The portions of the sacrificed animal which are offered to the demon. Also the state of a house for a period after the performing of certain sacrifices, during which the entrance of outsiders is prohibited.

Thangchhuah.—Lushai. A man who has given a series of feasts to his village. The expression is also used for the series of feasts. Honour in this world and comfort in the next are the reward of the Thangchhuah.

Thian.—A woman who receives part of the bride-price, and acts as friend or trustee to the bride.

Thir-deng.—Lushai. Blacksmith.

Tlangau.—Lushai. Chief's crier.

Upa.—Lushai. Chief's minister.

Zawlbuk.—Bachelor's hall and guest house.

THE LUSHEI KUKI CLANS

THE LUSHEI CLANS

PART I

CHAPTER I

GENERAL

THE Lushei chiefs now rule over the country between the Kurnaphuli river and its main tributary, the Tuilianpui on the west, and the Tyao and Koladyne river on the east, while their southern boundary is roughly a line drawn east and west through the junction of the Mat and Koladyne rivers and their most northerly villages are found on the borders of the Silchar district. Within this area, roughly 7,500 square miles, there are only a few villages ruled over by chiefs of other clans, and outside it there are but few true Lushei villages, though I am told that there are villages of people very closely connected with the Lusheis, on the southern borders of Sylhet, in Tipperah and in the North Cachar Hills, and there are a few in the Chittagong Hill tracts. 1. Habitat

All the Lushai Kuki clans resemble each other very closely in appearance and the Mongolian type of countenance prevails. One meets, however, many exceptions, which may be due to the foreign blood introduced by the many captives taken from the plains and from neighbouring tribes; but these are not worth considering, and the description of the Kuki written by Lt. Stewart close on 80 years ago cannot be improved on. "The Kukis are a short, sturdy race of men with a goodly development of muscle. Their legs are, generally speaking, short in comparison with the length of their bodies, and their arms long. The face is nearly as broad as it is long and is generally round or square, the 2. Appearance and physical characteristics.

B

cheek bones high, broad and prominent, eyes small and almond-shaped, the nose short and flat, with wide nostrils. The women appear more squat than the men even, but are strong and lusty." In Lushai clans both sexes are as a rule rather slighter made than among the Thado and cognate clans, whom Lt. Stewart was describing. Adopting the scale given in the handbook of the Anthropological Institute, the colour of the skin varies between dark yellow-brown, dark olive, copper-coloured and yellow olive. Beards and whiskers are almost unknown, and a Lushai, even when able to grow a moustache, which is not often, pulls out all the hairs except those at the corners of his mouth. The few persons with hairy faces may, I think, be safely said to be of impure blood.

The hair is worn, by both sexes, in a knot over the nape of the neck, and carefully parted in the middle. The young folk of about the marrying age devote much care to their hair, dressing it daily with much pigs' fat. Later in life they grow careless, and widows allow their hair to hang as it chooses. Children's hair is left to grow as it likes till it is long enough to tie up. Curly hair or hair with a pronounced wave in it is uncommon, and is much objected to.

The women are prolific, five to seven children being about the average, but the mortality among the children is so great that few parents can boast of more than two or three grown up children.

Both men and women are good walkers and hill-climbers, which is only natural, but for a race which lives exclusively on the hilltops the number of good swimmers is very large. Most men are not afraid of the water, and manage rafts very skilfully, making long journeys on them in the rains.

Abortion is not infrequently resorted to when a widow who is living in her late husband's house, and therefore, as described later, expected to remain chaste, finds herself enceinte. Suicide is also rather common, poison being the usual means chosen. The cause is generally some painful and incurable disease, but very old persons with no one to support them sometimes prefer the unknown future to the miserable present.

3. History. The existing Lushei Chiefs all claim descent from a certain Thang-ura, who is sometimes said to have sprung from the

union of a Burman with a Paihte woman, but, according to the Paihtes, the Lusheis are descended from Boklua, an illegitimate son of the Paihte Chief Ngehguka. The Thados say that some hunters tracking a serao noticed the foot-marks of a child following those of the animal, and on surrounding the doe serao they found it suckling a child, who became the great Chief Thang-ura, or, as they call him, "Thangul." From Thang-ura the pedigree of all the living chiefs is fairly accurately established. The Lusheis, in common with the Thados and other Kuki tribes, attach great importance to their genealogies; and pedigrees, given at an interval of many years, and by persons living far apart, have been found to agree in a wonderful manner. From comparison of these genealogies and from careful enquiries lasting over many years, I estimate that Thang-ura must have lived early in the eighteenth century. His first village is said to have been at Tlangkua, north of Falam. It is probable that he personally ruled over only a small area. From him sprang six lines of Thang-ur chiefs:—(1) Rokum, (2) Zādeng, (3) Thangluah, (4) Pallian, (5) Rivung, and (6) Sailo. To the north the country was occupied by the Sukte, Paihte, and Thado clans. These appear to have been firmly established under regular chiefs; but to the west the hills appear to have been inhabited by small communities formed largely of blood relations and probably each at feud with its neighbours. Therefore when want of good jhuming land and the aggressions of the eastern clans made it necessary for the Thang-ur to move, they naturally went westward. The Rokum, the eldest branch, are said to have passed through the hills now occupied by the Lushais, and some of their descendants are said to be found on the Tipperah-Sylhet border. The Zādeng followed the Rokum, and, passing through Champhai, moved westwards and about 1830 ruled some 1,000 houses divided into four villages situated near the banks of the Tlong or Dallesari river, round the Darlung peak. In alliance with Sailo chiefs of Lalul's family, they attacked and defeated successively the Hualgno (a Lushei family settled between Tyao and Manipur rivers) and the Pallian, who were their allies against the Hualgno. Subsequently the Zādeng quarrelled with Mangpura, then the most powerful Sailo chief, who, dying about that time, bequeathed the feud to his relatives, one of whom, Vutaia, prosecuted it with such vigour that the Zādeng, in spite of an alliance with the Manipur Rajah—who, however, proved but a broken reed—had to flee southwards, and their last independent village, numbering only 100 houses, broke up on the death of the chief, which occured at Chengpui, near Lungleh, about 1857. The Zādeng chiefs are reputed to have been cruel and arbitrary rulers, whose defeat was not regretted even by their own followers. Their descendants have retained these qualities, and, in spite of much assistance, have failed to regain their position in the world.

The Thangluah and Rivung took a more southerly course. The latter penetrated into what is now the Chittagong Hill tracts, and a chief named Vanhnuai-Thanga had a very large village on the Longteroi hill, between the Chengri and Kassalong rivers. He died about 1850, and shortly after his death the village was destroyed by Vutaia. The remnant of the Rivungs fled to Hill Tipperah, where Liantlura, a great-grandson of Vanhnuai-Thanga, had a village up till a few years ago, and there is one small hamlet under a Rivung chief in the Aijal sub-division of the Lushai Hills.

The Thangluah penetrated as far as Demagri and Barkhul, where Rothangpuia (Ruttonpoia) became known to us, first as a foe, and then as a faithful ally. Rothangpuia's son Lalchheva, fretting at our control, moved his village across our boundary, in spite of a warning that Government could on no account protect him if he did so. Very shortly after this move he was attacked by Hausāta, a Chin chief, and his village totally destroyed, many persons being killed and more taken captive. All the mithan (tame bison) were driven off and the chief escaped with little more than the one cloth he was wearing, and now the once prosperous Thangluah clan is represented by only a few poverty-stricken hamlets round Demagri.

The Pallian followed the same route as the Zadeng. The best known chiefs of this clan are Sibuta (Sheeboot) and Lalsuktla (Lalchokla). Sibuta is said in Mackenzie's "Eastern Frontier" to have thrown off the Tipperah yoke with 25,000 houses. He died close to Aijal, and his memorial stone is at the first stage on the Aijal-Lungleh road. It is extremely doubtful whether he ever was really subject to Tipperah, though it is certain that all these Lushai clans had dealings with the Tipperah Rajahs and feared them greatly. Among the tales in Chapter V. will be found one which exemplifies this.

Lalsuktla (Lal chokla), captured by Captain Blackwood in 1841, was a greatgrandson of Sibuta's. *Purbura* is said to have been a very powerful Pallian chief and at one time to have received tribute from almost all his contemporary Thangur chiefs. He had a large village, said to contain 3,000 houses, on the Dungtlang, whence he moved as far westwards as Pukzing, where his village was destroyed by a combined force of Zādeng, Sailo, and Chuckmahs. This attack took place somewhere about 1830. Purbura rebuilt his village, but died soon after, and his descendants were attacked frequently by the chiefs of the Rolura branch of the Sailo family, and now only two small hamlets, close to Aijal, remain to remind us of this once powerful clan.

The *Sailo.*—These chiefs are descended from Sailova, a greatgrandson of Thang-ura's. They came into prominence last, but have crushed all their rivals, and have developed such a talent for governing that they hold undisputed sway over representatives of all sorts of clans, over nearly the whole of the area now known as the Lushai Hills.

This great family has often come in contact with the British Government, but from the fact that our dealings with them have generally been through illiterate interpreters, they appear in our records under various names. The Howlongs, who caused much anxiety on the Chittagong frontier from 1860 to 1890, Lalul's descendants, whose doings fill the records of Silchar for nearly a century, Vonolel, Savunga, and Sangvunga, against whom the two columns of the Lushai Expedition of 1871–72 were directed—all these were Sailos.

As above remarked, it seems most probable that the country into which the various Thangur chiefs moved, under pressure from the Chins, was almost entirely occupied by small communities having no power of cohesion. The greater part of these were absorbed, and now form the majority of the subjects of the Thangur chiefs; but some fled north and west into Manipur, Silchar, Sylhet and Tipperah, where they are known as Kukis and where their appearance caused much trouble, as, from the very nature of the cause of their migration, much ill-feeling existed between them and the triumphant Lushais. In Stewart's notes on Northern Cachar, it is stated that the Old Kukis made their appearance in Cachar about the end of the eighteenth century. These Old Kukis include the Biate (Beteh) and Hrangchul (Rhangkol) and other cognate clans who are now known to us as Khawtlang. They claim the hills round Champhai as their place of origin, and the sites are still known by their names. We have seen that the Lusheis claim to have sprung from a village south-east of Champhai, and that the Zādeng passed through Champhai on their westward move, which ended so disastrously for them. The advance of such tribes would be slow, and would be largely regulated by the rate at which they exhausted the cultivable land near their village sites; therefore the appearance of the Biate and Hrangchul in Cachar at the beginning of the nineteenth or end of the eighteenth century fits in well with the date I had assigned for Thang-ura, the first Lushei chief, before I had read Lieutenant Stewart's book. These Khawtlang clans to this day have little power of cohesion, and they naturally gave way at once before the well-organised Lushais, and fled north and north-west into Cachar and Manipur, passing through the territory of the Thado clans and suffering considerably at their hands. When the Thangur had firmly established themselves, and the capable Sailo chiefs had come to the front, they felt equal to fighting the Thado clans, which were as highly organised as themselves. The Sailo chiefs triumphed, and hence the eruption of the New Kukis, alias Thados, and cognate clans, into Silchar about 1848.

In Colonel Lewin's "The Hill Tracts of Chittagong and the Dwellers Therein," page 109, is given an account of the "Cucis or inhabitants of the Tipperah mountains," written by J. Rennel, Chief Engineer of Bengal in 1800. With very slight alterations, this account is applicable to the Lushais of to-day, and I have no doubt that the Cucis therein described were the Rivung, the advance-guard of the great Lushai invasion.

On the Chittagong side, we find, as early as 1777, records of frontier disturbances ascribed to " Kookies, men who live far in the interior parts of the hills, who have not the use of firearms, and whose bodies go unclothed ' (Lewin's "The Hill Tracts of Chittagong and the Dwellers Therein," page 21). These Kukis were allies of the Chuckmahs, and we have seen that about fifty years later the Chuckmahs joined with the Zādeng and the Sailos in an attack on Purbura.

The various branches of the Sailo family were frequently at war, the cause almost invariably being a dispute as to land. About 1856 a war, known as "The War of the North and the South," broke out and lasted about three years. The Northern combatants were the descendants of Lallula, their opponents being Cherra's family. The bone of contention was the Piler hill, and this quarrel was on the point of breaking out again in 1892, when Mr. McCabe and I, appearing on the scene from Aijal and Lungleh respectively, " frightened both the heroes so they quite forgot their quarrel." The war ended in a victory for the North, who surprised Konglung, a village on the top of a very precipitous rock, and captured the young chief and his mother, who later were ransomed for many necklaces.

In 1874 the Southern Lushais fell out with the Thlantlang (Klangklang) chiefs. Vandula, head of the Lushais, had raided Vaki, a village on the Arracan border, and brought away as part of the loot a brass bowl and a big earthenware vase, which the Thlantlang chief claimed as being part of the promised price of his daughter, who had recently been married to the son of the Vaki chief. As Vandula refused to give up the articles, the Thlantlangs attacked a Lushai piquet on the Koladyne, killing some men. To revenge this insult, the Lushais attacked Bunkhua, with disastrous results, as is described in Chapter III, Para. 5, and had to make an ignominious peace.

Later the Northern chiefs quarrelled among themselves, and the war of the East and West broke out and lasted several years. The cause is said to have been a girl called Tuali, for whose affections Liankhama and Khalkhama were rivals. It is unnecessary to go into the history of our dealings with the Lushais, which have ended in the whole of the Hills being annexed, and a stop put to all such wars, but when we occupied Lungleh in 1889 we found the Fānai clan coming into prominence, and there is little doubt that, but for our intervention, that clan would shortly have attempted to eject the Southern Lushai chiefs.

4. Affinities. The Lushais are more or less closely allied to all the tribes now living in their vicinity, but some who show this most strongly, such as the Chiru, Kom, Aimol, are now settled in the Manipur State, while the intervening country is occupied by clans belonging to the Thado, Paihte, and Khawtlang families, which, though no doubt of the same stock, are more distantly connected. It seems certain that the former clans lived near the Lusheis when the Thangur commenced their victorious career, and it may well be that it was fear of absorption by their more powerful neighbour that drove these clans northwards, while the Lusheis took a westerly direction.

The connection between the Lusheis and their eastern neighbours is apparent both in their language and in their customs, but the eastern tribes, known to us generally as Chins, are of finer physique and, owing to their having permanent villages, the differences between clans have become more marked than among the semi-nomadic Lushais and Kukis. The feuds between different clans, which are always found where permanent villages exist, tend to widen the breach between communities and to accentuate every accidental variation of custom, so that the common origin is soon lost sight of. Nevertheless there is no doubt that the Kukis, Chins, and Lushais are all of the same race.

Less apparent but still quite traceable is the relationship between the Lushais and the Kabuis and Manipuris, though the latter nowadays try in every way to disown all connection with their poor relations.

5. Dress. The men's dress could not well be simpler, consisting as it does of a single cloth about 7 feet long and 5 wide. It is worn as follows:— One corner is grasped in the left hand, and the cloth is passed over the left shoulder, behind the back, under the right arm across the chest and the end thrown over the left shoulder. Although it would appear probable that clothing so loosely worn would be continually falling off, yet, as a matter of

fact, accidents of that sort seldom occur. In cold weather, one or more cloths are worn, one over the other, and also a white coat, reaching well down the thigh but only fastened at the throat. These coats are ornamented on the sleeves with bands of red and white of various patterns. When at work, in hot weather, the Lushai wraps his cloth round his waist, letting the ends hang down in front, and should he find the sun warm and if he is wearing two cloths, he will wear one as a puggri. Puggris are sometimes worn when out in the sun for long, and some affect rather a quaint style, twisting the cloth round the head so as to make an end stand up straight over each ear.

All these garments are of cotton, grown locally and manufactured by the women of the household. The cloths in general use are white, but every man likes to have two or three blue cloths ornamented with stripes of various colours.

The Lushais have a very strong objection to getting their heads wet, and therefore in the rain wear hats made of strips of bamboo or cane plaited and lined with smoked leaves. The original hats were almost flat and circular, but nowadays these have been discarded in favour of very clever imitations of helmets and solar topis. In the southern portion of the district the people use, as a protection from the wet, a large shallow basket-work tray, shaped like an oyster shell, and made waterproof by being lined with smoked leaves; the narrow end rests on the wearer's head, while the broad end reaches down well below the waist, so that, while bending down weeding in the jhum, the head and body are kept dry. This form of waterproof is not much used in the northern portion of the Lushai Hills, but is common among the Chiru and other allied clans in Manipur. As the Lushai has no pockets, he carries, wherever he goes, a haversack made of some pretty coloured cotton cloth slung over his shoulder by a strap of the same material. In this he carries his flint and steel and his tobacco, in neatly made boxes carved out of solid pieces of wood and fitted with lids of the same material, or of leather moulded into shape by being stretched over a block. His pipe is generally in his mouth; it consists of a bowl made out of a particularly hard kind of bamboo which is only found in the Chin hills—whence the Lushais claim to have sprung—with a long stem made of a

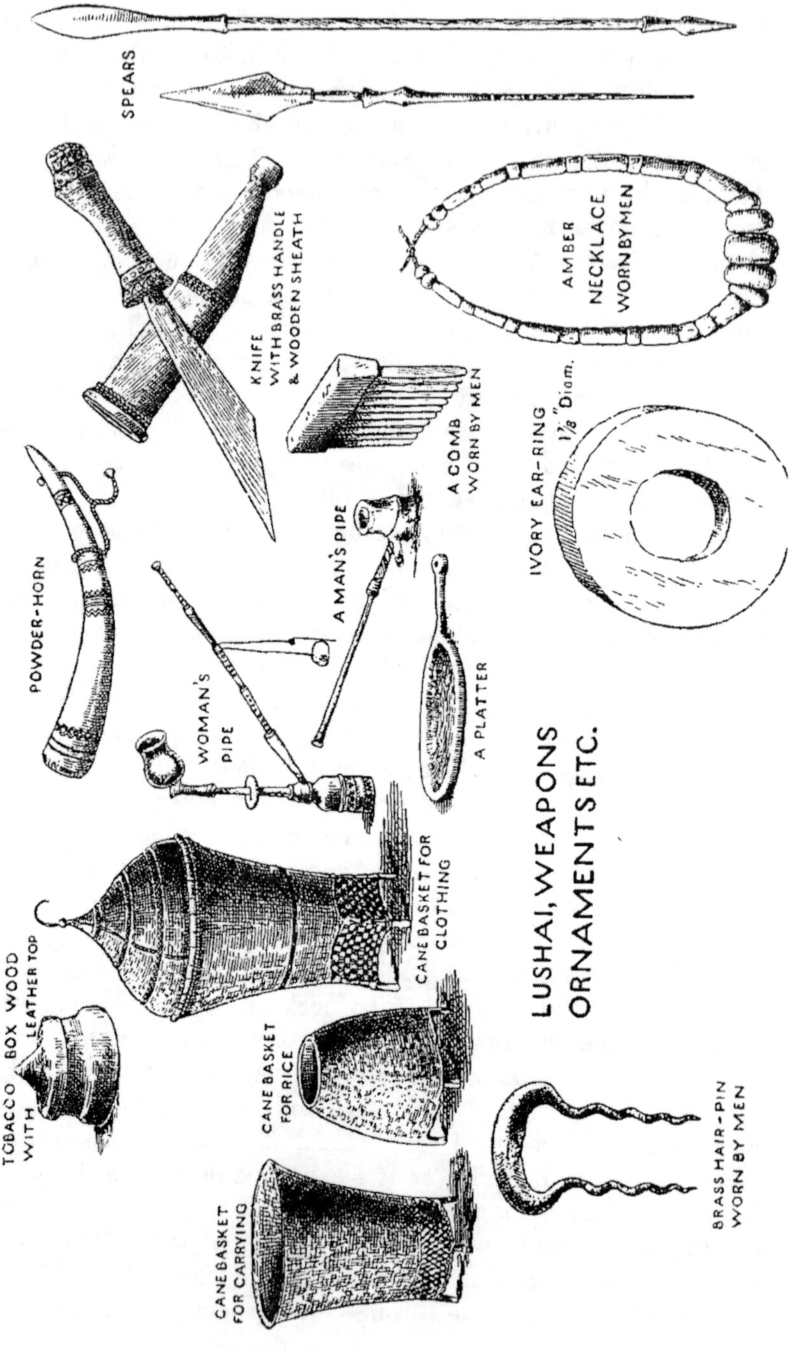

LUSHAI, WEAPONS ORNAMENTS ETC.

reed-like variety of the same plant. When not in his mouth, this also reposes in his haversack along with his "tuibur," a small gourd to hold the water which has been impregnated with nicotine in the pipe of his wife or sweetheart. A little of this evil-smelling concoction he takes into his mouth from time to time and, having kept it there a few minutes, he spits it out and declares that it has a stimulating effect. In his haversack you will also find his knife, the wooden sheath tied to one of the shoulder straps so that the handle is always convenient to his hand. The blade is about four or five inches long and nearly an inch wide at the handle, but comes to a sharp point; the edge is straight and ground like a chisel.

The dress of the chiefs is the same as that of the common people, except on occasions of ceremony, when they wear dark blue cloths, with red lines of a particular pattern, and plumes, made of the tail feathers of the king-crow, in their hair knots. These plumes are very much prized and are kept most carefully in bamboo tubes with leather caps. The cloth referred to above can also be worn by anyone who has given certain feasts, as described later on.

Dress in War-time.—When the Lushais were fighting us in 1892 I was much struck by the whiteness of their garments. The men who ran away from the stockades as we rushed them were always dressed in nice clean coats and cloths, and crowds of similarly attired warriors used to assemble every morning just out of range and challenge us to come and fight. I was told that it was considered the correct thing to come properly dressed when there was fighting on hand, but a raiding party I once came across was dressed far more suitably. A single cloth wrapped tightly round the waist, a haversack protected by a bear or tiger skin guard over one shoulder, and a fighting dao or dah over the other, and a gun in his hand completed each warrior's equipment. It will be seen from the above description that the Lushais are not fond of dress, and this is another point in which all Kuki clans differ from those of Naga stock.

Special Attire.—A man who has earned the title of "Thangchhuah" (*v.* Chap. IV, 9) is allowed to wear a cloth of a certain pattern and those who have killed men in war have special head-dresses, known as "chhawndawl" and "arke-ziak."

The Women's Dress.—The women are no more addicted to fine clothes than their men-folk. All women wear the same costume; a dark-blue cotton cloth, just long enough to go round the wearer's waist with a slight over-lap, and held up by a girdle of brass wire or string, serves as a petticoat which only reaches to the knee, the only other garments being a short white jacket and a cloth which is worn in the same manner as the men. On gala days the only addition to the costume is a picturesque head-dress worn by girls while dancing. This consists of a chaplet made of brass and coloured cane, into which are inserted porcupine quills, and to the upper ends of these are fixed the green wing-feathers of the common parrot, tipped with tufts of red wool. At the back is affixed a horizontal bar from which hang strings of glistening wing covers of green beetles. The women smoke as much as the men and have a special form of pipe, a miniature hookah about 9 inches high with a clay bowl, the water container being of bamboo much ornamented with patterns roughly scratched. The water when thoroughly impregnated is transferred to the "tuibur" gourd of some male relative or admirer. Children of both sexes begin smoking very young. I have seen a woman take her pipe from her mouth and put it into that of the baby on her back.

6. Tattooing. This is not much practised. The only patterns employed are circles on the forearm and breast, which are said to be mementoes of love affairs in happy bachelor days, and rude representations of a metna's head, which is said to have no particular meaning.

7. Ornaments worn by men. The Lushai wears a variety of articles in his hair knot. The commonest is a brass two-pronged pin with a head shaped like a G. The prongs are drawn out to sharp points and vary in length from three to eight or nine inches. These very long pins are a recent innovation, and their use seems to be restricted to the young dandies of the hamlets round Aijal. Skewers of ivory, bone, and metal about six or eight inches long are also worn. Of the two former there are two patterns, one four-sided, about a quarter of an inch thick at two thirds of its length, tapering to a point at each end, the other being flat, pointed at one end and about half an inch broad at the other. Both are ornamented

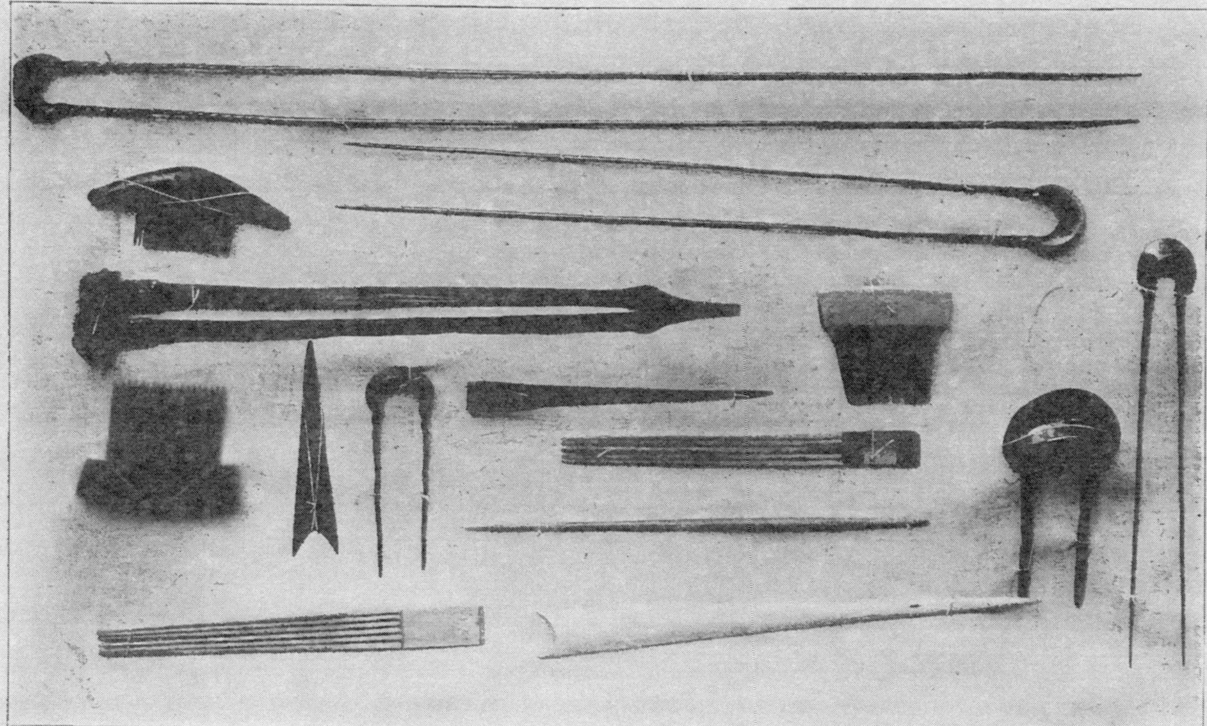

Photo by Lt.-Colonel H. G. M. Cole. I.A.

LUSHAI MEN'S HAIR ORNAMENTS.

with engraved circles and lines. The metal skewers are quite plain and more for use in scratching the head than for ornament; a piece of the rib of a broken umbrella is now often used. The hair comb is also an ornamental article; it consists of a piece of ivory or wood about three inches long, half an inch thick and an inch or so wide, into which are inserted, very close together, teeth of strips of bamboo about two inches long. If the back is of wood it is generally crescent-shaped and lacquered red and inlaid.

With reference to the comb I may quote from Colonel McCulloch's descriptions of the Thados in his "Account of the Valley of Manipur":—"Their attention to genealogy, the distinction of clans, and the respect paid to seniors, I have already noticed. Out of this may have sprung the only exclusiveness shown by the Khonjai (Thado), namely, in the point of who would be entitled to use his comb and whose comb he might use. This, though amongst them a very important matter, I cannot find to have any religious importance attached to it, but there is an indication of the superior rank in respect of descent or by connection, or of estimation in which an individual is held or holds himself to be found to whom he would refuse his comb, or amongst whom his comb is common." My Lushai informant says that the use of the comb is restricted, as headaches are communicated by the comb. He also adds, "A higher clan man is contaminated by a lower clan man using his comb. Thus a Renthlei may not use a Sailo's hair comb, and a Chawngthu may not use that of a Pallian."

Earrings.—Most men have their ears pierced, and wear either small wooden studs, with flat heads about half an inch in diameter, and coloured red, or cornelians suspended by a piece of string. The stones are barrel-shaped and unpolished, the surface being pitted with minute holes and circular marks. These are valued very highly, and are passed on from father to son, or given as a daughter's dowry. Some of them have names connecting them with some story of bygone days. These naturally fetch higher prices. I know of stones valued at Rs. 400/-.

Necklaces.—Both sexes are fond of necklaces; those of amber are most valued, and any that have histories attached to them fetch prices which to us seem absurd. I remember a chief, who was offered Rs. 60/- for his necklace, replying that if the Sahib wanted the necklace he would give it him, but that he would not sell it for Rs. 1000/- as it had been the property of his ancestors. The old necklaces are made of very dark amber, beautifully clear, and the beads are sometimes two to three inches long and over an inch in diameter. There is some doubt as to where these beads came from, but it is probable that they came through the Chin hills from Burmah. Besides amber, agate, cornelian, and various sorts of bead necklaces are worn, or, failing all these, white shirt buttons are acceptable.

A tiger's tooth is often hung round the neck as an ornament and is also thought to have magical properties. The young dandies are fond of hanging round their necks tufts of white goat's hair bound together with red thread; these are now worn as ornaments, but undoubtedly the custom arose from the idea that cures are effected by hanging round the affected part a piece of the skin or feathers of the animal or bird sacrificed to the demon, who is thought to be responsible for the illness.

Bracelets are not much worn and are generally plain brass rings.

Ornaments Worn by Women.—With the exception of their earrings, the Lushai women affect the same ornaments as the men. The earrings, however, are quite distinct, and, in order to be able to wear them, much preparation is necessary. When quite a child the girl has her ears pierced, and small wooden plugs are inserted. These are replaced by larger ones, which in turn give place to still larger ones of clay, the size of which is gradually increased till the real earring, which is an ivory disc some inch or inch and a half in diameter, with a hole in its centre, can be inserted. Widows remove their earrings, and slit the lobes of their ears when they abandon all thought of re-marrying.

8. Weapons. The Lushais have been in possession of firearms for the last sixty or seventy years. These weapons are flint-locks bearing the names of many European makers; many are Tower muskets,

and guns bearing the marks of the French Customs Department are not at all rare. These guns came into the country in the first instance chiefly through Burmah, though no doubt some came through Chittagong, and much money must have been made, for the demand was large. When the weapons first began to appear, the Lushais and other western tribes used to obtain them from the tribes on the Burmah border, giving slaves in exchange, a strong male slave being equivalent to two guns. The other weapons in use are spears and dahs. The former are inferior weapons with iron laurel-leaf shaped blades about a foot or fifteen inches long, very insecurely attached to the shaft, which is of hard wood, often a piece of sago palm; at the other end of the shaft is a long iron spike which is stuck into the ground when the user halts. A special spear is used for sacrificial purposes, the blade of which is much longer and diamond-shaped. The spike at the other end is also much elongated, so that sometimes the wooden shaft is only six or seven inches long. The dah is a more serviceable weapon, being copied, as its name "kawlnam" denotes, from the Burmese weapon, but the blade is shorter, the handle is of wood lacquered black and red, and ornamented with brass bands and a brass knob at the end. In former days oblong shields of bison-hide eighteen inches wide and about two feet long, adorned at the two upper corners with tassels of goat's hair dyed red, were carried. The upper half of the shield was sometimes covered with discs of brass, while from a string crossing the centre of the shield hung a row of brass cones about two inches long, from each of which depended a tassel of red goat's hair, reaching to the base of the shield. Bows and arrows have entirely gone out of use, but were formerly used, especially in the chase, when the arrows were poisoned. The bows were small and made of bamboo, the string being of bark. The arrows were furnished with barbed iron points, and were carried in a bamboo quiver with a leather cap to it. Among weapons we must class the bamboo spikes with which a retreating foe or villagers expecting an attack rendered the ground almost impassable to a bare-footed enemy. These spikes were of two kinds, one used round the village or block house, and the other, carried in a neat little cane-work quiver, and stuck in the path when returning from a raid to delay pursuit. The former were simple bamboo spikes of various lengths, while the latter were carefully smoothed bamboo spikes about six inches long, and no thicker than a knitting needle; each sort was nicked so that it might break off after entering the flesh. To a bare-footed foe these spikes form a very serious obstacle, and even our troops have suffered from them, the spikes being sometimes long enough to reach to a man's knee.

CHAPTER II

DOMESTIC LIFE

THE entire population may be classed as agriculturists, as only a few people, as will be afterwards described, live on contributions of rice given them in exchange for services rendered to the community. There are no shop-keepers, and, except the blacksmith, no craftsmen, each household being capable of existing on its own labours. The men build the house and cut the jhum, they help in the weeding and harvesting, and procure fresh meat by their skill in setting snares and hunting. Periodically they visit the nearest bazar, often a journey of several days, to purchase salt and the few requisites that their own industry cannot produce, consisting chiefly of brass cooking pots, iron to be made into daos or finished daos. Nowadays, it is true, the wants of the people are slowly increasing, and looking-glasses, umbrellas, needles, and Manchester goods are finding their way into the most remote villages. The women folk fetch the wood and water, cook the food and do the greatest part of the weeding and harvesting; they also make all the clothing for the whole household from cotton grown in the jhums, which they themselves gather, clean, spin, and weave into strong cloth. I. Occupation.

A Lushai woman has to rise early, fill her basket with empty bamboo tubes, and trudge off before daylight down to the spring, which is generally some way down the hill, and the supply of water is frequently so scanty that it takes her some time to fill her bamboos. Having conveyed her basketful to the house, she has to set to work cleaning the rice for the day. The necessary amount of unhusked rice has been dried the previous day on the shelf over the hearth, and this she now proceeds to pound in a mortar in the front verandah, and winnow on an oval bamboo tray till it is clean enough for use. The breakfast of rice has then to be cooked, and by the time it is ready her husband is awake. After the meal the real work of the day begins. In the cold weather the women settle themselves to some of the operations connected with cloth-making, while the men prepare to pass a day of complete enjoyment, lying in the sun and smoking, the younger ones combining this with courting any of the pretty clothmakers; while the children play around entirely uncontrolled, save when a shrill-voiced mother calls one of them to assist her in some domestic operation. About noon there is a meal of rice and herbs, after which work is resumed and continued till the evening, when the housewife has to make another journey to the spring, and on her return the pigs must be fed with a mixture composed of rice husks and a species of edible arum bulb, mashed and boiled together, the fowls enticed into their baskets, and finally the family collected for the evening meal, which varies little from the two previous ones, but some garnish, a little meat, dried fish, or some savoury vegetable is generally added. As soon as it is dark, all the female members of the family gather round the hearth, and carry on such work as can be carried on by what light they can get from the fire; though in villages near fir forests some pine splinters are generally kept handy for use when an extra bright light is required for a few minutes. The men either gather in the "zawlbuk" or in some house where there is drink going, but the young bucks sneak off to court their lady loves, which the girls' parents give them every facility for doing. In the other seasons of the year, that is from March to December, the people are engaged in their jhums from the morning to the evening meal, as is described later on.

Lushai parents are very fond of their children, and fathers are often seen carrying their infants about. In times of scarcity, what rice can be got is reserved for the young children, the rest of the people living on yams, jungle vegetables, and the pith of the sago palm. The children assist their parents as much as they can, tiny girls accompanying their mothers to the spring, and bringing up one or two bamboos of water, while the lads help their fathers in cutting the jhum. No one, however, takes any care of children, and they are allowed to run about the village as they like, in all weathers, which no doubt accounts largely for the heavy mortality among them, as their clothing is of the scantiest.

Teknonymy is very common. The parents of a child called Thanga will generally be known as Thanga-Pa and Thanga-Nu, and I have come across old widows whose real names were unknown. There is a strong and general dislike among all Lushais to saying their own names. When we first occupied the hills, a man would not tell you his name; if asked he would refer to someone else and say, "You tell him." The following explanation, given me by a Lushai, seems to me scarcely satisfactory:—"Lushais are shy of saying the name of their father and mother and their own names. Because it is their own name they are shy of saying it. Some people are shy because their names are bad. Their parents' names—because they are their parents they never call them by their names, therefore they are shy of saying them. Their own names also they never say; just for that reason they are shy of saying them. The names of their brothers and friends they are always saying, therefore they are not shy of saying them." Long ago another explanation was given me. When a man kills another, he calls out his own name: "I, Lalmanga, have killed you!" so that the spirit of the dying man may know whose slave he will be in Mithi-Khua, the dead man's village; it was suggested that it was unlucky to say one's name on less important occasions.

2. Weights and Measures.

In every village there is a small flat basket, the size of which is fixed by the chief, which is used for all retail dealings in rice and such goods, but large quantities are measured by the number of loads, a load being about 50 lbs. After the harvest the unhusked rice is piled in a conical heap. A Lushai will tell you that his crop is "chhip-zawn," that is, the heap is level with the top of his head; "silai-zawn," that is, level with the end of his gun held up perpendicularly over his head. This is about a record crop; lesser quantities are denoted by the height of his hand or hoe or axe held up. Time he measures by the time a pot of rice takes to cook—*i.e.*, about an hour—or by the time he can hold a sip of nicotine in his mouth; he has terms for each period of the day, denoting the usual occupation; he also divides the year according to the agricultural occupation proper to it. Terms expressing measures of length are very numerous. Short lengths are expressed by reference to the human body, as we speak of a span; but the Lushai has sixteen or seventeen of these, extending from "chang-khat"—*i.e.*, from the tip to the first joint of the first finger—to "hlam," which is the distance a man can stretch with both arms extended. Longer distances he expresses by terms such as the distance of the nearest jhum, the distance of the furthest jhum, the distance a mithan will wander during the day, the distance a man can travel before his mid-day meal, &c.—terms which, though well understood by the people, are a little perplexing to strangers. Measures of weight are scanty; a curious one is "chuai"—*i.e.*, as much as can be supported if suspended from the tip of the first finger palm downwards. Many of the stars and constellations have received names; most of them have some story attached to them. The months are lunar months, and some have names, but these are but little known or used.

3. Villages. The Lushai likes to perch his village on the top of a ridge or spur, partly because, hillsides being steep, it is difficult to find sites elsewhere, partly for the sake of the climate, but chiefly, I think, in order to get a good defensive position. His migratory habits disinclining him to make the elaborate defences over which the Chins, Nagas, and other dwellers in permanent villages took so much pains, he therefore sought for a site which was difficult of approach. When we first occupied the country, every village was surrounded by one or more lines of stockade made of timber, with several rows of bamboo spikes outside it. At each gateway was a block house, and others were built at suitable places on the roads along which enemies were expected to come, and were occupied whenever an attack was apprehended. Tradition speaks of villages of 3,000 houses, and, though this is probably an exaggeration, still from an examination of the sites it is evident that they must have been very large, and even when we occupied the country

villages of 400 and 500 houses were not uncommon, and there were two or three of 800 houses.

Now that all fear of being raided has gone for ever, people no longer feel the need of living together in large communities, and the size of villages is steadily decreasing. The peculiar vagabond strain in the blood of the Kuki-Lushai race, if not controlled, leads to villages splitting into hamlets and hamlets sub-dividing, till in the Manipur Hills we find single houses in the midst of dense jungle, several miles from the next habitation. This could never happen among tribes belonging to the Naga group, with whom intense love for the ancestral village site is a leading characteristic. A short distance outside the village by the roadside there generally are several platforms of logs with posts round them adorned with skulls of animals, gourds, rags, and old pots. These are memorials of deceased heroes, and will be more fully dealt with later on.

The gate itself was composed either of two large slabs of timber, or of a number of stout saplings suspended from a cross bar by holes cut through their upper ends; during the day these were drawn aside, but at night they hung perpendicularly in the gateways and were firmly secured between two cross bars. Passing through the gate, one finds oneself in a sort of irregular street leading up to the highest point of the village, where there is generally an open space, from which other streets branch off. On one side of this space will be the chief's house, with the "zawlbuk," or bachelors' hall, opposite it. The villages of powerful chiefs are beautifully laid out in regular streets which follow the natural features of the ground. When Colonel Lister in 1850 captured the village of Shentlang he was so impressed with the regularity with which the villages within sight were laid out that he was easily led to believe these were cantonments inhabited solely by warriors. If the village is a large one and contains a mixed population, it is divided into several quarters, or "veng," which are generally inhabited by people of the same clan, and each will have its zawlbuk, a large building constructed by the united labour of the men of the veng or the village. As the mithan or gyal (tame bison) belonging to the village pass the night under the zawlbuk, it is generally built on rather a steep hillside, so that the natural fall of the ground may allow ample room for the animals under the raised floor and ensure good drainage. It is built, as are all other buildings in the village, of timber and bamboos, tied together with cane and thatched with either cane leaves or grass—if the former, then the ridge of the roof is straight and gable-ended; if the latter, it is far higher in the centre, whence it curves down somewhat abruptly to each gable. Access to the building is obtained by a platform of rough logs at the uphill end, where the front wall commences some 3½ feet above the platform. Having stooped under this wall you are confronted by a low matting partition, surmounted by a huge log, the whole some 3 feet high, over which you scramble and find yourself in a large bare room varying from 15 to 50 feet long and 15 to 30 feet wide, according to the size of the village, with a square earthen hearth in the centre on which a few logs are always smouldering, and at the far end is a raised sleeping platform extending the whole width of the building. The young boys of the village have to keep up the supply of firewood for the zawlbuk, this duty continuing till they reach the age of puberty, when they cease sleeping in their parents' houses and join the young men in the zawlbuk. Until that time they are under the orders of the eldest or most influential boy, who is their "hotu," or superintendent. The zawlbuk is the particular property of the unmarried men of the village, who gather there in the evening to sing songs, tell stories, and make jokes till it is time to visit their sweethearts, after which they return there for the rest of the night. Travellers not having any friends in the village use the zawlbuk as a rest-house, but eating and drinking are seldom, if ever, carried on there. The zawlbuk is an institution common to many tribes, but among the clans I am dealing with it is confined to the Lushei and the clans most nearly allied to them. Its appearance among the Chiru and Vaiphei emphasises the close connection between these clans and the Lusheis.

The houses all abut on the street, but small gardens are often found at the back, in which sugar cane, beans, cucumbers, &c., are grown. The houses of the chief's advisers and wealthy men are generally grouped near his, but should the chief have more than one wife, or should he have some less fortunate

Zawlbuk, or Young Men's House.

relations dependent on him, their houses will be found scattered through the village, each forming a centre of a quarter or a veng, from the inhabitants of which the chief allows them to collect the dues, which are his by right.

The steepness of the hillside is no obstacle to house building, and frequently the roof of one house will be lower than the floor of the one immediately above it. The Lushais have been nomadic ever since their ancestors started on their western trek some 200 years ago. The method of cultivation which they follow is very wasteful, and a large village soon uses up all the land within reach, and then a move becomes imperative. Their custom of burying their dead within the village tends to make a site unhealthy, especially as the water supply is usually so situated as to receive the drainage of the village, and when the rate of mortality rises unduly high, a move is at once made. In old times these moves were often of considerable length—sometimes as much as two or three days' journey—and sometimes a halt for a whole season would be made at some temporary site, the people living in huts alongside their cultivation. The selection of a new site is a matter of much thought, and before a final decision is arrived at, a deputation of elders is sent to sleep at the proposed site, taking with them a cock. If the bird crows lustily an hour before daybreak, as all good cocks should, the site is approved of. Sites of villages which have been burnt by enemies are eschewed as unlucky, and a chief when re-occupying a site of some other chief's village generally tries to establish himself slightly to one side or other, in hopes that the new site will bear his name for many years.

As soon as the move has been decided on, arrangements are made for cutting the jhums near the new site, and during the rains all the workers live either in the jhum houses, or in temporary shelters built near the new site, to which, after the harvest, they laboriously carry all their belongings on their own backs, as they own no beasts of burden. These constant moves have had a great share in moulding the Lushai character, for when you have to carry all your worldly goods from your old to your new house every four or five years, it is not strange if you are disinclined to amass more than is absolutely necessary, and gradually become content with very little, and prefer ease and idleness to toiling in the hopes of being able to add to your worldly possessions. This I believe to be the explanation of the difference between the Lushai and the Chins, the latter being eager to earn money by work or trade, while the former far prefer to lie smoking in the sun.

4. Houses. The house of a commoner consists of three parts, the front verandah, approached by a rough platform of logs, the main room, and a small closet partitioned off at the far end, beyond which there will sometimes be a small bamboo platform. The verandah is termed "sum-hmun," from the "sum," or mortar in which the paddy is cleaned, which has its place here. On one side the careful housewife stacks her firewood, and the front wall of the house is the place on which the householder, if he is a sportsman, displays the skulls of the animals and birds he has slain; among them hang baskets in which the fowls lay, and even sit on their eggs, hatching out as numerous and as healthy broods as do the most pampered inhabitants of model poultry farms. The fowls spend the night in long tubular bamboo baskets, hung under the eaves, access to which is gained by climbing up an inclined stick from the front verandah. Hens with broods are shut up each night in special baskets with sliding doors.

From the verandah a small door, about 2½ feet by 4, with a very high sill, opens into the house. This door is placed at the side furthest from the hill, and consists of a panel of split bamboo work attached to a long bamboo which slides to and fro, resting in the groove between two other bamboos lashed on to the top of the sill, in which there is generally a small opening, with a swinging door, for use of the dogs and fowls when the big door is closed. Immediately inside the door, in one corner, are collected the hollow bamboo tubes which take the place of water pots; opposite will often be a large circular bamboo bin containing the household's supply of paddy. Next to this is a sleeping platform, known as "kum-ai," beyond which is the hearth of earth, in the centre of which three stones or pieces of iron are fixed, on which the cooking pot rests. The earth is kept in its place by three pieces of wood, that in front being a wide plank with the top carefully smoothed, which forms a favourite seat during cold weather. The earth is put in wet and well kneaded, and eventually becomes as hard as brick. Along the wall an earthen shelf serves the double purpose of keeping the fire from the wall and affording a resting place for the pots. Over the hearth are hung two bamboo shelves, one above the other, on which to-morrow's supply of paddy is dried, and various odds and ends are stored. These shelves also serve to keep the sparks from reaching the roof. Beyond the fireplace is another sleeping place, called the "kum-pui"—*i.e.*, big bed—which is reserved for the parents, while the young children and unmarried girls use the kum-ai; the bigger boys and young men, as has already been stated, sleeping in the zawlbuk. Beyond the kum-pui comes the partition dividing off the small recess used as a lumber room, and often as a closet. The beds and hearth are always on the side of the house nearest to the hillside, and do not usually extend quite to the centre, the rest of the floor being vacant, and, in order to avoid obstructing this, the posts which support the ridge are placed slanting, passing through the floor in line with the edge of the hearth. Along the wall opposite to the hearth are lashed two or more bamboos, forming convenient shelves, while a platform of the same useful plant is constructed from one cross beam to another. Forked sticks tied to the wall or to the uprights form hooks, and the large bamboos, wherever used, have openings cut in them which convert each joint into a tiny cupboard. At the far end of the house, opposite the front door, is a similar door opening on to a small platform, whence a notched log serves as a means of descending to the garden or the street. Many houses have bamboo platforms adjoining the front verandah, on which the women folk sit and do their weaving, while the young men lie at their ease and flirt with any girls who are good looking.

The houses of the chiefs are very similar to those of their subjects, only a good deal larger. Entering from the front verandah, the visitor finds himself in a passage running along one side of the house, off which open several small rooms inhabited by the married retainers; the other end of the passage opens into a large room with several sleeping platforms and sometimes two or more hearths, but otherwise similar to that above described. Beyond this is the usual closet, while beyond that is a wide verandah partially closed in, which is especially reserved for the chief's family. These verandahs, called "bāzāh," are forbidden to all except chiefs or wealthy

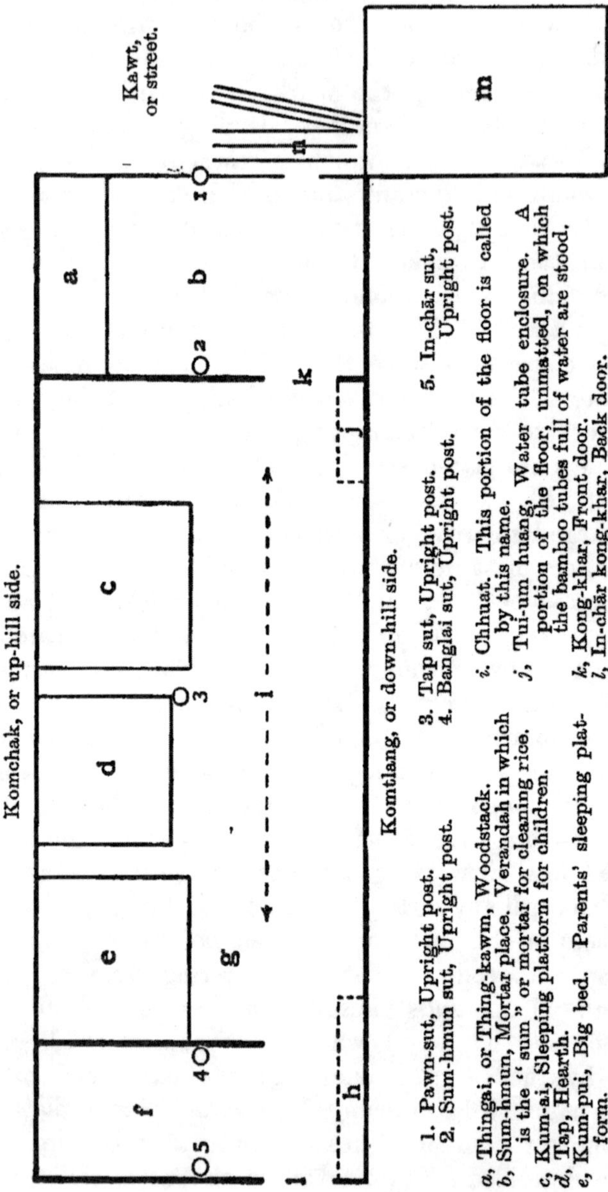

1. Pawn-sut, Upright post.
2. Sum-hmun sut, Upright post.
3. Tap sut, Upright post.
4. Banglai sut, Upright post.
5. In-chār sut, Upright post.

a, Thingai, or Thing-kawn, Woodstack.
b, Sum-hmun, Mortar place. Verandah in which is the "sum" or mortar for cleaning rice.
c, Kum-ai, Sleeping platform for children.
d, Tap, Hearth.
e, Kum-pui, Big bed. Parents' sleeping platform.
f, In-chār, Closet and lumber room.
g, Kum-pui lu, Head of big bed. The portion of the floor is known by this name.
h, Chhuar, A shelf level with the wall plate.
i, Chhuat. This portion of the floor is called by this name.
j, Tui-um huang, Water tube enclosure. A portion of the floor, unmatted, on which the bamboo tubes full of water are stood.
k, Kong-khar, Front door.
l, In-chār kong-khar, Back door.
m, Luka-pui, Big "luka," The raised platform, for weaving, sitting, and drying things on.
n, Luka, Platform of logs approached by "kai-ten" or "kai-lawn," a log ladder.

persons who have given certain feasts. A similar prohibition exists regarding windows, which are one of the prerogatives of the "Thangchhuah," as will be described in Chapter IV, para 1. Openings in the side of the house are viewed with suspicion, as likely to bring misfortune, and a most progressive chief told me he had refrained from making any but the authorised ones, in deference to the strong public feeling that the whole village would suffer for such an innovation.

The materials of which all the buildings are constructed are the same—*viz.*, timber for uprights and cross beams, bamboos for the framework of the floor, walls, and roof, split bamboos for the floor, walls, and if cane leaves are used to cover the thatch; the whole being tied together with cane. The uprights consist of sections of hard wood trees, which are split longitudinally and left to season for as long as possible. The cross beams which rest on the wall plates appear to us unduly heavy, while the wall plates seem very weak. The Lushais claim that the weight of the cross beams gives the house stability in high winds. The broad bands of split bamboo laid on top of the cane leaf thatch from eave to eave, secured at intervals by longitudinal bamboos tied down with cane, give the roof a semi-circular appearance from the outside. When cane leaves cannot be obtained, thatching grass is used, but its extreme inflammability makes it unpopular. When cane leaves are used, holes for the passage of cane ties cannot be avoided, and beneath each of these a bamboo split in half is secured as a drain pipe to convey the drippings beyond the walls.

5. Furniture. Owing to their nomadic habits the Lushais have not much furniture. Even in the houses of powerful chiefs but little will be found but a few rough and low wooden stools, some wooden platters, some earthenware beer pots, strengthened by plaited cane coverings, some brass pots, and many baskets in which valuable or perishable articles are preserved. Property which can be safely buried is often concealed in this way, a custom which is fast dying out now that raids are things of the past.

6. Implements. *Agricultural.*—The Lushai's cultivation being confined to cutting down the jungle, burning it, and dibbling in the seed among the ashes, he does not require many or elaborate implements and is content with a dao, an axe, and a hoe. The dao is a knife with a triangular blade, about 3 inches wide at the end and 1 inch or so at the handle. It is ground with a chisel edge, the broad end being also sharpened. This is used for clearing the jungle, and the broad end is used for grubbing the holes in which the seeds are placed. The axe heads are of iron only about 1½ inches wide at the edge, and taper almost to a point; the handles are simply pieces of bamboo, the heads being thrust through the tough root portion. The hoes very closely resemble the axes, the heads being a little lighter and broader.

Musical Instruments.—The commonest are gongs and drums, but a kind of mouth-organ known as "rotchem" and a fiddle made out of a piece of bamboo are sometimes used. The gongs are mostly imported from Burma, as much as Rs. 150/- being paid for large ones, but the most prized are sets of three small gongs, each with a separate note, on which three skilled performers can produce something resembling a tune. The drums are sections of trees hollowed out, the ends being covered with metna hide caps laced together. The rotchem, which is found in all Lushai-Kuki clans, consists of a gourd into which nine hollow reeds are inserted, one to serve as a mouthpiece; the others, which are of various lengths, have small holes cut in them. The performer blows into the mouthpiece, and, by closing and opening the holes with his fingers, he can produce various notes, but the music is dull and monotonous. The fiddle is a very rough affair, produced in a few minutes by loosening a strip of the outer skin of a bamboo, without detaching it at its ends, and raising it up and inserting a piece of stick to act as a bridge; the bow is made out of another piece of bamboo. The sound of a bugle is very cleverly imitated by blowing through several lengths of bamboo inserted one into the other.

Household Utensils.—Besides the articles enumerated under furniture, earthenware cooking pots and bamboo spoons complete the utensils used inside the house.

7. Manufactures. *Basket Work.*—This is chiefly carried on by men. The patterns are very numerous, each being adapted to some particular use. The material is generally bamboo. The "thul"

is a basket with four short legs, about twelve inches square at the bottom, widening till the mouth is a circle with a diameter of about thirty inches; this basket is supplied with a conical lid and is chiefly used to keep valuables in. The outer layer is of finely split bamboo closely woven, and this is lined with broad leaves well dried, which are held in their place by an inner layer of bamboo more loosely woven. These baskets are quite waterproof.

For carrying goods there are the "deron," a truncated cone 30 to 36 inches long with a diameter at its mouth of about 24 inches, holding about 50 lbs. of paddy; the "em," similar to the deron, but about half the size. The "bomrang," an open-work basket with an oval mouth, 15 inches by 12, is used for carrying goods on long journeys. The "pai-kawng" similar in shape to the em, but with open-work sides, is for conveyance of wood, water tubes, &c. There are also several sorts of flat baskets for holding grain, each with its particular name. The containing power of these is approximately constant, and they are used as measures of quantity.

Pottery.—The women make clay pots, moulding them by hand. There are only two kinds in use—a small circular pot with a mouth some 6 to 8 inches in diameter, used for cooking, and a large jar, about 24 inches high and 15 inches in diameter, tapering to about 9 inches at the mouth, which is used for brewing beer in.

Brass Work.—Occasionally one comes across rough specimens of moulding in this metal, which show considerable if untrained talent, but they are very rare, and I attribute them to captives taken from the plains of India or Burma, or to persons who have learnt from them. The method followed is to make a model in wax and cover it with successive washes of clay till a sufficient thickness is obtained, the whole then being baked till the clay is hard, and the wax has all run out through a hole left for this purpose. Into this mould the molten brass is then poured. The commonest use of this work is for the semi-circular tube required to connect the two arms of the syphons used in drawing off the rice beer. These tubes are sometimes surmounted by quite elaborate designs, a hunter approaching his quarry, a tree with many hornbills perched among the boughs, and on one which I bought are represented Vutaia and his "kawnbawl," or minister, with leg irons on. The latter carries on his shoulder an elephant's tusk, which formed part of the ransom of his master, who, in the ups and downs of the troublous times in which he lived, had been captured by the Kamhaus.

Iron Work.—The blacksmith is one of the village officials described in Chapter III, para. 2. The forge is placed in the middle of the widest street to lessen the risk of fire; it is only a rough shed with a log platform in front, which is as favourite a resort for loafers as is the forge door in England. The bellows consist of two hollow wooden cylinders in which pistons fringed with feathers are worked up and down. The lower ends of the cylinders are buried in the ground, side by side, and from them two bamboo tubes converge, meeting just behind a stone through which there is a hole; the charcoal fire is placed in front of this stone, and when the pistons are worked smartly a very strong draught is obtained. The blacksmith does little more than make and repair the simple agricultural implements of the village, but I have heard rumours of some who are capable of making gun locks. I think the form of bellows and the art of working iron have been introduced by captives, as the same type of bellows is found in the adjoining plains.

Cloth Manufacture.—Cotton is grown in the jhums. It is cleaned in a home-made gin, consisting of a frame holding two wooden rollers, one end of each being carved for a few inches of its length into a screw, grooved in the opposite way to the other, so that on the handle being turned the rollers revolve in opposite directions, and the cotton is drawn between them, the seeds being left behind. The cotton is then worked by hand into rolls a few inches long, whence it is spun into the spindle of a rough spinning wheel, or occasionally a bobbin is used, which, being given a sharp twist, draws the cotton into a thread by its own weight. This method admits of diligent ones spinning as they go to and from their jhums. The thread having been spun, it is thoroughly wetted and then hung in loops some three or four feet long over a horizontal bar, and stretched by several heavy bars being suspended in these loops.

Weaving.—The warp is prepared by passing the thread round two smooth pieces of wood, one of which is fastened to two uprights, while the ends of the other are attached to the ends of a broad leather band, which passes behind the back of the weaver as she sits on the ground and, by leaning back, stretches the threads to the requisite degree of tightness. The woof is formed by passing to and fro bamboos round which are wound different coloured threads, which are beaten home with a well polished batten made of the sago palm.

A very serviceable form of quilt called "puanpui" is made by passing round every fourth or fifth thread of the warp a small roll of raw cotton and drawing both ends up. A row of these cotton rolls is put in after every fourth or fifth thread of the woof, so that on one side the quilt is composed of closely placed tufts of cotton.

Dyeing.—The commonest dye is obtained by boiling the leaves of the Assam indigo (*Strobilanthes flaccidifolia*). Many immersions are required to render the colour permanent, and as the plant, which is cultivated near the villages or in the gardens, does not grow luxuriantly, it is seldom possible to obtain enough leaves in any one year for more than two immersions, so that the whole process may take two or three years.

Several red and yellow dyes are known, but they are little used, and most of the thread, excepting the blue and white, is obtained from the bazars.

Ornamentation.—Cloths are ornamented almost entirely by lines of different colours. White cloths have blue and red stripes down the centre and sometimes one transversely about a foot from either end. Coloured cloths are mainly blue, with stripes of red, yellow, and green. Zigzags are not uncommon, and short lengths of this pattern are placed haphazard on cloths and coats. The stems of women's pipes are ornamented with spirals and coils.

8. Domestic animals.

The most valued animal is the mithan; these tame bison wander all day at will in the jungle round the village and towards dusk return spontaneously, each animal going to its owner's house, round which it loiters till it receives a little salt, after which it joins the rest of the herd under the zawlbuk. The animals are only used for slaughter. They interbreed freely with the wild mithan, and the hybrids are, I believe, not sterile. The other domestic animals are pigs, goats, fowls, and dogs. The pigs are the scavengers of the village, but are generously fed on a species of arum and rice husks boiled together. The fowls are of a small breed; pure white, brown, and black are the commonest colours, but there is also a handsome spangled breed. The dogs have bushy tails, which curl tightly. Dogs are eaten freely, but their chief value is derived from the demand for sacrificial purposes. The goats are splendid animals with long silky hair and very large horns.

9. Agriculture. The only form of agriculture practised is that known to us generally as jhuming, and it consists in felling a piece of jungle and when it has completely dried setting fire to it. The ground is thus cleared and manured by the ashes at the same time. Timber which isnot entirely burnt is dragged to the side of the plot and made into a rough fence to keep deer out. The surface of the jhum is lightly hoed over and then there is nothing more to be done till the gathering clouds warn the cultivator that the rains are about to break, then everyone sallies out, each with a small basket of seeds slung over one shoulder and the square-ended dao in hand. Line is formed at the lower end of the clearing, and the whole family proceeds slowly upwards, dibbling shallow holes with their daos and dropping into each a few seeds. It is considered very lucky to get well soaked while sowing. The chief crop is rice, but the maize, ripening as it does in August, is eagerly looked for by the improvident Lushais who have probably used up more rice than was prudent in the manufacture of beer. The rice does not ripen till November or December, though a little early rice is grown which ripens in September. Between the sowing and the end of the rains in October the crop requires constant weeding, a duty which falls on the women folk if the family contains enough of them. In each clearing a small house is built, well raised off the ground, in which the cultivators stay during the time the work is heaviest. The other crops grown are millet, Job's tears, peas, and beans. Tobacco and cotton are also grown for home consumption. The rice is cut very high as the straw has no value. It is threshed on a piece of ground specially levelled near the jhum house. Threshing is done in

Photo by Lt.-Colonel H. G. M. Cole, I.A.

A Rest by the Way—on the Way to the Jhums. Lushais and Pois.

LUSHAIS THRESHING RICE

two or three ways. The ears are thrown on to the threshing floor and trodden out by persons dancing on them, or are beaten with sticks till the grains have all fallen out. Both these methods are rather wasteful, and a better one, which is much used in the northern part of the hills, is to construct a platform about 7 or 8 feet from the ground on which a circular bamboo bin is fixed, into which the ears of rice are thrown and a young man with a girl as a companion dance merrily among them, singing all the while, the split end of the bamboos of which the platform is made keeping up a cheerful clatter. The grain is quickly separated from the ear and falls in a golden cone on to the threshing floor, whence it can be easily collected and stored in large round bins in the jhum houses or in specially built granaries in some sheltered nook at a convenient distance from the village.

Jhuming is certainly a very wasteful method of cultivation, as seldom more than two crops are taken off the same piece of land, which is then allowed to lie fallow till it has again become covered with jungle, which will take three or four years in the case of bamboo, and seven to ten if the jungle be trees. Tree land is said to give better crops, but the labour of felling is greater than in the case of bamboo and more weeding is required, and if the land is jhumed too frequently the trees give place to coarse grass, which the Lushais refuse to jhum, whereas bamboos only grow thicker for cutting.

All the hill men are very fond of fresh meat, and are clever 10. Hunting and fishing.
at trapping game. Long lines of rough fencing are run through the jungle, with small openings at intervals, in which snares are set. Pheasants, jungle fowl, &c., coming to one of these fences will always run along it till an opening is found, and thus get snared. Porcupines are killed by a bamboo spear fastened to a sapling bent back like a spring alongside a run and so arranged that it shall be released just as the animal is opposite the spear point. Tigers are caught under a platform of heavy logs, which is supported in an inclined position by a strong cane passed over a cross piece held up by two uprights. In a hole under this platform is placed a pig in a basket; on the tiger pulling at the basket the heavy platform falls and squashes him, while the pig, being in a hole, escapes. Deer,

wild cats, &c., are caught in snares, a noose being arranged so that on the animal's stepping in it a sapling to which the noose is attached, and which is held down in a bent position, is released, thus hoisting the animal up into the air. The method of releasing the bent sapling or causing the platform to fall is in all cases the same. Two uprights are driven into the ground and a bar securely tied across near their tops. The string or rope which supports the platform or keeps the sapling in a bent position has a wooden toggle tied to it. The string is drawn between the uprights and one end of the toggle is hitched under the bar and the other end drawn down between the uprights until it is perpendicular, in which position it is held by a movable piece of wood being slipped across the uprights, just behind its lower end. In this position the pull of the string is on the upper cross bar, and a very slight touch will remove the lower one and set the toggle free; then up goes the string and down comes the platform or the noose is tightened. The removal of the lower bar is achieved in several ways. The bait or one end of a string stretched across the run may be tied to it, or it may be made to support one end of a tiny platform, on which the unwary quarry treads as it passes.

Pitfalls constructed in former times for the capture of elephants are found all over the hills, generally on a narrow ridge between precipices. To catch monkeys some rice is placed on a small platform at the end of a partially severed bamboo standing at a right angle to the hillside. The monkey, attracted by the rice, springs on to the platform and is precipitated on to a number of bamboo spikes which have been stuck in the ground beneath it. The same device with suitable alterations is sometimes employed to destroy tigers and bears.

The Lushai is also very fond of shooting, and with his old flintlock accounts each year for a good number of bears and tigers. If a village is much troubled by a tiger systematically waylaying its livestock, a general hunt is ordered, guns are borrowed from the neighbours, and the tiger, having been tracked into a piece of jungle, is approached by a shouting mob, from which he flies. Every effort of his to turn from the path selected for him is defeated by well posted crowds, who turn him back with shouts and beating of drums, till, wearied out, he comes to bay and falls a victim to a volley from all the guns present, but before he dies he has often severely mauled several of his tormentors.

Large hunting parties make lengthy expeditions into the uninhabited parts in search of elephants and wild mithan. To kill an elephant with their flintlocks is not an easy task. A volley is fired at the selected animal, which is then followed for days, being fired at when an opportunity occurs, till it falls from sheer exhaustion. The following graphic account of an unsuccessful hunt was written for me by a Lushai. The Kongpuishiam and funeral ceremonies will be described in the proper place further on.

"When Hmongphunga's village was at Kanghmun, they intended to go out shooting. They performed the Kongpuishiam ceremony; they placed the ashes in the middle of the road. Early next day they went and looked at them, and in the ashes they saw the footmarks of a tiger, an elephant, and a man. They started on the hunting expedition, carrying plenty of rice with them. They certainly found the elephants and fired a volley at one of them. One of the party was called Hrangkunga. The elephant ran away. They found it in a narrow ravine. Hrangkunga was about to shoot at it from above when the earth gave way and he rolled down close to the elephant, which picked him up and carried him to a level place close by, and threw him down, and trampled on him and broke up his gun and powder horn. His friends fired at the animal, and it went off; they could not kill it. When the elephant had gone they took up Hrankunga and buried him close by in the jungle, and set out for their village, near which they shot a tiger. When the people in the village heard of their approach they came out to meet them with 'zu.' The hunters wrapped up grass and leaves in a cloth to represent the corpse of their friend. Outside the village they fired guns and put down the effigy, which was buried by the elders of the village. Shortly after this they went out shooting again, and after going some way they saw Hrangkunga's ghost on the branch of a tree and were very frightened, and went home."

Fishing is carried on with the ordinary casting net, and fish are sometimes killed with spears or daos by torchlight, but most reliance is placed on the "ngoi." This is a weir built of timber and bamboos reinforced with stones, which stretches from side to side of the river. At one side an opening is left through which the water rushes with great force into a long bamboo shoot, which curves slightly upwards and ends in a deep receptacle, also of bamboo. The fish are carried into this by the force of the water which escapes between the bamboos, and are unable to leap out. Close by is placed a hut, well raised off the ground, in which the fishermen live for several days at a time and smoke the catch. Any chance openings in the weir are closed with conical baskets which detain small fish, prawns, &c. These weirs are constructed by the united labour of the whole village, and any villager can make use of them, but he has to pay a toll in kind to the chief. Certain spots are peculiarly adapted for these weirs, and each is by prescriptive right the property of the village occupying a certain site in the vicinity, any infringement of which will lead to a serious quarrel.

Deep pools in the smaller streams are sometimes poisoned by having a decoction of a certain herb called "kokur" or of a bark called "ru" poured into them. This stupefies the fish, which float to the surface and are easily captured. The mixture is said to be harmless to human beings or cattle.

11. Food and drink. The Lushai when speaking of food always means rice. Though he is fond of meat and likes vegetables and seasonings, he only considers them as a garnish to his rice. When a mithan is killed to feast the village, the flesh is boiled in earthen pots in the street and the contents emptied out on to plantain leaves, whence the feasters help themselves with their fingers, washing down the savoury morsels with the water in which they have been boiled, but this banquet in no way takes the place of the regular meal of rice.

Flesh of all animals is eaten, and is not objected to even when considerably decomposed. The flesh of leopards and tigers is only eaten by children, but in spite of many enquiries I have been unable to ascertain why adults abstain from this article of diet. Rats of the white-bellied variety are considered a luxury. Dogs, especially puppies, are a favourite dish. Next to rice, maize may be considered the most important staple. It is eaten boiled, never being ground into flour. Besides the

KHĀMLIANA, SAILO CHIEF

grains and herbs which he grows in his jhums, the Lushai finds many edible roots and herbs in the jungle. The young shoots of the bamboo are by no means unpleasant eating, and a salad of those of the sago palm is quite a luxury, while the pith of the latter is much eaten in times of scarcity. When a large animal has been killed at any distance from the village the flesh is cut into strips and dried over a slow fire, after which it remains edible, according to Lushai ideas, for a very long time. Boiling is the only culinary art known.

As regards his drink, the Lushai has very simple tastes. With his meals he drinks nothing but the water in which the food has been boiled, which he sips sparingly, washing the meal down with a draught of cold water. Intoxicating drinks he only takes when he has full leisure to enjoy them and in company with a party of friends.

There are two kinds of such drinks, both home-made, from rice. The commonest is known as "zu," and is a simple partially fermented drink ; the other, called "rakzu" or "zuthak," is distilled. This is very seldom used, being only made on special occasions. The still is a very simple contrivance, generally consisting of an earthenware pot on the top of which a gourd is fixed securely, the joint being made airtight with rags and clay; through the top of the gourd is passed a bamboo which is swathed in rags which are kept wet so as to condense the vapour from the pot. Zu is a very important article with these people. It is required for the due observance of every ceremony; a child's birth is an occasion for entertaining its relations, no marriage can be celebrated without the consumption of zu, while after his death a Lushai's friends and relatives drown their sorrow in all the zu they can obtain.

Has a demon to be propitiated, the return of a raiding or hunting party to be celebrated or a friend to be welcomed, in every case zu is indispensable.

Good zu takes some time to prepare. After being well bruised, paddy is damped and packed away in several layers of leaves and kept for some months—the longer the better. When the zu has to be brewed the bundles are opened and the contents placed in a large earthen jar and well pressed down, with a layer of leaves on top, and the jar filled up with water.

After standing a few minutes the liquor is drawn off by a syphon into a brass or wooden bowl, out of which it is handed round to the guests in horns or small bamboos. The principal guest is served first, and as he tosses off the cup he names the one in whose honour he drinks, who in duty bound must drink next, naming another to follow him. While the important personages are thus ceremoniously entertaining each other the rank and file sitting round in a circle are each in turn receiving a brimming horn full. As the supply in the jar gets low, more water is added, so that the quality of the liquor steadily deteriorates. Occasionally, instead of drawing off the zu, a tube is inserted and each toper in turn sucks up his allowance, the appearance of the top of a peg, inserted in the layer of leaves, giving him a hint when to leave off.

Should the zu not have been kept long enough, a cake of yeast prepared from rice may be required to start fermentation. Well prepared zu is by no means an unpalatable drink. It contains much nourishment, and Savunga, one of our opponents in the 1871–72 expedition, whom I found still living in 1898, was said to have taken little else during the last two years of his life. The drink naturally varies much in strength, but even at its strongest it is not very intoxicating, and it has not the exciting effect which the drink brewed from maize and millet seems to have on the eastern tribes, among whom violent crimes, committed during drinking bouts, are very common.

12. Amusements. The songs which the folk seem never tired of singing are slow, solemn dirges sung by the whole party to the accompaniment of a drum or gong, and are generally in praise of some former home of the tribe or some departed hero.

The dances also are very slow and monotonous. A single male performer enters the circle of drinkers and postures slowly, keeping time to the drum or gong. There are one or two exceptions, such as the dances in which the performer imitates a monkey or a bird, but generally speaking they are most uninteresting.

The men are fond of putting the weight; the stone used is a light one weighing 10 to 12 lbs. and the thrower is allowed to follow on as much as he likes. Jumping and running races are never indulged in, and, though I have often prevailed on the young men to try, the results were always very poor.

The Lushais are very badly off for games. Girls play a game with a large, flat bean, called "koi." The players divide into two parties, each in turn placing their kois in a row on the ground to serve as a target for those of the other party, which are held between the thumb and first finger of the left hand and propelled by the middle finger of the right. Should the target not be struck the first time, each firer goes to where her koi lies and again aims at the target, but this time the missile has to be propelled in another manner. Sometimes it is placed between the knees and jerked forward by a sharp jump, or it is balanced on the cheek or forehead and then projected by a jerk of the head, or it may be balanced on the instep and kicked towards the mark. This game is played among the Manipuris, who call it "Kang sanaba." The koi bean of the Lushai is called "kang" by the Manipuris, but the latter now usually use round discs of ivory instead of the natural bean.

A game played by both sexes is "Vai lung thlān."[1]

The players sit on the ground on opposite sides of two parallel rows of shallow holes. In each row there are six holes and in each hole five small stones are placed. Each player in turn picks up all the stones in any hole in the row nearest him and, commencing from the hole next on the left, drops one in each hole along his row and then back along that of his opponent. If at the end of a turn one or more of the holes last dropped into is found to contain only one stone, the player removes these single stones and places them aside. The game continues till all the stones have been thus removed, and the winner is he who has taken most. Counting the stones in the hole before removing them is not allowed, and considerable skill is required to judge accurately the number of stones, so as to select a hole containing the number of stones which when distributed will leave the maximum number of holes with single stones in them. This game, under the name of "Mancala Bao" and "Warri," is played by the Negroes in many parts of Africa, but on elaborately carved boards.

[1] Lung = stone; thlān = grave; "vai" may mean "foreign" or be short for "vai phei," the name of an old Kuki clan.

Boys and young men are very proficient with the pellet bow, and many a bird and squirrel falls victim to the sun-dried pellets shot from their bamboo bows, with strings of cane. The other amusements of the children consist chiefly in imitating their elders, the building of model houses forming a favourite pastime. Swinging is also popular, the swing consisting of a creeper suspended from the branch of a tree or from two poles stuck in the ground and tied together at the top. The swinger holds on to the end of the creeper, or places one leg through a loop, or sits astride a big knot tied at the end of it.

CHAPTER III

LAWS AND CUSTOMS

THE population of a village ruled by a Thangur chief at the present time is composed of representatives of many tribes and clans, which have all more or less adopted the language and customs of their rulers. I have already described the rise of the Thangurs and the process by which they either ejected or absorbed into their communities the other inhabitants of the country. 1. Internal structure.

Our arrival in the country put a stop in certain cases to this process of absorption. For instance, many chiefs held considerable numbers of Paihte or Vuite and Khawtlang in a species of semi-slavery. These were captives or descendants of captives made in war, and nearly all have availed themselves of the Pax Britannica to return to their own people. Again, we found certain villages ruled over by non-Lushei chiefs, who were living under the protection of powerful Lushei chiefs. In the process of pacification these non-Lushei chiefs regained their independence and have gathered round them many of their clansmen, who formerly were scattered among the Lushei villages, and who, if we may judge by what has undoubtedly happened in other cases, would in a short time have become completely absorbed. Inquiries lasting over many years have convinced me that these clans are little more than enlarged families. In most cases the dialects of the minor clans have been entirely forgotten, and the only differences remaining are the manner of performing the "sakhua" or domestic sacrifice, the position occupied by the corpse at the funeral feast, and such other minor points.

A stranger might live for a long time in a Lushai village without knowing that such divisions existed. Every clan is further subdivided into families and branches. Thus the Lushei clan has several families. One of these is the Thangur, and the Thangur family has six branches—Rokum, Zādeng, Rivung, Thangluah, Pallian, and Sailo—but none of these branches has any further sub-division, though the descendants of certain powerful chiefs are sometimes collectively spoken of by their ancestor's name, showing how these clan, family, and branch names have arisen.

During the census of 1901 an unsuccessful attempt was made to get a complete list of the clan families and branches. The causes of the failure were the ignorance of the people themselves as to what clan or family they belonged to and the tendency to claim to be true Lushais.

Everyone knew the name of the branch to which he belonged, and as a rule the family name would be correctly given, but in many cases the clan name was altogether omitted, or Lushei was entered against families which had no real claim to that distinction.

An old Lushai once asked me why I was troubling myself about family and branch names, and on my explaining that I hoped to make a complete list of them he muttered, "Can you count the grains in that basket of rice?" and turned from me to the zu-pot.

As a sample of the constitution of a clan I give in the Appendix a list of all the families and branches of the Lushei clan.

My enquiries lead me to believe that practically all the clan and a great many of the family and branch names are eponyms. In some cases the name of a village site has been given to its inhabitants, first probably by outsiders and eventually adopted by the people themselves, but even in these cases as often as not enquiry will show that the village site was first named after some famous chief who lived there.

Before the Thangur chiefs had risen to their present predominant position there were many consanguineous communities scattered over the hills, living under headmen of their own and each using a dialect of its own. Some of these communities appear to have had separate corporate existence for long periods and in consequence to have been sub-divided into many families and branches, while others were quickly absorbed by the Thangur and consequently have few sub-divisions.

I have been accused of deriving "Lushei" from 'lu," head, and "shei," long. If in the salad days of my sojourn among these folks I was ever guilty of this folly, I hereby publicly repudiate it. There is no doubt that Lushei, in common with the other clan names, is an eponym.

A versatile and imaginative writer has recently derived "Sailo," the name of the branch of the Lushai clan to which the present chiefs belong, from "sai" elephant, and "lo," a jhum, alleging that because the elephant is the biggest animal, therefore "Sailo" means the biggest jhum and that the name refers to the excellence of the jhum land between Burkhal and the source of the Kornaphuli river, where he says the Sailos formerly lived. There are some objections to this theory; to begin with, the Lushais never use "sai" as a prefix meaning greatness, and secondly half the area mentioned was never inhabited by Sailo chiefs, and thirdly only a small and little considered branch of the great Sailo family ever entered this land of fatness and not till long after the family name had been generally accepted; further the name of the common ancestor of all the Sailo chiefs is known to have been Sailova, which is a common name still in the family.

2. Tribal organisation of the Lushais.

Among the Lushais, each village is a separate State, ruled over by its own "lāl" or chief. Each son of a chief, as he attained a marriageable age, was provided with a wife at his father's expense, and given a certain number of households from his father's village and sent forth to a village of his own. Henceforth he ruled as an independent chief, and his success or failure depended on his own talents for ruling. He paid no tribute to his father, but was expected to help him in his quarrels with neighbouring chiefs; but when fathers lived long it was not unusual to find their sons disowning even this amount of subordination. The youngest son remained in his father's village and succeeded not only to the village, but also to all the property.

Our rule has tended to increase the independence of the

young chiefs; for in former days, when might was right, it behoved a son to follow the advice of his father, or the latter's help might not be forthcoming when danger threatened.

The chief was, in theory at least, a despot; but the nomadic instinct of the people is so strong that any chief whose rule was unduly harsh soon found his subjects leaving him, and he was therefore constrained to govern according to custom.

To assist him each chief appoints one or more elderly men, known as "upa." These form a sort of council which discusses all matters connected with the village, and decides all disputes between people of the village, for which they receive fees termed "salām" from the party who loses the case. These fees are their only remuneration. The chief presides over this council, which is generally held of an evening in the chief's house, while the zu horn circulates briskly. The chief receives a portion of each fine levied, a practice found to prevent undue leniency.

Besides the upas the chief appoints the following village officials—"rāmhual" and "tlangau." The former, of whom there may be several, are advisers as to where the jhums shall be cut, and are allowed first choice of land for the purpose, but have to give the chief five to seven baskets of paddy instead of two, which is the portion due from other subjects.

The tlangau is the crier, whose high-pitched voice is heard after dark, when every good householder is at home, proclaiming the chief's orders.

He also arranges how the work of the village is to be divided, who are to go and make a road, who are to repair the zawlbuk, &c.

In return for his labours he receives a small basket of rice from each house in the village.

Besides the rāmhual and the tlangau, no village is complete without at least one "thirdeng," or blacksmith, and a "puithiam," or sorcerer. The former receives one basket of rice from each householder whose tools he repairs; the latter receives the same amount from each householder for whom he performs the sacrifices connected with his cultivation.

The chief receives one hind leg of every wild animal shot by any of his men, and when the killing of elephants was allowed

ZATAIA, SAILO CHIEF AND FAMILY

he took one of the tusks if his villagers were lucky enough to slay one of those animals.

The villagers build the house of their ruler, and formerly they also cut his jhum, but I regret to say that nowadays they have ceased doing so, and this is an unsatisfactory sign of how, without any desire on our part to do so, our rule has weakened the authority of the chiefs.

The chief held rather an anomalous position. Nominally he was a despot—I am speaking now of the state of things which existed prior to our occupation of the Hills—but in reality his power was very much circumscribed, and his subjects could so easily transfer their allegiance to some rival chief, who would probably be willing, for a consideration, to champion the cause of his last recruit, that every ruler had to use tact as well as force. In fact the amount of power he wielded depended almost entirely on the personal influence of the chief. A strong ruler, who governed mainly according to custom, could do almost anything he liked without losing his followers, but a weak man who tried petty tyrannies soon found himself a king without any subjects.

The chiefs naturally tried their best to stop people leaving their villages, and it was customary to confiscate the paddy of any person who left the village without permission, but leave was seldom refused if the emigrant intended moving to the village of a friendly chief; and if the fugitive took refuge with a more powerful ruler it was extremely likely that a demand for the prompt surrender of all his property would be made with such a show of force that it could not be ignored.

I add here two extracts from Colonel Lewin's book, "The Hill Tracts of Chittagong and the Dwellers Therein," page 100.

"The village system among the Kookis, *i.e.* (Lushais) is best described as a series of petty states, each under a Dictator or President. To illustrate the position of the chief or President I may mention that in 1866, when on a visit to the village of one of the leading chiefs among the Looshai, I was standing talking with him in the path that ran through the village. While we were thus standing a drunken Looshai came stumbling along, and finding us somewhat in the way, he seized the chief by the neck and shoved him off the path, asking why he stopped the road. On my asking the chief for an explanation of such disrespect being permitted, he replied, 'On the war-path or in the council I am chief, and my words are obeyed; behaviour like that would be punished by death. Here, in the village, that drunkard is my fellow and equal.' In like manner any presents given to the chief are common property. His people walk off with them, saying: 'He is a big man, and will get lots more given to him. Who will give to us if he does not?' On the other hand, all that is in his village belongs to the chief; he can and does call upon people to furnish him with everything that he requires.

"To collect his people, or in fact to authenticate any order, the chief's spear, which is usually carved and ornamented, is sent by a messenger from village to village. Should the message be a hostile one, the messenger carries a fighting dao, to which a piece of red cloth is attached. Another method is by the 'phuroi,' which is a species of wand made out of strips of peeled bamboo, about eight inches long, in this shape (†). If the tips of the cross pieces be broken, a demand for blackmail is indicated, a rupee to be levied for each break. If the end of one of the cross pieces is charred, it implies urgency, and that the people are to come even by torch light. If a capsicum be fixed on to the 'phuroi,' it signifies that disobedience to the order will meet with punishment as severe as the capsicum is hot. If the cross piece is of cane, it means that disobedience will entail corporal punishment."

The "Boi" Custom.—Among the Thados and Chins real slavery used to exist, and men and women were sold like cattle. Among the Lushais this has never been the case, but there is a class known as "boi" who have been miscalled slaves by those ignorant of their real condition.

Among the Lushais no one but a chief can have boi, who are divided into the following classes:—

(1) Inpuichhung (Inpui = big house, chhung = within), Lal-chhung, or Chhungte—*viz.* those who live in the big house or chief's house. (ii.) chemshen boi (chem = dao, shen = red); (iii.) tuklut boi (tuk = promise, lut = to enter). The first class consist of all those who have been driven by want of food to take refuge in the chief's house. Widows, orphans, and others

who are unable to support themselves, and have no relatives willing to do so, form the bulk of this class of "boi," but it is not unusual, if a young widow remarries, for her second husband to insist on his predecessor's children being put into the chief's house, unless any of their father's relatives will take them. The inpuichhung are looked on as part of the chief's household, and do all the chief's work in return for their food and shelter. The young men cut and cultivate the chief's jhum and attend to his fish traps. The women and girls fetch up wood and water, clean the daily supply of rice, make cloths, and weed the jhum, and look after the chief's children. In return the boi get good food and live in the chief's house, and often wear his ornaments and use his guns and weapons. They have to do very little more work than they would have to do if they were independent, and, on the other hand, they are free of all anxiety as to the morrow.

As all the chiefs are of the same family, a boi is at liberty to move from one chief's house to another. If a chief or his wife treats a boi very badly, the injured one goes off and seeks for a new master, and, as a large number of boi is considered to increase a chief's importance, every chief is willing to receive him, and therefore boi are generally well treated. In former days powerful chiefs like Sukpuilala and Vutaia only allowed their boi to go to one of their own relations, but even then a boi very often would manage to find an asylum with some equally powerful chief.

When a person has once entered the chief's house, he or she can only purchase freedom by paying one mithan or its equivalent in cash or goods. The fact that a boi can ever do this shows that he is allowed to acquire property. When a male boi reaches a marriageable age, the chief generally buys him a wife, and he lives with her for three years in the chief's house: should he marry a female boi, the couple have to live six years in the chief's house. After this period, he sets up a house of his own and is known as "inhrang (in = house, hrang = separate) boi," and works for himself, but is still in some respects a boi. If he kills any animal he has to give a hind leg to the chief, and failure to do so renders him liable to a fine of one mithan or its equivalent. If the chief is in want of rice he can call on his boi to help him if they have any surplus, and if a boi is in want he can look to the chief for assistance.

Regarding the children of such a boi, customs differ somewhat. Some chiefs have made it the rule that only the youngest son, who inherits his father's property, is a boi, the remainder of the sons and all the girls being entirely free. Others insist that all the children are boi, and that the chief is entitled to the marriage prices of the daughters. They give, as a reason for this, that the chief has paid for the boi's wife and so is entitled to consider the children as boi. In either case the children are inhrang boi.

A female boi is allowed to marry, and the chief receives the marriage price, and when this has been paid in full he has no further claim on the woman or her children during her husband's lifetime, but should she be left a widow, she is sometimes forced to re-enter the chief's house; but as a rule, if she behaves decently, she is allowed to remain on in her husband's house, and manage his property on behalf of his children, who are never considered boi. Should she re-marry, the chief will again receive whatever sum is paid as her marriage price.

It will be seen that the inpuichhung are by no means badly off, and the custom seems in every way suited to the circumstances of the case. Many a clever young man rises from being a boi to being the chief's most trusted adviser, and it is by no means unusual for a chief to take a favourite boi into his own family by the ceremony called "Saphun" (see under Adoption, page 54).

(*ii.*) *Chemsen Boi* (*Red Dao Boi*).—These are criminals who, to escape from the consequences of their ill deeds, take refuge in the chief's house. Murderers closely pursued by the avengers of blood rushed into the chief's presence and saved their lives at the expense of their own or their children's freedom. Debtors unable to pay their creditors sought the chief's protection, and he released them from their debts on condition that they and their children became boi. Thieves and other vagabonds avoided punishment by becoming the chief's boi. Civil disputes were unblushingly decided in favour of the party who volunteered to become the chief's boi. It is evident that the custom in these cases has grown up by degrees from the chief's granting sanctuary to those who, having committed serious crimes, were in danger of being killed by those they had injured or their relatives.

Chemsen boi do not live in the chief's house or work for him. Their position is similar to that of an inhrang boi, but all their children are considered bói to the same extent as their parents. The chiefs generally take the marriage price of the daughters of such Boi.

(iii) Tuklut (Enter by Promising) Boi.—These are persons who during war have deserted the losing side and joined the victors by promising that they and their descendants will be boi. A tuklut boi can purchase his freedom for a mithan, and if there are three or four persons in one household one mithan will release them all. As a rule the daughters of tuklut boi are not considered boi. A tuklut boi does not live in the chief's house, and is in most respects in the same position as an inhrang boi.

Chemshen boi have not been recognised by our officers, and whenever one has claimed protection he has been released. The tuklut boi have also not been formally recognised, but their duties weigh so lightly on them that they seldon claim their release, and in their case, as in that of the "sāl," the class, receiving no fresh recruits, will soon cease to exist. As regards the inpuichhung boi, the custom seems well suited to the people and provides for the maintenance of the poor, old, and destitute, and it would be extremely unwise to attempt to alter it.

When we first visited Kairuma in 1891, we found some 80 houses of Thado, Biate, and other clans living in his village (in a species of serfdom) very much on the footing of the tuklut boi, only that Kairuma received a mithan out of the marriage price of each of the daughters as well as the other dues. These people were remnants of conquered clans and were not allowed to leave the village. I was assured that, if any of them tried to run away, a party of young men would be at once sent off to kill or bring back the fugitives. When Kairuma's village was burnt, owing to its continued contumacious behaviour, all these people made their escape to the villages of their own clans.

Sāl.—Persons captured in raids are called "sāl"; their position is quite different from that of any of the classes of boi. They are the personal property of their captors, and I am told that when guns first made their appearance in the hills the western tribes used to exchange their sāl with the eastern tribes for guns, one strong sāl being worth two guns. As a rule only children and marriageable women were taken captive, and the latter were disposed of in marriage, the lucky captor acting *in loco parentis* and taking the marriage price. The children grew up in the captor's house as his children, and as a rule were so well treated that they seldom wished to return to their former homes.

3. Marriage. The Lushais have wide views as to matrimony. A young man is not hampered in his choice by any table of prohibited degrees, nor is his choice confined to any particular family or clan; in fact, he can practically marry any woman he chooses except his sister or his mother. There is, however, a certain amount of prejudice against first cousins on the father's side marrying, but the reason generally given for this is that when a girl's parents have to consider the question of her marriage they naturally try to dispose of her outside the family, in order that her price may increase the wealth of the family, not merely transfer it from one brother to another. I have, however, been told that girls object to marrying their "brothers." Among the chiefs the desire to marry another chief's daughter limits the young man's choice, and marriage among first cousins is more frequent than among commoners. Marriage among nearly all the other clans dealt with in this monograph is endogamous as regards the clan, but exogamous as regards the family. When we consider the composition of the following of the Thangur chiefs, we see at once the cause of this difference, for any restrictions on intermarriage would have interfered with that fusion of clans which was so necessary for the establishment of their power.

Regarding the number of his wives also the Lushai has great latitude; in fact, it is simply a matter of money. Experience has taught them that two wives in one house is not conducive to peace, and consequently polygamy is almost entirely confined to the chiefs, for few others can afford to keep up two establishments. Marriage is purely a civil contract, although, as is described in Chapter IV, para. 7, a pseudo-religious ceremony is performed.

Among Lushais the following sums constitute the price which has to be paid for a wife:—

(*i.*) *Manpui* (*Principal Price*).—This is paid to the bride's nearest male relative on the father's side. In case the bride's father is dead and she has brothers these divide the manpui, but if any one of them has contributed more than the others to the girl's support, or has provided her "thuam"—*i.e.*, her trousseau—he receives a larger share of the manpui than the others.

The manpui is always reckoned in mithan, and varies according to the family of the bride. Thus a Thangur maiden is valued at ten mithan, while less aristocratic girls are worth less, the lowest price being three. A custom seems springing up of counting the manpui in "tlai" = Rs. 20/-. If the bride's "thuam," or trousseau, is a good one a sum of Rs. 20/-, called "tlai," is added to the manpui, but should the woman die without issue, this sum will not be paid, as the thuam will return to her father's family. If she has children these inherit the thuam, and therefore in such cases the tlai must be paid. The thuam consists of necklaces, earrings, and superior cloths, not articles for everyday use.

(*ii.*) *Pushum.*—The perquisite of the nearest male relative on the mother's side or of a person specially chosen as the bride's "pu" or protector. It varies between Rs. 4/-, and Rs. 10/- but in the case of a chief's daughter it is a mithan.

(*iii.*) *Pālāl.*—The bride or her relations select some trusted friend, who may be of any family, whom they appoint her "pālāl," or trustee, and he is expected to look after her interests throughout her whole married life. His fee varies in accordance with the pushum.

(*iv.*) *Niman* (*Aunt's Price*).—A sum equal to the pushum which has to be paid to the bride's aunt on her father's side. If there are several aunts the eldest takes the "niman" of the eldest niece and the second aunt that of the second niece and so on. It is possible for a niece to refuse to allow her aunt to take the niman and to select another person of her own family.

(*v.*) *Thian.*—The "thian," or friend, is a female pālāl, but she only receives a small sum from Rs. 10/- downwards.

(*vi.*) *Nau Puan Puak Man* (*Price of Carrying the Younger Sister in her Cloth*).—Each sister receives this from the husband of her next younger sister. Among Sailo it varies from Rs. 20/- to Rs. 40/-; in other families it is only Rs. 3/- or Rs. 4/-. In the case of the eldest sister it is taken by some near female relative.

These sums are never paid down at once; in fact, they are allowed to remain unpaid for many years, but, as a rule, in each family it is the custom to pay a certain amount of the manpui before the marriage; this is called "sum hmā hruai," "price before taking."

Divorce.—The bonds of matrimony are extremely loose and are very easily slipped off. If a couple disagree they simply separate. The woman returns to her parents and the man renounces all claim to any portion of her price which he may have paid, unless the woman agrees to its being partially returned. If the man turns the woman out for no fault he must pay up her full price, if he has not already done so. If a woman commits adultery or leaves her husband against his will, however unfaithful he may have been, the whole of her price has to be refunded.

If a pair who have separated by mutual consent wish to make it up they can do so. If the overtures are made by the man he is expected to pay the woman a small sum up to Rs. 20/- If, however, the woman makes the advances the man has nothing to pay.

Widow Re-marriage.—There is no objection to a widow remarrying. If a woman has a son and there is any property, it is proper for her to remain unmarried and look after her son and his interests; should she, however, wish to remarry there is nothing to prevent her, but her late husband's relatives will take charge of the children and all the property. Should a widow be left with daughters only, it rests with her husband's nearest male relatives whether she shall continue to live separately or shall enter his house. It is not unusual in such cases for the widow to be allowed to bring up her daughters, utilising, with the heir's approval, whatever property has

Photo by Lt.-Colonel H. G. M. Cole, I.A.

LUSHAI GIRLS.

been left, but the marriage prices of the girls will be taken by their father's heir. In olden times a widow had to remain unwashed and with her hair uncombed for a whole year from the death of her husband, but the period has been reduced to three months, out of pity for the women, and after that time remarriage is allowed. A widower who remarries before three months has passed since his wife's death used to be fined, but this excellent custom has dropped out of use. Should a woman elect to live in her late husband's house and bring up his children, she is considered as still married to him, and should she be detected in an intrigue her relatives will have to refund her marriage price just as if her husband were alive.

4. Female chastity.

The unmarried girls are not very strictly looked after, and, if they conduct their intrigues with a fair amount of secrecy, nothing is said. As has been described in Chapter II, 3, there is a sleeping place on each side of the hearth, that furthest from the door—kumpui—being reserved for the parents, the other—kumai—being for the girls and young children. Sometimes, however, if the family is large, one of the girls sleeps with her parents. If a young man is found on the kumai nothing is said to him; if, however, he trespasses on the kumpui he is fined. In some villages if he even crosses the centre of the hearth he is fined. The fine varies in different villages, but it is about Rs. 10/-. If a girl becomes pregnant, the man responsible is at once surrounded by her relatives, who demand a mithan as the price of his indiscretion. This is called "sawn man," "the price of the bastard." This has to be paid even in the case of the child being born dead and in cases of premature births where the legs and arms are complete.

When the father has paid the sawn man he can claim the child as soon as it is old enough to leave its mother.

In cases in which the girl has been prodigal of her favours, no sawn man can be demanded.

In case a man should have a second illegitimate child by the same woman, he is not expected to pay more than Rs. 10/- and often nothing at all. For a third child he would, however, have to pay a mithan. In case when asked to pay sawn man, the man at once expresses his desire to marry the girl, he would not have to pay the fine in addition to the usual marriage price. If, however, he delays in marrying her, he must pay both. In this matter, however, custom varies considerably in different villages.

5. Inheritance. The general rule is for the youngest son to inherit, but occasionally the eldest also claims a share. With chiefs it is usual for each son, as he comes to a marriageable age, to be given a certain number of households and allowed to set up a village of his own, but the youngest generally remains with his father, and inherits his village and his property.

Adoption.—Persons of property who have no son sometimes adopt a near relative, but there is no special ceremony; it is a purely private arrangement. The custom known as "Sā-phun," is in some respects akin to adoption. Should a chief have a very favourite boi, he sometimes grants him admission into his own clan. The "puitiam" being called, a fowl or a pig is sacrificed, after the appropriate prayer has been said, and a few of the hairs or feathers are tied round the man's neck, and he is henceforth considered to belong to the chief's clan. Anyone can thus admit another to his clan, but in practice it is seldom done, except by chiefs. I think the sacrifice is made with a view to propitiate the Sakhua of the clan which the man is abandoning.

6. Offences regarding property. Certain articles are said "man a nei," "to have a price," and the theft of any of them is punished by a fine of one mithan, quite irrespective of the actual value of the article stolen. These are—rice cleaned or unhusked, cloths, guns, brass pots, domestic animals, and wild animals, or birds which have been killed or trapped. The theft of other articles is punished by fines of from Rs. 1/- to Rs. 5/-, which are taken by the chief and his upa, and termed "salām." Restitution of the articles stolen is always insisted on.

To steal or even to retain a hoe or axe found on the road is most unlucky, and is supposed to be followed by the death of the finder's child.

7. Offences connected with the body. The punishment in these cases rested originally with the aggrieved party or his relatives, who were allowed to exact summary vengeance. Thus a husband was at liberty to kill an unfaithful wife and her paramour, but if he did not take

refuge in the chief's house, becoming a chemsen boi, the families of the victims were also entitled to kill him whenever they got an opportunity. Very shortly after our occupation of the Lushai Hills, two lads deliberately cut down a man who, they were told, had murdered their father many years before. The deed was done in broad daylight, in the middle of the village, and apparently attracted but little attention. The boys both entered the chief's house, and I should never have heard of the occurrence had they not applied to be released from service to the chief.

To cut off the ears or nose of the paramour was a favourite way for a husband to avenge himself, and he did not always wait to be sure that there was anything to avenge. A man of Lianphunga's village passed the night in Tlungbuta's village, and, having been very hospitably treated by a friend, mistook the house of a very jealous husband for that in which he was to sleep, and was promptly ejected and deprived of his ears. Lianphunga, being a more powerful chief than Tlungbuta, exacted ten mithan as compensation for the injury done to his man, who, however, received absolutely nothing. The chief kept eight of the animals and killed two to feast the village, but the unfortunate victim was too ill even to share in the feast.

Rape or sodomy were punished in the same way, but the latter, if committed with the consent of the pathicus or with an animal, was not considered a crime, and there is no doubt that the class of men known as Tuai, who dressed as women and did women's work, indulged habitually in this disgusting vice. Fortunately the class, never very large, has almost died out, but I fear the vice is far from extinct.

8. Decisions of disputes.

The chief of each village, assisted by his upa, was the one and only court of justice in the village, and from their decisions there was no appeal, but nevertheless an unsuccessful litigant found a way of getting his case reheard. If the matter in dispute were of sufficient value to make half of it worth a great chief's acceptance, the would-be appellant could generally find some powerful chief who would accept him as a subject and take up his quarrel on those terms. The custom of settling disputes by ordeal or by oaths, which is so common among the Naga tribes, is almost unknown to the Lushais. During the fourteen years I was among them I have only twice heard a party to a case offer to accept the other's oath.

In ordinary cases, a man wishing to be believed will take an oath holding a tiger's tooth, saying, "If I lie, may a tiger eat me as I now gnaw this tooth"—suiting the action to the word.

An oath of friendship between chiefs is a serious matter. A mithan is tied up to a post and the parties to the oath, grasping a spear with their right hands, stab it behind the shoulder with sufficient force to draw blood, repeating a formula to the effect that until the rivers run backwards into the earth again they will be friends. The animal is then killed and a little of the blood is smeared on the feet and forehead of the oath takers. To make this oath more binding they both eat a small piece of the liver raw.

9 War and head-hunting. The true Lushai method of making war was to raid the enemy's villages and carry off as many captives and as much loot as possible. In this they form a great contrast to the Chins, whose plan of action was systematically to ambush the paths in the enemy's country and kill as many passers-by as possible. The Lushais consider this unsporting and say pathetically, "How can men live if for fear of ambushes no cultivation can be carried on?" The Chins were fully aware of the effectiveness of their method of warfare and resorted to it whenever they wished to extend their boundaries, piqueting the coveted piece of land so effectually that it was soon abandoned to them.

The essence of success in Lushai tactics was surprise, and no disgrace attached to a party of warriors which, on finding the enemy on the alert, quickly returned home without attempting any attack.

The wars between the different Lushai clans lasted sometimes for several years, but were not very energetically prosecuted. Thus in a war between the Thangluah and Sailo chiefs which lasted from about 1833 to 1850, about six villages were destroyed on each side, but, except on one occasion, but few lives were lost. The exception was the massacre of Thaurang, a Sailo chief's village, which is still spoken of with pride by the descendants of the perpetrators. The people of Thaurang were celebrating a great feast, and in all the principal houses in the village zu was being dispensed to all comers. There had been no hostilities of late, and the guards gradually abandoned their posts and joined the groups round the zu pots. With song and dance the night passed merrily, and by two or three in the morning no one was in a fit state to notice that a large number of strangers, whose drunkenness was only assumed, had mingled with the crowd. Suddenly a gun-shot gave the signal, and, drawing their dahs, the Thangluahs fell on their enemies, who, too drunk to know friend from foe, were slaughtered without mercy. Having burnt the village, the successful warriors returned dragging with them many captives. The Sailo chiefs tried to play the same trick on the Thangluah when some time later the latter were celebrating their victory with a large feast, but their intelligence department was inefficient and the attack was not delivered till some days after the feast.

At that time there were but few guns in the country, and so little was the use of those they had understood that the wad on the top of the bullet was often omitted, with the natural result that when the time for firing came there was no ball in the gun, and hot were the arguments as to the value of this new-fangled weapon. In those days also they had not acquired the art of making stockades, which they subsequently copied from the Chins, and consequently there was but little chance of resistance if the surprise was successful, and the shouts of the assailants were a signal for a general stampede on the part of the whole population. The attack was always delivered just before daylight, and, if successful, but little time was lost; as many captives as could be caught were collected and loaded with as much loot as they could carry without retarding the retreat, and the whole party set off and seldom halted till they had travelled forty-eight hours. As a rule only strong women and children who could keep up in the retreat were taken, all other captives being killed on the spot, and should any captive lag behind a spear thrust quickly ended her career, and her head was taken on to form an ornament in the raiders' village. Occasionally a few young men were carried off to be killed during the festivities which were held in honour of the success of the raid. If the raiders' chief had a son too young to accompany them, a captive was frequently reserved for him to slaughter and thus prove his bravery.

Having put what they considered a safe distance between them and any possible pursuers, the party proceeded more leisurely. sending on messengers to announce their success, whose arrival set the village in a ferment, and everyone commenced preparations for the ensuing feast. As the brave warriors were seen in the distance the whole population rushed out to meet them with horns of zu for their refreshment, beating drums and gongs, and shouting praises of their bravery. The following is an accurate translation of an account given me by a Lushai of the proceedings which followed the return of a successful raiding party:—

"Formerly the Lushais raided the Tipperahs and captured about ten and dragged them back to their village, and killed them either in the street or just in front of their houses. Presently they said, 'Let us dance.' They danced before the heads of the slain, and a crowd collected and watched. The heads were placed on posts around the open space in the village, and those who had killed men came out into the space in the centre of the village with their guns and fighting dahs, wearing their 'chhawn' head-dress, and the girls came with beautiful plaits of red and black cotton thread and tied them round the knots of the young men's hair. This is called 'arkezen.' Then the young men danced beautifully. 'We are very magnificent,' they said. In the middle of the open space a platform had been built of bamboos like those in front of the house. On this everyone collected any number of eggs, and those who had killed their enemies and those who had felt no fear ate up the eggs as fast as possible. This is called 'mālchawh.' Very tall 'thingsia' and 'phulrua' (kinds of bamboo) are put up in front of each man's house and called 'rālngul,' and they hang to the end of the phulrua, by a piece of cane called 'vawmhrui,' a circle of pierced pieces of wood; these are called 'hrangkhual.'"

In wars between Lushais it was considered wrong to kill chiefs. This, of course, was due to the chiefs being all of the same family.

When starting on a raid each man provided himself with cooked rice for several days. This was rammed down very tightly into pieces of bamboo, so that several days' food could be conveniently carried without fear of any being lost on the road. Sections of bamboos were also employed as water bottles, the bamboo being cut above one joint and below the next and a small hole made just below the joint on one side, which could be easily plugged with a roll of leaves; for sake of lightness the bamboo would be whittled down as much as could be safely done. These raiding parties travelled immense distances. About 1850, Vuta, whose village was then at Hweltu, suddenly appeared at Pirovi's village on the Soldeng, and, taking the people entirely by surprise, made many captives, among whom were the chieftainess and her infant son. Many others were killed and much loot rewarded the daring savages. The distance between the two villages is about seventy miles in an air line and at least twice that by the jungle paths. Although guns quickly became common in the Hills, the style of warfare did not change. In the war between the Northern and Southern Chiefs, which lasted from 1856 to 1859, each side only made three successful raids, and the actual number killed in action appears to have been very small. I once asked one of the chiefs who had been very prominent in one of the later wars how many men he had killed with his own hand, and, on my expressing surprise at his admitting that he killed none, he naïvely remarked, "You see, we chiefs always go last, shouting 'Forward, forward!' and by the time I reached the village the people had always run away." Though the Lushais were able to turn the Thados and other clans of their own kindred out of their possessions, yet when they came in contact with the Chins they were invariably defeated. In 1881 a large force of Southern Lushais raided Bunkhua, a Chin village to the north of the Tao hill. They burnt the village without much trouble, but the Chins refused to acknowledge this as a defeat and kept up a hot fire on their assailants, killing one of their bravest warriors. When the Lushais set out on their return journey they found the whole country up, and in a gorge they were greeted with a volley which laid forty of them low, and the remainder fled in all directions, and, had it not been for heavy rain, which washed away the bloodstains and made tracking difficult, but few would have reached their homes.

Although when fighting among themselves the ambushing of cultivators and travellers was disapproved of, they resorted to it freely when fighting us, but our casualties were not very great, as the ambushers were so anxious about their own safety they generally fired too soon. These ambushes were always arranged below the road, where the ground fell away very sharply, and, having fired, the brave fellows hurled themselves down the hill, ignoring all cuts and scratches in their anxiety to escape.

Head-hunting.—It used to be considered that all inhabitants of these Hills were head-hunters. In fact, so great an authority as Colonel Lewin derives the name "Lushai" from "lu," "a head," and "sha," "to cut." This, of course, is a mistake, as the name of the clan is not Lushai, but Lushei, and though "sha" does mean "to cut," it does not mean "to cut off," and could not be used of cutting off a man's head; but that such a mistake should have been possible shows how firmly rooted was the belief that head-hunting was one of the peculiarities of the population of these Hills. I believe that as far as the Lushais and their kindred clans are concerned, head-hunting was not indulged in. By this I mean that parties did not go out simply to get heads. Of course, a man who had killed his man was thought more highly of than one who had not, and, therefore, when a man did kill a person he brought the head home to show that he was speaking the truth; but the raids were not made to get heads, but for loot and slaves. The killing and taking of heads were merely incidents in the raid, not the cause of it. I think that the Chins or Pois are an exception to this, and, as far as I can gather, the glory of bringing in a head was sufficient to send a young man and his friends off on the raid.

I have also made careful enquiries in all parts of the Hills as to whether there is any truth in the commonly accepted theory that on the death of a chief a party was at once sent off to kill people in order that their heads might adorn his memorial and their ghosts wait on his spirit in the other world, but I never heard anything which lent any colour to the idea, and, as regards Lushais, I believe it to be a pure invention; but it was undoubtedly a Thado custom. If a single person is killed in a raid every person in the attacking party is entitled to all the honours pertaining to a slayer of a man.

CHAPTER IV

RELIGION

PRACTICALLY all divisions of the Lushai-Kuki family believe in a spirit called Pathian, who is supposed to be the creator of everything and is a beneficent being, but has, however, little concern with men. 1. General form of religious beliefs.

Far more important to the average man are the numerous "Huai" or demons, who inhabit every stream, mountain, and forest, and to whom every illness and misfortune is attributed. The "puithiam" (sorcerer) is supposed to know what demon is causing the trouble and what form of sacrifice will appease him, and a Lushai's whole life is spent in propitiating these spirits.

In addition to Pathian and the Huai there is a spirit known as Khuavang, who is sometimes spoken of as identical with Pathian, but is generally considered to be inferior to him, and more concerned with human beings. Khuavang sometimes appears to people, and his appearance is always followed by the illness of those who see him. A Lushai will say, "My Khuavang is bad," if things are going wrong with him, and he will also tell you that you are his Khuavang, meaning that his fate rests with you. I have also been told that there are two spirits called Mivengtu, watchers of men. One of these is a good spirit and guards people; the other is a bad spirit who is always trying to sell men to the Huai. Similarly each person is said to have two "thlarao," or souls, one of which is wise, while the other is foolish, and it is the struggles between these two that make men so unreliable. If a man hits his foot against a stone, he attributes it to a temporary victory of the foolish spirit.

In addition to all these spirits, there is another. Each clan has a special spirit presiding over its destinies. The spirit is known as "Sakhua," and all sacrifices to him have to be performed by a puithiam of the clan, and only members of the family can be present.

The Lushais believe in a spirit world beyond the grave, which is known as Mi-thi-khua—*i.e.*, dead man's village—but on the far side of Mi-thi-khua runs the Pial river, beyond which lies Pial-ral, an abode of bliss. Access to this is not obtained by a life of virtue while on earth, but the due performance of sacrifices and the killing of men and certain animals and success in the courts of Venus. The following account of the common belief was written for me by a Lushai, who embellished his essay with a map. It will be noticed that in the latter he has inserted the Kristian's (Christian's) village and their heaven, the road to which is under Isua (Jesus), while the roads to the Lushai's Mi-thi-khua are watched by Seitana (Satan). This incorporation of the teaching of the missionaries with the indigenous belief is not without interest, showing a broad spirit of tolerance in the author, who, without abandoning the faith of his forefathers, is ready to admit the truth of Christianity and its suitability to those who profess it, and sees no difficulty in providing in the unknown lands beyond the grave a special country for each race, just as there is in the world he knows of.

Translation of a Lushai's account of the World beyond the Grave

"The first man is said to have been Pupawla; then he died before all those born after him. Then Pupawla, this man who died first, shoots at those who have died after him with a very big pellet bow, but at some he cannot shoot. Hlamzuih (see below, para. 8) he cannot shoot at. Thangchhuah he may not shoot at. Then he may not shoot at a young man who has enjoyed three virgins, nor at one who has enjoyed seven different women, even if they were not virgins; but women, whoever they may be, he always shoots at. They say that there is a road between the Mi-thi-khua and the Rih lake. [This lake is on the left bank of Tyao river 1½ miles from the place where the Aijal-Falam road crosses the river.] To go there, they say, there are seven roads, but Pupawla has built his house where the seven roads meet. Then after Pupawla has shot them, there is a hill called Hringlang hill, and then there is the Lunglo river [heartless, feelingless, which removes feelings] the water of which is clear and transparent, and the 'hawilopar' [look back no more flowers] flourish there. The dead pluck hawilo flowers and place them behind their eyes and drink of the Lunglo water, and have no more desire for the land of the living."

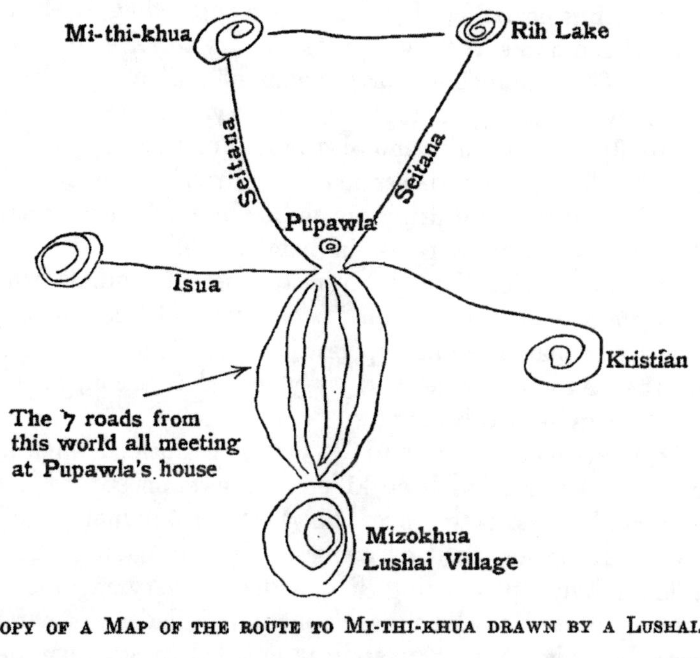

COPY OF A MAP OF THE ROUTE TO MI-THI-KHUA DRAWN BY A LUSHAI.

The Thangchhuah, mentioned above, are those who have slain men and certain animals and have given a series of feasts to the village, which will be found described in para. 9 of this chapter.

Those whom Pupawla hits with his pellet cannot cross the Pial river and are doomed to stay in Mi-thi-khua, where life is troublesome and difficult, everything being worse than in this world, the metna of Mi-thi-khua being no larger than crabs.

The proud title of Thangchhuah, which carries with it much

honour in this world as well as the right of admission to Pial-ral after death, can only be obtained by killing a man and each of the following animals—elephant, bear, sambhur, barking deer, wild boar, wild mithan—and by giving the feasts enumerated below; but it is well also to have killed a species of snake called "rulngan," a bird called "vahluk" and a species of eagle called "mu-vān-lāi" (hawk in the middle of the sky). A Lushai gave me the following account of the journey of Thangchhuah to Pial-ral.

"After death the dead man holds the horns of the sambhur while sitting on its head, the rulngan will wind itself round him and the horns, the mu-vān-lāi will try to seize the rulngan, but the Thangchhuah can drive them off. That is why they always fly screaming so high in the sky. The vāhluk shade him by flying above him and also hide him from Pupawla, and thus the Thangchhuah is carried to Pial-ral."

In Pial-ral food and drink are to be obtained without labour, which to the Lushai appears the height of bliss.

The omission of the tiger from the list of animals which a Thangchhuah must have killed is curious, and I cannot explain it as the Lushais have no superstitious objection to killing tigers and the "Ai" of a tiger is a very special function, as will be seen in para. 4 of this chapter.

This ceremony called "Ai" is always performed when a man or a wild animal has been killed. It is supposed to give the performer's ghost power over the ghosts of the man or animals killed. He is described as going to Pial-ral leading the ghost of his enemy on a string like a dog. Every member of a hunting party in which an elephant is killed or of a raiding party in which a man is slain is entitled to say that he has killed an elephant or a man. This simplifies admission to Pial-ral, and now that the killing of men and elephants is prohibited by an unsympathetic Government, it is popularly supposed that this qualification will not be insisted on.

Many people profess to have seen Mi-thi-khua in their dreams, but none claim to have seen Pial-ral. Should a person dream of his parents and in his dream accept rice from their hands he will die without fail in a very short time.

I have been told that the spirits of the dead sometimes are

Khawtlang Posts Erected to Commemorate the Slaying of Mithans at a Feast.

reincarnated in the form of hornets and sometimes in the form of dew, and if this falls on a person the spirit is reborn in his or her child.

2. Ancestor worship.

Though this can scarcely be said to be the religion of the Lushais, yet they firmly believe that the spirits of the dead are constantly present and need to be propitiated, and one of the principal Thangchhuah feasts is in honour of the dead. This is described in para. 9 of this chapter.

At every feast or sacrifice a small portion of flesh, rice, and a little zu is placed on a shelf under the eaves for the spirits of the dead members of the family. This is called "rao-chhiak."

A little of the first fruits of each crop is always placed on the wall under the eaves, above the spot where the water tubes are stacked, as an offering to the cultivator's parents. This is called "Mi-thi-chhiah," but there is another more important Mi-thi-chhiah. It is supposed that the spirits of the departed are very fond of coming to watch the Kut festivities (see para. 9 of this chapter) and on such occasions the spirit of a mother will enter her daughter's body and the daughter then goes off into a trance. The Lusheis say, "Mi-thi in a thluk" (The dead has taken her place). To cause the spirit to depart and restore the girl to consciousness it is necessary to perform the ceremony called Mi-thi-chhiah. Necklaces, earrings, cloths, petticoats, rice, and zu are placed in a heap on the floor where the corpse of the deceased was seated during the funeral feast. Then the worst cloth and petticoat of the girl are burnt in the forge and she forthwith returns to life. One reason given for the behaviour of the spirit is that sufficient attention to the adornment of the corpse at the funeral feast had not been paid. The spirit is supposed to be able to brood over the slight put on its late tenement; hence the collection of all sorts of cloths and ornaments on the spot where the corpse had been seated.

3. Worship of natural forces and deities.

The Lushais do not worship the sun or moon or any of the forces of nature, though when wishing to emphasise a statement they frequently say, "If what I say is not true, may the sun and moon desert me." But they believe the hills, streams, and trees are inhabited by various demons. These are known as "Huai," those inhabiting the water being called "Tui-huai," and those residing on land being known as "Rām-huai." These spirits are uniformly bad, and all the troubles and ills of life are attributed to them, and the sacrifices described in the next part are supposed to appease them.

The following account of the doings of one of these Huai was given me by Suakhnuna, one of the most intelligent of the Lushei chiefs:—

"A Rām-huai named Chongpuithanga used to live near the ford over the Sonai. He said he was the servant of the King of the Huai and was always on the look out for men along the banks of the river. He spoke through a girl called Ziki, who was often ill, and used to go into trances. He demanded a pig and professed to have caused the deaths of ten persons of the village." The following is another story which the teller fully believed. "About six years ago Hminga, of Lālbuta's village, was looking at a ngoi (fishing weir) and saw some Rām-huai. These wore the chawndawl (headdress worn by slayers of men), and round these were strings of babies' skulls. On his return home he got very ill, and all his family kept on asking him what was the matter, but when he was going to tell them the Rām-huai would seize him by the throat so that he could not tell them. If he managed to say a few words he got a pain in the head. He did not die, but recovered." Again, "A woman of Lālbuta's village went out of her house at night for purposes of nature. Her name was Mangāmi; she was enceinte. The Huai of the Tuitlin precipice caught her, and forced out the immature child and then carried her off down the rocks. The young men of the village went to search for her and found her naked in the jungle at the foot of the precipice, where the Rām-huai had left her. She knew nothing about it. She recovered."

The following story gives rather a different view of the Huai:—"A man called Dailova, who may be alive now, did not know that it was time for him to perform his Sakhua sacrifice. He and his son went down to fetch 'dhan' from the jhum house, and slept there among the straw; in the night the boy, feeling cold, went into the jhum house and slept among the paddy, but Dailova covered himself up in the straw and kept warm. Towards morning two Huais came along, one of whom was called Lianthawnga, and the other, Rām-huai, called to him, 'Where are you going to, Lianthawnga?' and he replied 'I am going to Lungzawl.' Then Dailova, from under the straw, called out, 'Where are you going to, Lianthawnga?' Then the Rām-huai came into the straw and wrestled with Dailova. When they had finished wrestling it was daylight, so they ate their rice and came home, and Rām-huai followed them and wrestled with Dailova. Sometimes the Rām-huai appears as a tiger and sometimes as a man. Dailova kept on saying, 'I will wrestle again with him,' and at last he called out, 'I have conquered.' Then the Rām-huai told him that his Sakhua sacrifice was overdue and he performed it at once." In the last story the Rām-huai is represented in much the same aspect as Khuāvāng has been described to me by others, one of whom told me that once, returning from a drinking bout at the chief's house, he had found a man of huge stature sitting by his hearth, who after staring at him for a moment or two disappeared. Another, who also had been at a feast, while on his way home saw huge men with enormous heads passing through the jungle. In both these cases the narrators assured me that they were perfectly sober; in fact, one of them alleged as a reason for being sure that the figure which he saw was Khuāvāng was that, in spite of having drunk a great deal, he did not feel intoxicated. In each case the vision was followed by a severe illness.

There is a lake called "Dil," between the southern border of the Lushai Hills and the Arracan hill tracts, which was credited with being the abode of many savage Tui-huai. No hill man would go within sight of the water, and when I first went there I had great difficulty in getting men to accompany me. The story is that some foreigner visited the place once and climbed into a tree overhanging the water, whence he dropped his knife into the lake and sent one of his men down to fetch it. The diver returned without the knife, but with tales of wonderful beings beneath the water. The foreigner fired his gun into the lake, whereupon numbers of Tui-huai emerged and chased the whole party of intruders, catching and carrying off all except their leader, who made good his escape.

Every form of sickness is attributed to the influence of some Huai or other, and all tales about Huais either begin or end, "There was much sickness in our village." At the time of an epidemic there is probably some hysterical girl, such as Ziki appears to have been, whose mind has been imbued with tales of Huais, who works herself up into a frenzy and believes herself possessed of a devil. This theory receives confirmation from the facts recorded in the next chapter regarding Khawhring. Not every Huai is known by name, and the sacrifices about to be described are offered to all Huais of a particular class.

Lāshi.—Although the Lāshi are not considered as demons or divinities, yet this seems an appropriate place to deal with them. A Lushai describes them thus:—"The Lāshi folk are spirits which live in the Lur and Tān precipices. Formerly a Lushai young man went shooting alone. Beneath the Tān precipice a most beautiful Lāshi maiden was weaving, and on seeing her the youth became love-sick and could not go away, so he stayed and courted her all day, till it began to grow dark; then the Lāshi maiden, wishing to go to her house, asked him to roll up her weaving for her, but he would not. Then she said to him, 'What animal would you most like to shoot?' and on his saying an elephant she at once caused him to kill one and he bore its head back in triumph, while the Lāshi maiden and her mother rolled up the cloth and disappeared into the precipice." My informant assured me that had the young man rolled up the weaving he would never have escaped. In another tale a Lāshi youth falls in love with the daughter of a man called Lianlunga, to whom he appeared in a dream and offered to place in his tobacco box the fur of many wild animals and to enable him to shoot every animal the fur of which was in the box. In return for this Lianlunga agreed to the match, and both he and his wife were given the power of decoying wild animals. Lianlunga's wife would pinch her pig's ear, and if it made no noise Lianlunga would go out shooting and Chawntinleri, a younger sister of the Lāshi son-in-law, would drive all the animals past him, and he shot what he liked, for the Lāshi had tamed all the animals. Lianlunga, however, came to a tragic end through trying to dispense with the services of the Lāshi. He enticed a wild metna under his house and then tried to spear it through the floor, but only wounded it and the animal escaped. This offended the Lāshi, who "made the barb of an arrow come out of his heart so that he died." The Lāshi seem to be only concerned with wild animals, over whom they are believed to have complete control.

In this part I propose only to deal with the various sacrifices which play so important a part in a Lushai's existence, but the festivals described in para. 9 are, to a certain extent, religious ceremonies, and are performed with the idea of pleasing the gods. Suakhnuna explained to me, when giving the description of the Thangchhuah feasts, that Pathian resided in the sky and that these feasts were supposed to please him. Similarly, the carrying about of the effigies of their ancestors in the "mi-thi-rawp-lam" is supposed to be acceptable to the spirits of the departed. In these feasts I think we may safely trace the rude beginnings of the magnificent pageants performed by the Manipuris and called by them "Lai-harauba"—*i.e.*, "Pleasing the god." Before describing the various sacrifices it is necessary to explain some of the terms used. **4. Religious rites and ceremonies.**

Hrilh closely approximates to the Naga "Genna." The meaning is that those to whom it applies must do no work, except necessary household tasks, and must not leave a prescribed area. The "hrilh" may apply to the whole village or only to the household of the performer of the sacrifice, and the area in which those under "hrilh" are allowed to move about may be either their own house and garden, or the village limits.

Sherh.—This term is used to describe the portions of the animal sacrificed, which are reserved for the god or Huai. These portions vary slightly in different sacrifices, but, generally speaking, they are the extremities and some of the internal organs, such as the heart, liver, or entrails. In every case the extremities are included. I believe the Khasis offer these to the "thlen."[1] I have found the Manipuri iron-workers when about to work a new deposit, also offer the hair from the end of the tail and from the fetlocks, and a little blood drawn from the ear of the buffalo, to the local god. Having become Hindus, they can no longer kill the animal as their forefathers did, but still make this offering of the "sherh." "Sherh" is also used in the sense of tabu. Thus a house in which a sacrifice has

[1] *Vide* p. 99 of Colonel P. R. Gurdon's Monograph on the Khasi People.

been performed may be said to be "sherh," meaning that no one outside the household may enter it. Portions of the animal killed are kept for certain periods, during this time are "sherh," and cannot be touched by outsiders. A woman is "sherh," for some days after her confinement, and during that time must not go to the water supply.

Thiang-lo is translated by the missionaries as "unlawful," but I think "unlucky" more exactly represents the meaning, which is that a certain act will be followed by some misfortune to the doer.[1]

The sacrifices made by Lushais may be divided into eight classes.

1. *Săkhua.*—A sacrifice to the guardian spirit of the clan or family.
2. *Khăl.*—These are sacrifices to Huai supposed to frequent the village and houses.
3. *Daibawl.*—These are to propitiate the Huai in the jungle, streams, and mountains.
4. Various sacrifices in case of sickness.
5. Sacrifices to cure barrenness in women.
6. *Nao-hri.*—These sacrifices should be performed once in a lifetime in a particular order.
7. Sacrifices connected with hunting and killing animals.
8. Sacrifices connected with jhuming.

1. Săkhua. From the chant given below a good idea is obtained of what the word "Săkhua" means to the Lushais.

Each clan has a special chant or invocation, and though in almost every case the animal sacrificed is a big sow, yet the method and place of the sacrifice and the disposal of the "sherh" vary in each clan, and uniformity in this respect is looked on as proof positive that two families belong to the same clan.

Among the Lushei clans the sacrifice must be performed by a pui-thiam of the clan, and the pig is killed outside the house, but is brought in to be cooked and eaten. The legs and ribs have to be kept for three days above the rafters, and during this

[1] Compare Major Playfair's *The Garos*, page 114, where the word "marang" is said to have the meaning of "unlucky" and "unlawful."

time they are "sherh," and if they are touched by anyone of another family, someone of the household performing the sacrifice will suffer in some way, unless another pig is quickly killed. The skull of the animal is hung on the centre post inside the house. The sacrifice is generally made about once in four years, unless the pui-thiam advises the performance more frequently on account of sickness. The following is the chant or invocation used by the pui-thiam at this sacrifice Each invocation begins and ends with a long drawn out note. The refrain "And accept, &c.," is repeated after each line.

Ah—h. Arise from the village. Aw—w.
And accept our sacrifice.
Ah—h. Arise from the open spaces in the village. Aw—w,
And accept our sacrifice.
Ah—h. Arise from your dwelling places. Aw—w.
Ah—h. Arise from the paths. Aw—w.
Ah—h. Arise from the gathering mists. Aw—w.
Ah—h. Arise from the yam plots. Aw—w.
Ah—h. Arise from Bualchuam hill. Aw—w.
Ah—h. Arise from Khawkawk hill. Aw—w.
Ah—h. Arise from Buhmām hill. Aw—w.
Ah—h. Arise from above the road. Aw—w.
Ah—h. Arise from below the hill. Aw—w.
Ah—h. Arise from Vāhlit hill. Aw—w.
Ah—h. Arise from Muchhip hill. Aw—w.

The spirits of three more hills are invoked.

Ah—h. Arise from the new village site. Aw—w.
Ah—h. Arise from the shelf over the hearth. Aw—w.
Ah—h. Arise from the village. Aw—w.
Ah—h. Arise from the floor. Aw—w.
Ah—h. Arise from the earth. Aw—w.
Ah—h. Spirits prayed to by our ancestors,
Accept our sacrifice.
Bless Luta's spirit (the householder's name),
Bless us with sons, bless us with daughters,
Bless us while in bed, bless us round the hearth.
Make us to flourish like a sago palm,

Make us to flourish like a hai tree.
Bless us while the sun shines,
Bless us while the moon shines.
May those above bless us, may those below us bless us.
Guard us from our enemies, guard us from death.
Favour us with flesh. (May we have success in the chase.)
Favour us with the produce of the jungle.
For ten, for a hundred years bless us.
Bless us in killing man, bless us in shooting animals,
Bless us in cultivating our jhums, bless us in cultivating the beans.
Guard us in the presence of men, guard us in the presence of animals. Bless us in our old age,
Bless us when our heads are bowed down.
Guard us from the spear, guard us from the dah.
Those whom our grandmothers worshipped guard us,
Those whom our grandfathers worshipped guard us.
Bless us in spite of the faults in this our chant,
Bless us in spite of the faults in this our worship."

Bualchuam hill is the hill in which the first men built their first village, Buhmām the hill on which the first bird's nest was built by a crow. The other hills mentioned give a clue to the village sites of the first Lushei chiefs. The omission of a prayer to be preserved from the danger of gunshots shows that the chant has remained unaltered in spite of the gun having superseded the dah and the spear.

2. Khāl. There are many sorts of Khāl. The following are some of the most important.

Vok-te-Khāl.—A small pig killed near the head of the parents' sleeping platform, flesh cooked inside the house, and the skull hung over the sleeping place. The sherh consisting of the heart and liver and fat, are kept for the night in a pot with salt and rice and then thrown away. The day of the sacrifice and the night following are "hrilh" for the household.

Ar-Khāl.—Similar to the Vok-te, but a red cock is killed, and instead of the head, the long feathers from above the tail, called "fep" by the Lushais, are strung on a cane and hung over the parents' sleeping place. The sherh, consisting of the head, feet, heart and liver, and wings, are placed in a small basket and thrown away in the morning.

Kel-Khāl.—A goat is killed in a place where the water tubes are kept; its flesh is cooked inside the house. The sherh are hung on a cane in the front verandah. The hrilh lasts three days, and during that time no intercourse must be held with strangers, nor must any of the household enter the forge.

These three sacrifices should always be performed soon after marriage, but poor persons postpone them till ill-health shows that the Huais will wait no longer. Dreams are also the means of notifying when a Khāl should be performed. If a person dreams of a beautiful stranger of the opposite sex who laughs constantly, then the Vok-te-Khāl should be performed, and if the dream is repeated often Ar-Khāl must follow or the dreamer will certainly get ill. Should a tiger bite the dreamer, Kel-Khāl is most urgently needed, and if not performed the dreamer will certainly die. Persons who dream this dream are so frightened that they will not leave their houses after dark, nor stir beyond the village during the day, for fear of a tiger seizing them.

Vān-chung-Khāl.—A white cock is killed on the hearth and the flesh cooked inside the house. The sherh are placed in a winnowing basket on the top shelf over the hearth with salt and a little rice taken from the pot before anyone has eaten. The next morning it is thrown away. Hrilh only for one night.

Khāl-chuang or *Mei-awr-lo.*—"Tail not worn"—because it is not obligatory for the performer to wear the tail on a string round his neck as is is done in Kel-Khāl.

A goat is killed as in Kel-Khāl and the sherh are treated in the same way, but the flesh must not be cooked till the next day, and it is "thiang-lo" to eat "thei-hai" fruit. Though this sacrifice is so very similar to the Kel-Khāl, yet it is considered more efficacious.

3. Daibawl.

The commonest of these is "Tui-leh-rām" (water and land). This sacrifice has to be performed at the outskirts of the village. It is to appease the demons inhabiting the woods and the streams.

A cock and hen are killed. Three bamboos are brought; of these "theibial" are made, which are pieces of bamboo about four inches long stuck into the ground. A small basket called "maichām" is also made, and some small square mats called "lengleh" made of a thin strip of bamboo bent round and round itself and kept in position by lacings of black and red threads. These are hung from small pieces of bamboo stuck into the theibial. The fowls' throats are cut and the blood allowed to flow on the maichām and theibial. Then three small stones are brought from the nearest stream and a shallow hole is dug at the place of sacrifice and lined with a wild plantain leaf. In this some water is poured and the stones and the sherh are placed in the water. The fowls' flesh may be cooked and eaten either on the spot or in the house.

Bawl-pui.—This is a very important sacrifice, which is seldom performed and only after all others have been tried. Two small clay figures are made, one to represent a man and the other a woman. These are called "rām-chawm."

The female figure has a petticoat of "hnahtial" (a plant which has tough leaves used for wrapping up food to be taken on a journey), and is made to bite the pig's liver.

The male figure is provided with a pipe and a necklace of the liver of the pig which is sacrificed. A small bamboo platform is made, and on it is put a clay model of a gong and other household utensils, and sometimes of mithan.

The pig's throat is cut and the blood allowed to flow over the platform, &c.

The pig's flesh is cooked on the spot. To take it into the house is "thianglo." Many persons come and eat it with the puithiam. If the patient does not die during the performance of the sacrifice or during the subsequent feast he will undoubtedly recover.

4. Various sacrifices in case of sickness.

Kāngpuizām.—This is a very important and efficacious sacrifice, and can only be performed by a certain wise man of the Khawtlang or Vuite clans. It costs Rs. 40/- besides the cost of the animals killed and zu drunk. In front of the house a sort of arbour is made of grass and boughs supported on four sticks. All round this are hung little balls made of split cane rolled up tight. This split cane is said to be much liked by the devils. All round the house strands of cane are stretched, the ends being tied to the arbour. The devils are supposed to be unable to pass these canes, so that the sorcerer has no fear of the devils who are already inside the house being assisted by recruits from the outside. Drinking of zu and reciting of charms goes on during the day, and after dark the sorcerer and his assistants get up on the roof of the sick man's house and commence marching up and down reciting charms and ordering the devils to leave the man, and offering them asylum in the bodies of a goat, pig, and dog which they carry with them. After some shouting and firing of a gun the party sit down on the roof over the front entrance of the house, and the sorcerer commences a long incantation over each of the animals in turn, beating them and stamping on them. Then some of the party come down and the rest retire to the back of the house, and each of the animals is brought in turn from the far end of the house, being made to walk on its hind legs to the front, and then is thrown down on to the entrance platform. Lastly a big bough is carried from the back of the house along the roof and fixed in a hole through the roof over the entrance. From this bough a cane is stretched to the arbour. Then all the rest of the party come down, and after many incantations and much shouting the animals are sacrificed and eaten by the sorcerer and his assistants, the usual useless portions being hung up in the arbour for the devils, who are supposed to have been driven either into the animal or along the cane into the arbour.

Ui-hring.—A full-grown dog or bitch is killed on the entrance platform and its flesh is cooked in front of the house. Blood is put on the sick man's wrist, inside his elbow joint, on his forehead, on his chest, at the back of the knee and ankle. Sherh and head are hung up on a post.

Hring-ai-tān.—Similar, but a different charm is muttered and the heart is roasted and eaten. The house is "sherh" for one day, leaves being hung in front of the door to warn outsiders. One day's hrilh is observed.

Khuavàng-hring.—Puithiam decides what animal shall be killed, and the sacrifice takes place on a platform before the house, the flesh being cooked in the street. Sherh and head are hung on a post in a small basket.

Thlako (The Calling of the Spirit).—Sometimes a Lushai returning from a shooting expedition experiences a sudden feeling of fear near the water supply, and on reaching his house feels ill and out of sorts. He then realises that he has lost one of his "thlarau," or souls, in the jungle. So he calls in the puithiam and requests him to call back the wanderer. The puithiam then hangs the head of a hoe on to the shaft of a spear and goes down to the water spring chanting a charm and calling on the spirit to return. As he goes the iron hoe head jingles against the iron butt of the spear and the spirit hears the noise and listens. The puithiam returns from the spring to the house still chanting and calling, and the spirit follows him, but should the puithiam laugh or look back the spirit is afraid and flies back to the jungle.

Epidemics.—The appearance of cholera, or any similar disease, is the signal for the evacuation of the village. The sick are abandoned and the people scatter, some families taking up their abode in the jhum huts, others building huts in the jungle. The neighbouring villages close their gates to all coming from the infected neighbourhood, and to terrify the Huai, who is supposed to be responsible for the epidemic, a gateway is built across the road leading to the stricken villages, on the sides and arch of which rude figures of armed men made of straw with wooden spears and dahs are placed. A dog is sacrificed and the sherh are hung on the gateway.[1]

5. Sacrifices to remove barrenness in women.

Chhim.—This is generally performed if a woman does not become enceinte in the first year of married life. A white hen has to be caught just as it has laid an egg, but as this is a somewhat difficult feat, and as the demons, though malevolent, are supposed to be easily imposed upon, a white hen is often caught and put into a nest basket with an egg and fastened there till the puithiam arrives and says, "Oh, ho! so your hen has laid an egg!" Then the hen is killed at the head of the sleeping platform (khumpi), under which the sherh are placed in a basket till sunrise next morning, when they are thrown away. The flesh is cooked on the hearth and eaten.

[1] For a somewhat similar instance of trying to ward off cholera, *vide* Khasi Monograph, p. 35.—P. R. G.

Nu-hrih.—A black fowl is killed and eaten as in the "Chhim" sacrifice. The sherh are wrapped in a wild plantain before being placed under the bed in a basket. They are thrown away in the morning. The feathers are bound with the thread used for tying the woman's hair and hung on the wall opposite the fireplace. Whether the couple cohabit on this night or not is immaterial.

The following sacrifices are performed some time during life, whenever a person is unwell. If a person keeps well they will not be made. Rich people often go through the whole course for their children as a precautionary measure. The sacrifices are done in the following order:— **6. Nao-hri.**

1. *Hmar-phir.*—Cock and hen killed on entrance ladder.
2. *Hmarchung.*—Cock killed on entrance ladder.
3. *Hmarkhat.*—Hen killed on entrance ladder.
4. *Vawk-te-luilam.*—Small pig killed outside house.
5. *Ui-te-luilam.*—Puppy killed outside house.
6. *Zinhnawn.*—Puppy killed outside house.
7. *Zin-thiang.*—Puppy killed outside house.
8. *Ui-ha-awr.*—Dog killed in front of platform, tooth worn round neck.

Kongpui Shiam (*Making a Big Road*).—This ceremony is supposed to make successful hunting probable; it also foretells the result. It is performed before a large hunting party starts and also annually about April. **7. Sacrifices connected with hunting and killing animals.**

TRANSLATION OF LUSHAI ACCOUNT.

"As soon as it gets dusk two men and the puithiam go a short way down the road which leads out of the village southwards taking a small pig with them, and there they make a fire, and kill the pig and cook its flesh. They drink some zu which they have brought with them in a gourd and also eat the flesh of the pig. Presently they say no one is to come this way, and the puithiam sweeps a place in the middle of the road and places some of the ashes from the fire there, and sings this magic chant:—

"'Animals come, animals of the Ri lake come, animals of the Champhai come, animals from the village come, animals of Aizawl come, you with the white tusks, you with the standing manes (bears), you with the branching horns come.'

"Then, picking up some small stones and putting them in their haversacks, they return. As they are about to enter the chief's house, they say, 'We are bringing men's and animals' heads.' The upas who are collected in the chief's house ask, 'Are you friends or enemies?' 'We are friends,' they reply. Then they open the door and put the stones which they have brought into a basket, and as they enter they are given zu."

The next day is "hrilh" for the whole village. In the morning, early, they go to look at the ashes, and are supposed to be able to see the likeness to footmarks in them, and thus to what animals will be killed in the chase. If a man's foot marks are seen, it is unfortunate, and a man will be killed.

Ai.—In order that a person after death may gain possession of the spirits of the men or wild animals he has killed here below, it is necessary for him to sacrifice a mithan, goat, or pig. This is called "Ai." After this feast, before the skull can be placed in the front verandah, a religious ceremony has to be performed by the puithiam. This is called "Sa-lu-an-chhuang" —*i.e.*, "Hoist the head of the wild animal." A small white fowl is given to him and the skull of the animal is placed in front of him. He then takes some zu in his mouth and spits it out over the skull, and, after muttering a charm in so low a tone that no one can hear him, he strikes the skull with the head of the chicken. If some of the feathers stick on the skull it is very lucky. After this the skull can be put up. As is stated further on, the Lushais believe that the spirit of a dead man cannot pass to Mi-thi-khua unless some animals are killed. These have to be provided by the heir, and no greater objection can be urged against a claim to inherit than a failure to provide the funeral sacrifice. This explains the reason of the Ai ceremony; the performer thereby enables the spirit of the dead animal to pass to Mi-thi-khua and in return acquires power over it. No Ai has to be performed for tame animals, presumably because they are the property of the slayer already. The word "Ai" has many meanings—among them are "to fascinate," "to obtain power over"; and there is also a plant of that name, which in one of the folk tales is said to have the magical property of driving away any evil spirit at which it is pointed.

The Ai of a man requires the sacrifice of a mithan and a small pig. If an enemy is killed and no Ai performed the slayer is very likely to go mad.

If you perform the Ai you can take your enemy with you (as a slave) when you die; if you do not perform the Ai you cannot do so, and the spirit of your deceased enemy will haunt you in this life.

Translation of a Lushai Account of the Sakei-Ai.

"When Bengkhawia's village was at Thenzawl, a tiger beset the village and in one day killed a mithan and two goats. The crier called on the people to surround it, and they did so. Thangbawnga shot it and performed the Ai ceremony; the night before he must not sleep. A young man cut its tail off; he also must keep awake all night. The next day he performed the Ai ceremony, sacrificing a mithan. Thangbawnga, who was performing the Ai, dressed himself up as a woman, smoked a woman's pipe, wore a woman's petticoat and cloth, carried a small basket, spun a cotton spindle, wore ivory earrings, let his hair down, and wrapped a mottled cloth, which was said to be of an ancient pattern, round his head as a turban. A crowd watched him and yelled with laughter, but it would have been 'thianglo' for him to laugh. Presently he took off his turban and carried it in the basket. Then he took off his woman's disguise and dressed himself as a man, and strapped on a fighting dah and carried a gun. He also took 'sailungvar' (white flints) and put them into the tiger's mouth while he ate eggs. 'You eat the sailungvar,' he said; 'who will swallow them the quicker?' 'I have out-swallowed you, you have not swallowed yours; I have swallowed mine. You go by the lower road; I will go by the upper. You will be like the lower southern hills; I shall be like the high northern ones. You are the brave man of the south; I am the brave man of the north,' he said, and cut the tiger's head three times with his dao. Then the men buried the body of the tiger outside the village." If the tiger has killed men, his eyes are gouged out with skewers or needles and thrown away; it is "thianglo" for the performer to laugh, so he holds a porcupine in his arms, and if he laughs by accident they say, "The porcupine laughed." The idea of the performer disguising himself as a woman is that the spirit of the dead tiger may be humbled, thinking that it has been shot by a woman; and the giving of the flints while the performer eats eggs is to show the power of the performer over the the tiger, as he eats the eggs easily, while the tiger is unable to chew the flints.

Haohuk Ai.—The Ai of a "haohuk," or gibbon, means a feast given to all who care to attend. Twenty pots of zu are required, but they are of a small size. A pig has to be killed and eaten. This Ai is especially necessary because of the superstition connected with the killing of these animals, which will be found in Chapter V.

8. Sacrifices connected with jhuming. *Lohman.*—When the jhum house has been completed, the sacrifice has to be performed by the owner of the jhum. The puithiam has to be called and two fowls killed by him. A small hole is dug in the ground under the house and lined with plantain leaves and then filled with water, and three small stones are dropped in. The puithiam cuts the throats of the fowls, allowing the blood to fall into the hole. The sherh are then cut off and hung under the house, and the rest of the flesh is cooked and eaten in the jungle. The next day is hrilh. The first day after this on which they work, some rice and vegetables are placed on the top of one of the posts of the house platform as an offering to the Rām-huai.

Fānodawi.—The chief prepares zu in his house. Puithiam and two upas go just outside the village on the road to the jhum and sacrifice a cock, and its wings are hung on either side of the road and the sherh are placed in the middle of the road. Next day is hrilh; no one goes out of the village except to carry water. This is to make grain fill in the ear, and is performed in July.

5. Priesthood. There is no regular priesthood; the nearest approach to priests are the puithiam (great knowers). These men pretend to be able, by feeling a sick man's pulse, to tell which sacrifice is needed. The only training necessary is to commit to memory the various "hla," or charms, which have to be muttered while performing the sacrifices. Any man who thinks he has a call

can acquire these from a puithiam on payment of a fee of a few rupees. His success in his calling appears largely to depend on luck.

There is generally one puithiam appointed by the chief, but there is no limit to the number there may be in a village. As has been said, the important Sakhua sacrifice requires the presence of a puithiam of the clan concerned, but other sacrifices can be performed by a puithiam of any clan. The services of a puithiam are not given gratis. For performing those connected with cultivation he receives a basket of rice; for other sacrifices he receives sums varying from a rupee up to ten rupees, but for some it is not customary to take payment, and the fees depend chiefly on the position of the person who has to pay them, as the puithiam, on the principle that half a loaf is better than no bread, will generally perform a sacrifice and take what he can get rather than get nothing. For the more important sacrifices, the fees, however, are always higher.

6. Ceremonies connected with child birth.

The particular sacrifices to be performed in connection with a child's birth vary considerably in different clans and families. Within seven days of the birth, the sacrifice known as the "Arte-luilam," consisting of a cock and a hen killed just outside the house, must be made; till this is done the woman cannot go to the spring and is "sherh," and had better not leave the house.

Should the woman not observe the custom the child will suffer in health. Three days after the birth of a child a small chicken and seven small packets of rice and vegetables are suspended under the edge of the front verandah. This is called "arte-hring-ban" or "khaw-hring-tir." The object is to satisfy the "khawhring" (*see* Chapter V, para 12) and prevent it entering the child.

If a woman has difficulty in bringing forth, a fowl is killed and divided equally. The portion with the head is put at the upper end of the village with seven pieces of cane rolled into bundles, the other half at the lower end of the village with five rolls of cane, and the woman is given a little water to drink. This is called "arte-pum-phelna"—*i.e.*, "to open the stomach with a fowl."

For seven days after a child's birth its spirit is supposed not to be quite at home in the little body and to spend some of its time perched like a bird on the parents' bodies and clothes, and therefore, for fear of injuring it, the parents keep as quiet as possible for these seven days. If either of the parents works during these seven days and a red rash appears on the child, the illness is called "borh," and the cure, which is called "borh keo," is as follows:—A certain creeper called "vomhrui" is brought and coiled round and round, forming a sort of cylinder, and into this the child is dipped three times. This is done at night after the fire is out, and no fire can be lit again till morning.

Two days after the birth of a child its parents give a big drink to their friends and relatives—this is called "nau"—and seven days later another big feast is given. Some families give the name at the first feast, some at the second. The proper custom is for the "pu" to name the child, but nowadays parents generally do this.

Should several children have died young, the parents will carry the next baby and deposit it in a friend's house, and then come and ask, "Have you a slave to sell," and purchase it for a small sum. This is supposed to deceive the Huais. Such children's names always begin with Suak,[1] and, judging from the frequency with which such names are met, the custom must be a very common one.

It is thought good to appoint a "pu." The pu kills a pig and a fowl and eats it with his friends. Some of the "fep" of the fowl are tied round the child's neck. The pu is a general protector, and he only can get the "pushum" of a girl. He also receives the "lukawng" (see Part 8). Should a woman die in childbirth, it was considered unlucky for another woman to rear the child, which was buried alive with its mother.

There are no ceremonies connected with attaining the age of puberty. A boy simply joins the young men in the zawlbuk. After this it is considered unlucky to cut the hair.

7. Marriage ceremonies. A young Lushai as a rule chooses his own bride, but the arrangements are made by the parents. The would-be bridegroom's parents select two male friends, called "palai," who go to the parents of the selected girl and arrange matters. If the

[1] "Suak" or "Suok" in most old Kuki dialects and in Thado means a slave.

parents are agreeable the palai go on another day with zu, and the girl's parents brew zu. The price to be paid is fixed by custom, as before explained, but the amount to be paid down has to be settled by negotiation, and this is often a long business, the palai urging the poverty of the bridegroom's family, while the bride's parents try to fix the sum as high as possible. When this difficulty has been overcome the palai go again with zu, and the girl's parents also provide zu. On that day the girl is escorted by her friends to the house of the bridegroom's parents. This is called "Loi." As they pass through the village all the children pelt them with dirt, but on arrival they are welcomed with brimming cups of zu, and the bridegroom says to the bride, "Oh! your cloth is dirty," and gives her a new one. After some time the bridegroom produces a fowl, and this is killed by the puithiam, who says certain charms while doing so. This fowl is called "rem ār"—*i.e.*, "the fowl of agreement"—and directly it is killed the bride and bridegroom pledge each other in zu. Then the bride and her young friends retire, while the rest of the party remain and have a great feast, consuming the "rem ār," and also the fowls and zu, which the bridegroom receives from the bride's aunt, pu, thian, and pālāl. The next day towards evening, the bridegroom's mother or other elderly female relative goes to the bride's house accompanied by two or three young girls, and they escort the bride to her husband's house and hand her over to him. The young companions of the bridegroom sometimes amuse themselves by collecting a number of fowls under the house, tying she-goats up in the verandah, while the kids are tied at the far end of the village, and throw stones at the house throughout the night, so that the happy couple get but little sleep. This is called "Ingaithlak." On the following morning the bride returns to her mother's house, and for some time, occasionally for several weeks, the bride will spend her days at her mother's house, only going to her husband's after dark.

Different clans have different methods of disposing of their dead. The following is the custom of all true Lusheis, whenever the means of the deceased's family are sufficient to meet the expenses. 8. Funerals.

Directly after death the corpse is washed, the hair dressed carefully, and then the body is attached to a bamboo frame, placed in a sitting position, and adorned with fine raiment, necklaces, &c.; if the deceased was a man his gun, dao, &c., are put near him. In Lushei families the corpse is put on the floor at the head of the kumpui. In other clans it is placed against the wall on one side. If the family be rich a mithan, a pig, a dog, and a goat are killed, but at least one of these must be killed. The flesh is then cooked in anticipation of the arrival of the friends and neighbours who are invited to a funeral feast, "Rāl," which is kept up with singing and drinking till the evening of the next day. Food and drink are offered at intervals to the corpse. The spirits of the animals killed are supposed to accompany the soul of the deceased to Mi-thi-khua. If these animals are not killed the soul of the deceased will either not reach Mi-thi-khua, or if it does will be very poorly off there. So far there is not much difference between the Lushei custom and that of other clans. The other clans, on the evening of the day after the death, bury the deceased outside the house, without any particular ceremony. The nearest male relative makes a short farewell speech wishing the deceased a pleasant journey and asking him to prepare things for those who have to follow him. With a man are buried his pipe, haversack, and flint and steel; with a woman only the two first. As regards the burying of food and drink and weapons the custom varies, but it is generally done.

The Lusheis, however, prefer not to bury their dead. The body is placed in a box made by hollowing out a log, a slab of wood is placed over the opening, and the joint plastered up with mud. This rough sort of coffin is placed in the deceased's house near to the wall. A bamboo tube is passed up through the floor and through a hole in the bottom of the coffin and into the stomach of the corpse. The other end is buried in the ground. A special hearth is made close to the coffin and a fire is kept burning day and night on this for three months, and during the whole of this time the widow of the deceased, if he leaves one, must sit alongside the coffin, over which are hung any valuables owned by the deceased. About six weeks after placing the corpse in the coffin, the latter is opened to see if the destruction of the corpse is proceeding properly, and if necessary the coffin is turned round so as to present the other side to the fire. The opening of the coffin is celebrated by the killing of a pig and the usual drink, and is known either as "en-lawk" or looking, examining.

When it is thought that everything but the bones has been destroyed, the coffin is opened and the bones removed. The skull and the larger bones are removed and kept in a basket, which is placed on a special shelf opposite the hearth. The remainder of the bones are collected and buried generally in an earthenware pot.

On the occasion of the final opening of the coffin—"khuang pai," "throwing away coffin"—it is customary for chiefs to kill a mithan; lesser people are content with the usual drink. Few Lusheis, except chiefs, can afford the expense incurred in this method of disposing of their dead, and in such cases the body is simply buried. It is customary for relations and friends of the deceased to send animals to be killed in his honour, and the spirits of these are supposed to belong to the spirit of the deceased in the Mi-thi-khua.

The skulls of all animals killed on such occasions are placed on poles round the grave if the body has been buried. If the body has not been buried, the heads will be placed on poles round the "lung dawh," or platform erected in memory of the deceased. These "lung dawh," in most cases, are merely a rough platform of logs placed beside the road just outside the village, but in the case of chiefs and of men who have killed men in war, the platform is built of stones. A big upright stone is placed in the centre, and on this various figures are roughly outlined, representing the deceased and sometimes his wife and children and the various animals he has killed. An indiarubber-tree is very often planted by a chief's grave. Sometimes a person who either has no near relatives, or who mistrusts those he or she has, will get the young men of the village to build the lung dawh during his or her lifetime.

An aged couple with no relatives expended all they had on a feast to the young men who brought and set up a big stone. The old people were carried in sitting on the stone and cheerfully superintended the feast, and a month later peacefully departed this life.[1]

Hlamzuih.—If the first child in a family dies shortly after birth, it is buried without any ceremony under the house, and it is called "hlamzuih" (hlam = after birth, zuih = to follow). Should other children subsequently die, however young they be, they will be honoured with a complete funeral. It will be remembered that the hlamzuih are exempt from being shot by Pupawla. (See above, page 62).

Lukawng.—On a person's death a sum, varying from Rs. 2/- to Rs. 20/- according to family custom, has to be paid by his heir to the pu of the deceased (see para. 6). A chief generally claims the "lukawng" of all his boi.

Sār-thi.—Deaths from accidents, in childbirth, or those caused by wild animals, or in war are termed "sār-thi," and the corpse must not be buried within the village; in some cases the corpse must not even be brought into the village, if the death occurred outside. Even if the corpse is brought into the village, it is often not allowed into a house, but deposited in the forge. In such cases no lukawng can be demanded. Should the injured person survive for any considerable time, the death will not be called sār-thi unless the person has been wounded by a tiger. The fact that tigers eat men is given as the reason for this. The graves of persons killed by tigers are watched by the young men of the village for several nights, lest the tigers, or their elder brothers the wild cats, should come and dig up the body.

In-thian, Thi-thin.—Three months after a death a small chicken is killed and placed with some rice on the shelf which runs along the wall. The family indulge in zu. This is apparently a sort of farewell to the soul.

9. Festivals. There are three feasts connected with the crops. They are all known as "Kut." The first is called "Chāp-chār-kut"; it is the most important of the three, and is held after the jhums are burnt, about the time of sowing, and is never omitted. It lasts three or four days. On the first day a pig is killed by each

[1] Can the fear of his heirs neglecting to put up a memorial stone have originated the "stone hauling" customs so distinctive of Maram and Angami Nagas?

householder who can afford it and zu is drunk. On the second day, about 4 p.m., the whole population gathers in the open space in the village, dressed in its best. Everyone brings platters of rice, eggs, and flesh, and tries to force the food down the throats of their friends. After dark the young men and girls collect in houses of well-to-do people with several daughters and dance "Chai" till daylight.

The Chai consists in all the young men sitting with their backs to the walls, each with a girl sitting between his knees with her back to him. Individual performers dance in the middle, the remainder singing and clapping hands. On the third day the young men and girls collect in the centre of the village and form a circle, every girl being between two youths, whose arms cross over her neck, holding in their hands cloths which hang down behind like a curtain. Inside the circle is a drummer or gong-beater, who chants continuously, the young people taking up the refrain, and treading a slow measure in time with the song, while cups of zu are brought to them in rotation. Fourth day, "Zuting-ni." The performance is repeated again if the liquor holds out.

In villages where there are many Rālte,[1] they kill their pigs the next day after the Lusheis and the other ceremonies are postponed one day.

Mim-kut.—Named after the maize, as it takes place when the crop ripens. It is of but little importance and seems likely to die out. Cakes of Job's tears are eaten and the next day is "hrilh."

Pawl-kut.—Held at harvest time. Fowls are killed and children, dressed in their finest clothes, are fed with the flesh mixed with rice and eggs. The next day is "hrilh."

The correct performance of the Chāp-chār-kut is thought to go far towards insuring a good crop for the year.

Thang-chhuah Feasts.—The feasts which an aspirant for the honours of Thang-chhuah must give are five in number and have to be given in the order named, as they involve considerable expenditure, but not within any specified time.

1. *Chong.*—The feast lasts four days, the first of which is called "In-chhia-shem-ni," (day for repairing the house). The floor in

[1] The Rālte clan is described in Part II, Chap. II.

the house is strengthened to make it safe for the large number of guests. The labourers receive a liberal allowance of zu in payment for their trouble. The second day is called "Zu-pui-ni," from the large amount of zu that is drunk. The next day —"Rawi-ni"—two boars and a sow are killed and there is a great feast. The last day is known as "Chang-do-ni," and on it the remains of the feast are finished up.

2. *She-doi*—The feast only lasts three days. The first day is "In-chhia-shem-ni," the second is known as "She-shun-ni" (mithan slaughter day), and a mithan is killed and eaten. The third day, known as "Sa-ru-che-u-ni," is similar to Chong-do-ni.

3. *Mi-thi-rawp-lām.*—Three months before the day fixed for the feast all the young men and girls of the village start cutting firewood, for cooking the flesh of the animal to be killed. A cane is stretched along from tree to tree beside one of the main approaches to the village for some 500 yards, and against this on alternate sides are rested the billets so that they may be thoroughly dry by the time they are needed. As a reward the young people receive a he-goat and a sow, which they consume with much merry-making, the skulls being placed on posts at each end of the line of billets. This collection of wood is called "sa-thing-zār" (flesh-wood-hangout). The actual feast lasts four days, which are known by the same names as in the "Chong" and are spent in much the same way, but on the Rawi-ni, besides the slaying and eating of mithan, effigies, supposed to represent their deceased relatives, are made and attired in the finest cloths and adorned with the best necklaces. These are strapped on a square bamboo framework, in the centre of which on a tall pole is an effigy supposed to represent the progenitor of the clan. The oldest living member of the clan then comes slowly from his house, bringing with him a gourd of zu, and gives each effigy in turn a little zu, muttering a charm as he does so; he arranges his tour so as to reach his own father's effigy last, and when he has muttered his charm and given it the zu he dashes the gourd down on the ground and, bursting into tears, rushes into his house, whence he must not emerge for a month. The effigies are then carried about the village with much shouting.

This carrying about of their effigies is supposed to be very pleasing to the spirits of the ancestors, and it is evident that the people consider that these spirits are able to influence them for good or for bad, though I have never had this view of the matter clearly explained to me. This carrying about of persons on a platform is considered an honour, and an instance of it will be found in the description of the Fa-nai. It also appears among the Aimol and Tikhup. Among the Manipuris or Meitheis the right to be carried in a "dolai," or litter, is much valued and is the prerogative of certain officials, but is sometimes granted by the Rajah as a personal distinction. The last day of the feast resembles the same day in the Chong.

4. *She-doi* as before.

5. *Khuang-choi.*—This is the greatest feast. Wood is collected three months before, as in the Mi-thi-rawp-lām, but the collectors get a mithan and a goat as their reward. The feast lasts four days, the names being the same as in the Chong. On the Rawi-ni at least three mithan must be killed. The Khuang-choi really completes the series, and the giver can now proudly wear the Thang-chhuah cloth and have a window in his side wall, but it is considered unlucky to stop, and after some time the She-doi is performed again under the name of "Tlip," followed in the course of a year or so by "Zānkhuān," a four days' feast similar to the Chong, but one or two mithan are killed. If the fortunate man's life is prolonged he will continue repeating these two feasts alternately. A man who has twice celebrated a Khuang-choi is allowed to build a raised summer house called "zao" a short distance in front of his living house.

After slaying a mithan in any of these feasts the giver of the feast is subject to various restrictions. Till he has performed the "In-thian" ceremony, he may not leave the house nor talk to anyone from another village. In some cases his movements are not so closely restricted, but he must in no case cross running water. I am told that should he infringe these rules his Sakhua would be offended and he or his family would get ill. The "In-thian" ceremony is performed some forty or fifty days after the killing of the mithan, and consists in the sacrificing of a cock. The prohibition of conversing with strangers is generally enforced only for three or four days, but on no account must they be allowed inside the house.

The skulls of mithan killed on these occasions are placed on posts to one side of the entrance to the house of the giver of the feast, and it is the highest ambition of the Lushai to have a long line of such posts in front of his house. Each post is cut out of a tree of considerable size, which is dressed until the lower 7 or 8 feet are only some 8 or 9 inches thick. Above this the tree is roughly cut into a plank some 8 or 9 inches thick, forming an irregular quadrilateral, the lower side being a foot or so long and the upper from 2 to 3 feet, while one side may be 18 inches and the other 2 feet or a little more; at each of the upper corners there is a perpendicular projection some 12 inches long terminating in a spike, a short distance below which a ring of wood is left. The skull is placed on the higher spike, while on the lower an egg is affixed by a thin peg of fir wood. This use of fir may be a survival of the time when the clan lived east of the Tyao, where fir forests are still found.

Posts are erected on similar occasions by many of the Kuki-Lushai clans. Among the Khawtlang the quadrilateral portion is only two or three feet from the ground, while the projections are far longer. Among the Vuite the custom is to put a thin straight post slightly carved on one side of the house and to plant a number of branches in a clump on the other. The Tangkhul Nagas, to commemorate the slaying of cattle, plant lines of dead trees in front of their houses.

The method of killing the mithan at these feasts is strictly laid down. After the puithiam has said a prayer, the giver of the feast stabs the animal behind the shoulder in the region of the heart, but only sufficient to draw blood. The poor beast is then despatched by other men with sharp bamboos or clubs; it must on no account be shot.

Buh-ai.—This is a feast given by a wealthy person who has had an exceptionally good harvest. It is not one of the feasts which a would-be Thangchhuah has to give, nor is there any idea of obtaining advantage in the next world, as there is in

Chief's House Showing "She Lu Pun," the Posts Supporting the Skulls of Mithan Killed at One of the Feasts.

the Ai ceremonies performed after the killing of animals or men, but it is a thank-offering for a good harvest. It is not worth performing Ai for a crop of less than 100 baskets. An old red cock and a pig are killed and much zu prepared.

There is a special pot of zu prepared on the platform in front of the house of which no one who has not performed the Buh-ai can drink, for others to drink of it is "thianglo." The person who gave the last Buh-ai feast is entitled to the first drink at this zu, which is called the "Buhza-zu" (the 100 baskets of rice zu). There is ordinary zu for the others to drink, and if it is not all finished the first day the guests return on the morrow.

The flesh of the animals killed is eaten by the guests. At night the girls and lads dance the Chai, as in the Chāp-chār-kut. To give such a feast reflects great glory on the giver and improves his standing in the village.

The Buh-ai is celebrated by nearly all the Lushai-Kuki clans and in some replaces the Thangchhuah feasts. Full particulars will be found in Part II.

CHAPTER V

FOLK-LORE

1. Legends. THERE are many tales common to all the Kuki-Lushai clans, though the names under which the various personages figure in them are not always the same. A numerous class of legends deals with the creation of the world and the first appearance of mankind thereon and other natural phenomena; another class accounts for the names of hills and rivers; a third class reminds one of Uncle Remus's tales of the doings of Brer Rabbit; but there are also a great many which are simply tales and which are generally a trifle obscene. The following are instances of the first class:—

Chhura is said to have shaped the world, beating it out fla with his mallet. There are many tales connected with Chhura some of which will be found further on. The following translation gives a Lushai's idea of an eclipse of the sun or moon:—

"Formerly the Hauhul chief swallowed the moon, having been changed during his dream into an awk, and many people were watching and said, 'The awk is swallowing the moon.' Then he awoke and his mouth was bleeding. A year later he died and his ghost was turned into an awk and went up into the sky, and the moon was full and big, and the ghost, which had been changed into an awk, could not swallow the moon, but the next day the moon was smaller and he swallowed it. Thus men knew for the first time that there was an awk."

When an eclipse occurs there is much excitement and beating of drums, &c. This is to frighten the awk, for the Lushais believe that once the awk swallowed the sun so effectually that general darkness prevailed. This awful time is called "Thimzing"—*i.e.*, the gathering of the darkness—and many awful things happened. Everything except the skulls of animals killed in the chase became alive, dry wood revived, even stones became alive and produced leaves, and so men had nothing to burn. The successful hunters who had accumulated large stocks of the trophies of their skill were able to keep alive using them as fuel, and some of their descendants still survive among the Thados, under which heading they will be found in Part II. As it was pitch dark, neither animals nor men could see at all, and tigers went about biting wildly at trees, stones, and people. A general transformation took place, men being all changed into animals. Those who were going merrily to the jhum were changed into "satbhai" (laughing thrushes), as can be known by their white heads, which represent the turbans worn by the men, and their cheery chatterings. People wearing striped cloths became tigers, the chiefs of those days being represented by the hornbills of to-day, whose bills represent the bamboo rods for stirring rice while cooking; but another version is that the chiefs became king-crows, whose long tail-feathers the chiefs value much and wear as plumes. The black hands of the gibbon prove clearly that his ancestors were dyeing thread when the Thimzing occurred. Another version ascribes the same origin to the crows. Similarly those who were carrying torches finding their way down stream beds were changed into fireflies. The Chongthu family are sometimes said to have been turned into monkeys, the Vangchhia into elephants; but another version says the elephants were old women who were wearing their "puanpui"—*i.e.*, cotton quilts—with the tufts of cotton outside. Wrestlers were suddenly transformed into bears, who to this day grapple with their foes.

The Paihte or Vuite clan became a species of squirrel, while the Rālte's ancestor was just saying, "Vaibel kan chep te ang nge?" "Shall we suck our pipes?" and was therefore changed into a sort of squirrel called "chepchepa," from the sound it is always making.

The domestic animals were changed into wild ones, but a number of large boulders in the Van-laiphai are said to represent Chhura's mithan which were grazing there at the Thimzing. After this terrible catastrophe the world was again repeopled by men and women issuing from a hole in the earth called the "Chhinglung," which appeared to me to be a disused "cache" in which some long forgotten chief used to hide his valuables on the approach of danger. Mithan reappeared from gourd seeds, as is shown by their bellow "um mu"—*i.e.*, gourd seed. Pigs issued from the Rih-lake, wherefore they come to their food when called "rih rih." Fowls were re-created from the mud, so to this day they answer to the call "chirih chirih," *i.e.*, "chir mud."

It is not quite clear how, if representatives of the different clans were changed into various animals, these same clans again issued from the Chhinglung, but our own legends are not always quite easy to follow.

The following is a translation of a Lushai account of the repeopling of the world and of a feast which is said to have taken place soon after:—

"The place whence all people sprang is called Chhinglung. All the clans came out of that place. Then two Rālte came out together, and began at once chattering, and this made Pathian think there were too many men, and so he shut down the stone. After a short time Thlāndropa was going to hold a Khuangchoi, and told them to call together all the people of the world, and when this had been done he held his Khuangchoi. They said to the sun, 'Do not shine, because we want our leader the Sā-huai (Loris) to lead us in the dance,' and the sun said, 'All right.' At that time the Sā-huai and all the animals could talk, and the bamboo rat was beating the drum, and they all danced, and in the middle of their fun the sun said, 'Oh, how I do want to look,' and shone out, and all the animals got hot, and could not dance any more, so the Sā-huai got angry and quarrelled with the sun, and won't even look at it nowadays. There was a great feast of flesh, but the owl got no meat, so he got angry, and went and sat on the bough of a tree, and Zuhrei, the big rat, chaffed him and said, 'Buka has eaten his fill.' Then the owl being still hungry, got angry and bit Zuhrei. Since that day they have been at war, and if the owl sees Zuhrei he assuredly bites him." The point of the allusion to the Rālte is that this clan is famed throughout the Hills for the loquacity of its members.

Another story connected with this feast is that Thlāndropa gave a number of presents: to the ancestor of the Poi or Chin tribes he gave a fighting dao, while the ancestor of the Lushais only received a cloth, which is the reason that the Poi tribes are braver than the Lushais. On my asking what the ancestor of the white man had received, I was told he had received the knowledge of reading and writing—a curious instance of the pen being considered mightier than the sword.

Thlāndropa appears to have been a great person in his day, for he is supposed to have received Khuavang's daughter in marriage, giving in exchange a gun, the report of which we call thunder. This legend puts Khuavang on a par with Pathian, and supports the theory that the differentiation is of comparatively recent growth.

There is a legend that the king of the Water Huai fell in love with Ngai-ti (loved one) and, as she rejected his addresses and ran away, he pursued her and surrounded the whole human race on the top of a hill called Phun-lu-buk, said to be far away to the north-east. As the water kept on rising, to save themselves the people threw Ngai-ti into the flood, which thereupon receded. It was the running off of this water which cut up the surface of the world, which Chhura had levelled, into the deep valleys and high hill ranges of which the whole world as known to the ancestors of the Lushais consisted.

As a sample of the second class of tale, the following story regarding the origin of the Tui-chong river, which joins the Kurnaphuli, near Demagri, may be taken:—

Nine miles from Demagri, on the Lungleh road, the traveller has to cross the Tui-chong river, one of the largest tributaries of the Kurnaphuli, on which Chittagong stands. This river, according to the Lushais, owes its origin to the self-denial of a girl called Tui-chongi, who, with her little sister Nuengi, was walking on the hills whence the river rises. It was April, and the sun blazed down on them. Nuengi began to cry for water. "How can I get you water on the top of a hill? Don't you know that all the springs are dry, for are not the jhums ready to be burnt?" "Water, water, or I shall die," wailed Nuengi. "Would you rather have water than me?" asked Tui-chongi.

"If I don't get water, I shall die, and then of what use would you be to me?" replied the spoilt child. So Tui-chongi, to satisfy her youngest sister's thirst, changed herself into a river, and Nuengi drank and was satisfied. But the water flowed down among the hills and burst its way into the country of the Bengalis. The king of the Bengalis was astonished to see so mighty a river flowing past his palace, and sent some of his people to find out whence it came. They journeyed many days, till at length they reached the source of the stream, and there sat Nuengi, who, now that her thirst was satisfied, would gladly have had her sister back again to show her the way home. The explorers were astonished to find so beautiful a maiden sitting thus in the middle of the jungle, and decided that it would be wise to take her back to their master, who liked pretty girls. So Nuengi was added to the harem of the king of Chittagong, and in time became the mother of a most lovely boy. The king's chief wife, on seeing the child, thought to herself, "If my lord sees this jungle woman's brat, he will assuredly love her more than me who am childless." So she had the child thrown into the river, which flowed under the palace windows, and frightened Nuengi into keeping silence on the matter. Tui-chongi, however, in spite of the change in her circumstances, remembered her little sister, and cherished the child so that he grew and throve. In the same way six more children were born and thrown into Tui-chongi's fostering arms. When they were grown up Tui-chongi told them the circumstances of their birth, and sent them to dance on the roof of their father's palace, who, hearing the noise, came out to see the cause of the disturbance. When he saw seven handsome young men he was much astonished, and asked them who they were. "We are your sons," they replied. "Why do you lie to me?" said the king; "liars have short lives in my kingdom." "Nay, O king, we lie not; we are Nuengi's sons"; and they told him their story. So the king smote off the head of the bad queen, and installed Nuengi in her place.

Of the third class the following are good examples, and admirers of Uncle Remus will be reminded of the doings of "Brer Rabbit and the other animals."

The Tale of Granddaddy Bear and the Monkey.

The Monkey made a swing and was always swinging in it. One day Granddaddy Bear saw him and said, "Oh, Monkey, let me have a swing." The Monkey replied, "Wait a minute till I have hung it more securely." Then he climbed up and bit the cane nearly through and jumped down again crying out, "Come on, Granddaddy Bear, have a swing." The bear got in and swung, the cane broke, and he fell down. The Monkey, intending to eat him, had gone and fetched some cooked rice (to eat with the bear's flesh). But though Granddaddy Bear fell down he was not killed. The Monkey, being terribly afraid, said, "Oh, Granddaddy Bear, hearing you had fallen I brought some rice for you," and gave him all he had brought.

The Bear's Water Hole.

The Bear made a dam to collect water, and put the Monkey to watch it. Every sort of animal came crying, "I am dry. Who has water which he does not want? I am dry." The Monkey always said, "The water belongs to Granddaddy Bear. If you dare to drink, drink; if you dare to suck, suck it up." Then the Tiger came along, saying, "I am dry. Who has water which he does not want? I am dry." The Monkey replied, "It is my Granddaddy Bear's water. If you dare to drink, drink; if you dare to suck, suck it up." The Tiger drank it all; he sucked the place dry. Then the Monkey went to the Bear and said, "Oh, Granddaddy Bear, the Tiger has drunk your water!" So the Bear rushed up and began to fight with the Tiger. They fought a long time and both died, and the Monkey took their bones. "Whose ever bones will sound, whether my Granddaddy the Tiger's or Granddaddy the Bear's," he said, and so, taking the bones which would sound, he made a rotchhem (see Chapter II, para. 6) out of them and he sat in the fork of a tree and played on it. The Quail, hearing the sound, came up. "Hallo, Monkey! let me play for a bit," he said. "Oh, ho!" said the Monkey, "you will fly off with the rotchhem." "If you fear that," said the Quail, "hold me by the tail." So the Monkey held him tight by the tail, and off he flew, but the Monkey pulled his tail clean out. Then the Quail came and begged for his tail, saying, "Do give me back my tail." But the Monkey replied, "You can ransom it by paying eight mithan." "Oh," said the Quail, "if I have to pay eight mithan for it, I'll just remain tailless," and flew away.

The following tale is interesting as showing the great prestige the Tipperah chief enjoyed among the Lushais, who call him "Rengpui." There are many versions of this tale, some of which are very long. I have been obliged to abridge it considerably.

Rimenhoiyi married Zawlthlia. Their house was of iron. They had an eight-fold iron door. They beautified the inside with iron and brass things. They also had a window (*i.e.*, Zawlthlia was Thangchhuah[1]) and a platform to sit on—in fact they wanted for nothing.

Rimenhoiyi planted flowers, but there was one flower she had not, called "nipuipar" (bright sun flower—a creeper with scarlet flowers). When her husband was about to go in search of it he said to her, "Please don't go outside the house," and having filled the brass vessels with enough water to last her many days, he went off. However, the supply ran short and the lady went to the stream to wash, and one of her hairs was carried down and swallowed by a fish, which was caught by the cook of the king near the mouth of the river; and from out of the fish the cook pulled this immensely long hair, and it filled a winnowing basket. The king sent for the owner of the hair, and after many episodes she was brought to him. Zawlthlia returning found his wife gone, but with the help of the domestic animals he traced her, and, on arriving at the foreign king's village he saw slaves fetching water; and, ascertaining that it was for the new queen, he put one of the nipuipar into the vessel, so Rimenhoiyi knew he had arrived. According to one version, they resorted to the same subterfuge that Abraham and Sarah employed when entering Egypt and lived happily till, the king's suspicion being aroused, Zawlthlia was summarily slain. According to another, Rimenhoiyi married them both, but as she showed a preference for Zawlthlia the king killed him.

With the help of a wise woman learned in charms Zawlthlia was brought to life in a more beautiful form, and the king was

[1] See above as to windows, page 27.

so struck by the improvement in his appearance that he asked to be allowed to undergo the same treatment, and was duly killed, but, unfortunately for him, was by some accident restored to life in the shape of a dog; but in this shape he seems to have found more favour in the fickle fair one's eyes, and a child called Uithovi was born, who, being very poor, begged for some land of Zawlthlia, who had become king of the Tipperahs, and was told to take as much as a buffalo hide measured. By cutting the hide into a very thin strip he was able to measure a considerable area of ground, but, not content with this, he voyaged far till he reached the place where money was to be found, and he became very prosperous. "Nevertheless it was said that to the present day Kumpinu (the Company's Mother—*i.e.*, the late Queen), who is a descendant of Uithovi's, cannot get the better of Rengpui (the Rajah of Tipperah). If the Sahibs fight against Rengpui, all their crops fail, and much sickness occurs among them. Pathian once threw down a cannon from the sky, and a great number of Kumpinu's sepoys tried to move it, but could not, while a few of Rengpui's men were able to drag it away."

Chhura is represented as a man of immense strength and stature, of an easy-going disposition, but not much blessed with brains. Thus one story tells of how, being on a visit, he was regaled with a crab stew, which he had not tasted before, and liked greatly. He inquired of what animal it was made. On his way home he forgot the name and commenced searching. Someone seeing him looking about asked what he had lost. "Stupid," replied Chhura; "if I knew, would I be looking?" The passer-by remarked that he smelt strongly of crab. "That's it! That's what I was searching for," cried Chhura much pleased, and went on his way. His mallet head, a roughly dressed cylinder of stone, about 30 inches long and 18 in diameter, is pointed out to the curious, lying beside the path between Leng and Lingvum, where it is said to have fallen when it flew off the handle while Chhura was flattening the earth in the Vān-lai-phai valley some five miles away. A large spherical stone in the same neighbourhood is pointed out as one of the pellets shot from his pellet bow when he was at Thenzawl, many miles distant.

There are many tales of this hero, who is especially honoured by the Khawtlang.

Mualsavata is another mythical hero of immense stature. The smoke from his pipe was like that of a jhum burning. His whetstone, some 18 inches long, lies beside the road near Chongthleng, where it fell from his haversack, which his wife had neglected to mend.

I have given so many tales in other parts of the monograph that I shall only add one more here.

The Tale of Him who Demanded His Sister's Price.

He went to the west to demand his sister's price. The debtor gave him a bamboo stirring rod. If you stirred an empty pot with this rod it was at once filled with rice. He returned towards his village. On the way he stayed the night in the house of a widow, and placed his stirring rod on the shelf over the hearth saying, "Granny, please don't stir your pot with my stirring rod." "All right," said she, but, while he was walking about the village, she stirred her pot just to see what sort of a stirring rod it was, and, behold, her pot was full of rice. "It is a very good stirring rod," she said; "I will just exchange mine for it"—which she did secretly. And the owner of the magic rod went on to his village, and on arrival there he called to his children, "Set the water boiling to cook the rice." His children replied, "We have nothing to cook. What is the use of boiling water alone?" "I have got rice, I've got rice," he said. So they boiled the water, and he stirred it hard with his rod, but nothing came. "If we stir more it will come," he said, but nevertheless nothing came.

Then he went off to demand the price from the debtor again, who gave him a goat which passed nothing but amber and cornelian beads, and said, "Take it carefully home." "All right," said he. He stayed the night at the same widow's house, and when he was going out to stroll through the village he said, "Granny, you will be careful not to kick my goat on the rump, won't you?" "All right," said she, but directly he was out of sight she kicked the goat and he passed many beads. "It is a good goat," she said, and secretly substituted her own goat for it. Her guest went off and directly he reached his house he called out, "Prepare strings for necklaces. Prepare strings for necklaces." His children replied, "Father, we have nothing to put on the strings. What is the good of the strings alone?" "I have got beads, I have got beads," he cried. So they prepared a winnowing basket full of threads. Then he gave the goat several good kicks on the rump, but it only passed filth and bleated loudly.

Then he went again to demand payment and was given a mallet and a piece of cane. "The name of this piece of cane is 'Ramdia,'" they said. He set off for home and again stayed in the same old woman's house and put Ramdia and his mallet down among the firewood, and as he started for his stroll he said, "Granny, don't touch this cane, will you? It is called Ramdia—and you won't touch the mallet either, will you?" "All right," she said, but no sooner was he gone than, saying, "They are valuable things," she touched them both. The cane wound round and round her and the mallet began to beat her. She was in terrible trouble and shouted to her neighbours; wherever she went the mallet beat her and beat her till she died.

2. Superstitions.

The Lushais are an extremely superstitious race; any unusual occurrence is considered as portending some evil results. The meaning of the word "thianglo" has been already explained in Chapter IV, para. 4. Certain acts, dreams, or sights are universally considered "thianglo," or unlucky, but should a Lushai see any unusual sight or hear an unusual sound he would at once consider that some misfortune was imminent and take advice from the puithiam as to how it could be avoided. The following are some of the superstitions connected with cultivation.

It is "thianglo" to find, in the proposed jhum, a gibbon's skull stuck on a tree stump. If in burning the jhum the flames make a peculiar huk-huk sound; if the khatchhat (nightjar) calls by day, the jhum had better be abandoned. Should the jhum cutter after his first day's work dream of water or rice all will be well, but should he dream of a mithan chasing him or tigers springing on him, he must not continue cutting the jhum, or he will certainly get very ill and probably will die. If on the site of the proposed jhum a "thing-lu-bul" is found, death will certainly claim the cultivator should he persist in jhuming anywhere near the unlucky object, which is a kind of abortive tree growth without boughs or shoots, but covered with bulbous excrescences, which sometimes remotely resemble the human form, and if cut exude a blood-red juice. Should a tree have a pendant protuberance, called "thingzang," the jungle near must not be cut. The rubbing together of two tree boughs is thought to denote the presence of a Huai, who must be appeased by the sacrifice of a cock and hen, the sherh being hung under the jhum house with some chips of the tree. Brackish springs, known as "sa-khi-shi" (barking deer springs), are supposed to be the abodes of Huai, who are generally satisfied with the sacrifice of a fowl, the sherh being hung in a basket over the spring, but if the Huai be greedy the jhumer will fall ill, and then a pig and a dog must be sacrificed in the same manner.

The following are some of the superstitions about animals:—

A Lushai named Kela visited Aijal; on the road he met a rat, which stood up in the middle of the road and held its paws to its head. "What a curious rat!" he said. Two days after he reached his home he died. To see such a rat is certainly "thianglo." This incident happened a short time ago; no one had ever heard of such a rat having been seen before, and the unusualness of the occurrence, coupled with the death of Kela, was, to the Lushais, proof positive of its being the cause of his death. The Lushais tell me that sometimes a muskrat will be followed by her whole family, each holding in its mouth the tail of the one in front; this they call "In tir mei kai," and whoever sees it will certainly die. Should a bear on being shot fall on its back, and lie with its legs in the air, the shooter will die. If a bird enters the house prompt measures have to be taken to avert misfortune. The puithiam is called and the bird captured. The house is festooned within with the leaves of a certain tree, and the bird is thrown out of the house by the puithiam, who, muttering various charms, advises it to take itself off and carry its witchcraft with it. I came across, in an old number of the *Outlook*, a translation of a Chinese poem said to be dated about 100 B.C. in which the following occurs:—"When a wild bird enters a dwelling it portends that the human occupant must go forth." The coincidence is curious.

The following translation of a Lushai's reason for considering the sight of an atlas moth "thianglo" shows the origin of such superstitions. Atlas moths are rare in the Lushai hills. The "keptuam" (atlas moth) was the letter bearer between Pathian and the Vai (foreigner); and once when he was carrying Pathian's letter to the Vai chief the keptuam made the letter into wings, and flew away and disappeared, and Pathian was much disturbed at the loss of his letter and at the disappearance of his messenger, and he made mankind hunt for the missing keptuam. Now the keptuam did not wish to be caught, so he said, "Whoever sees me will die"; but as mankind did not know this they hunted and hunted till at last one saw the fugitive and died, and so they learnt that to see a keptuam is "thianglo," and ever since if anyone sees a male keptuam he will probably die.

Should the fowls at midnight become terrified and make an unusual sound like "i-ak, i-ak" someone will die. Should gibbons be heard hooting during the night, they have seen the corpse of someone who will fall from a tree or be drowned. As the gibbon retires to rest even before the sun sets, it must be very seldom that their shouts are heard at night. It is "thianglo" to shoot a gibbon, because at the Thimzing a man and a wife were changed into those animals. The woman at the time was dyeing blue thread, and therefore the palms of the hands of the female gibbon are black, though the rest of the body is light coloured.

The rhinoceros is also safe from attack on account of a similar belief, the folds of his skin being supposed to be derived from the folds of the cloths of persons who were transmogrified. The natural result of killing one of these animals is that all members of the slayer's family sicken and die, but this can be avoided if the successful huntsman on his return to the village goes straight to the zawlbuk or forge and remains there a whole day and night, after which it is safe for him to enter his house, provided that he leaves his gun and haversack behind and has changed all his clothes.

It is, however, worth noticing that, though monkeys, elephants, tigers, bears, &c., are also said to have been men before the Thimzing, there is no reluctance shown to kill them, and in fact the chiefs wear plumes of the king crow's feathers, and hornbills' beaks decorate many a chief's verandah.

When building his house the Lushai must be careful that he does not put his hearth on the side of the house next to that on which his neighbour has his. To do so is "thianglo" and illness will follow. It is not difficult to guess how this idea has arisen. Lushai houses are generally built in lines one above the other on the sides of a hill, and therefore it is more convenient to place the heavy earthen hearth on the upper side where the posts are shorter. This causes the hearths of all the houses in one row to be on the same side, and, the custom once formed, any deviation from it is considered unlucky. To dream of the auction of a "hlang"—*i.e.*, the bamboo frame to which the corpse is strapped during the funeral feast—is unlucky, and the person seen by the dreamer to purchase it will certainly die.

The following translation of a Lushai account of "tualsumsu" is interesting:—

"There are 'tualsumsu' in dreams and also while people are in a trance; the latter are the worst. If two friends are sleeping and in their dreams one says to the other, "Go as "tualsumsu"'—*i.e.*, 'beating your head on the ground'—nothing will happen to the one who goes, but the man who sends him will die. If anyone goes without being told to go, and likes it, he will die, but if he says, 'Oh, how it hurts my head!' he will not die. Sometimes a person will go beating his head on the ground and when roused from the trance know nothing of it."

The following is another curious belief:—

"If a man dreams that with his friend they are going to fly like 'Chawifa,' and they, both carrying burning maize cobs wrapped in old cloths in baskets, intend flying from inside the house, and having come outside, his friend flies away, while he himself stands on the end of the roof and cannot fly, his friend who flew away will die quickly, while he who could not fly will live. And he that flew away knew nothing of it, and the corn cobs wrapped in old cloth were thrown up, and the people saw them blazing like fire. This is extremely 'thianglo.'"

The Lushais speak confidently of "Chawifa," and many say they have seen it. They describe it as a kind of meteor, which flies through the village blazing brightly, and if it alights on a house the owner must die. Compare the Lakher idea of "Chawifa," given in Part II., and the Manipuri "Sangaisel," in Mr. Hodson's book on the Meitheis, page 121.

3. Snake worship.

The Lushais do not worship snakes, but there are many tales of "rulpui" (the big snake). Colonel Lewin in his "Progressive Exercises" has written as follows:—

"Throughout the Lushai Hills, among all the tribes with whom I have come in contact, whether 'Toung-tha' or 'Khyoung-tha,' sons of the hill or sons of the river, I have always found that special attributes have been assigned to a certain description of snake or serpent that is found in these forests. I remember once we were camped peacefully beside the border of a small hill stream; the shanties of leaves and grass which form our *tentes d'abri* in this part of the world had been erected, and all the world (our world some 30 persons) was either smoking the pipe of peace or stirring the pot of rice that was to form the evening meal. Suddenly there arose a shout of 'Tchubba-gree! Tchubba-gree!' which is the Hill Arracanese for 'the big snake, the king-serpent.' Behold the camp in a ferment, each stalwart young fellow seizing his dao and tightening his waistband. We went forth, and indeed the snake was very big. His long sinuous growth was at least 20 feet in length and bulky in proportion; he moved slowly along, taking apparently no notice of the turmoil and confusion that soon filled the wood around him. The Hillmen swarmed around his length like ants, and in a few moments he was cut in pieces by dao strokes. I noticed that each of my combatants as they ran up to the snake spat at him before striking. On inquiring the reasons of this, I was informed that in attacking a snake of this description, if he spat at you first before you struck him, your fate was sealed, and strangulation was your doom; but if you were speedy in salivation and forestalled his action, then he was delivered a prey into the hands of his assailants. A similar superstition formerly attached to the basilisk or cockatrice, which was said to be able to fascinate or cause the destruction of man or beast if it first perceived its victim before it was itself perceived. Sir Thomas Browne, in discoursing 'Of the Basilisk,' says 'that veneration shooteth from the eye, and that this way a basilisk may empoison, is not a thing impossible; but that this destruction should be the effect of the first beholder or depend on priority of aspection is a point not easily to be granted.' The flesh of this snake (which is a species of python) is eaten by the Hill folk, and the fat of the reptile is held to be a sovereign cure for all cuts and wounds, as well as for more obscure diseases. In the household tales and fireside stories of the people 'the big snake' holds a prominent place, and is vested with attributes of power and knowledge."

Colonel McCulloch, in his account of the Valley of Manipur, 1859, page 32, mentions the belief of the Manipuris in a snake god, and in fact the royal family is supposed to have sprung from a snake god known as "Pakhangba." Colonel McCulloch also relates that a Kuki—*i.e.*, a Thado—who had left him in perfect health, "saw a black snake as large as his thigh, which uttered a sound like that of an ox bellowing." "On his reaching his home he became ill, his belly swelled, and he has not recovered his health." Compare this with the following translation of a statement made to me by Hrangzova, a Lushai political Chaprassie, in 1904:—

"When I lived at Thenzawl, I once saw a curious object about 18 inches long, and about 6 inches thick, like a snake, which kept standing up on its stumpy tail, and then falling forward. I called my friend, who also saw it. When I got home I told my father and mother, who were very frightened, and said it was 'thianglo.' They both died within the year. This was 12 years ago. The rulpui which I saw had not got feathers, but perhaps that was because it was not big enough, as I am told the real rulpui has feathers like that of a cock."

There are various places named after rulpui. On one hill the body of a large snake is said to have been raised up on a pole, and so big was it that its shadow fell on a hill many miles away, called thereafter "Rulpui-thlin"—*i.e.*, Rulpui's Shadow. The following is the translation of the story of the origin of "rulpui."

Chhawng-chili and the Rulpui.

Once upon a time there was a girl called Chhawng-chili, who was in her father's jhum. At the bottom of the jhum in a hollow tree a snake had its nest, and the snake loved Chawng-chili very much. Whenever they went to the jhum she used to send her younger sister to call the snake, who used to come up and coil itself up in Chhawng-chili's lap. The little sister was very much afraid of the snake and did not dare tell her father. When the girls were going to the jhum, their parents always used to wrap up some rice and vegetables for them to take with them. On account of her fear of the snake, the little sister could not eat anything. Then her sister and the snake ate up all the rice and the vegetables, and the little sister stayed in the jhum house all day and got very thin, and her parents said to her, "Oh, little one, why are you getting so thin?" but she always said, "Oh, father, I can't tell you"; but her parents pressed her to tell them, and at last she said, "My sister and the snake make love always; as soon as we get to the jhum she says to me, 'Call him to me,' and I call him, and he comes up and coils himself up on her lap, and I am so frightened that I cannot eat anything, and that is why I am so thin." So they kept Chhawng-chili at home, and her father and younger sister went to the jhum, and her father dressed himself up to resemble Chhawng-chili, but he put his dao by his side; then the little sister called the snake, who came up quickly and curled itself up in her father's lap, and he with one blow cut it in two, and then they returned to the village. On the next day Chhawng-chili and her sister went to the jhum and her little sister called the snake, but her father had killed it. So they came back to their house, and found their father lying on the floor just inside the door sill. Chhawng-chili said, "Get up, father, I want to scrape the mud off my feet" (on the door sill), but her father would not move. So Chhawng-chili scraped off the mud from her feet, and stepped over the sill, and her father struck up and killed her. In her stomach there were about 100 small snakes. They killed them and killed them, but one escaped and hid under a dry patch of mithan dung, and grew up and used to eat people, and when it got bigger it wriggled into the "rulchawm kua"—*i.e.*, "feed snake hole"—and people of all villages used to feed it. After a time it was not content with goats and pigs, but demanded children. One day a Chin who was travelling noticed his host and hostess weeping, and on asking the reason was told it was the day for giving a child to the snake. "I will kill the snake," he replied, and, being provided with a goat, he slew it, and wrapped its flesh round his dao and forearm and offered it to the ralpui. When his forearm had been swallowed, by a quick turn of his wrist he disembowelled the monster. The place where this took place is on the Aijal-Champhai road, some forty miles from Aijal. The Biate or Bete claim to have been the people who fed the snake.

If a "thingsir" (a snake of which the female is very light-coloured and the male dark) enters a house, it is very "thianglo."

The entry of any snake into a house is looked on with suspicion, and either portends misfortune or it denotes that the sacrifice to Sakhua is urgently needed. If this sacrifice is not performed speedily death may ensue.

To see a snake with legs is "thianglo." The Lushais believe there are such creatures. My informant says it is only nowadays that this is "thianglo," inferring that formerly such creatures were common and therefore attracted no attention. It is the unusualness of the thing which makes the Lushai think it "thianglo."

4. Omens. In the section dealing with superstition the subject of omens of misfortune has been fully dealt with, and there is no need to say much more, but the following extract from "Asiatic Dissertations," II, 1792, is interesting—it is from a description of the "Mountaineers of Tipra."

"If at any time they see a star very near the moon they say, 'To-night we shall undoubtedly be attacked by some enemy,' and they pass the night under arms with extreme vigilance."

This belief may be accounted for by the superstition that projects undertaken on such occasions are likely to succeed.

Once when starting on a night expedition to capture a rebel chief, I noticed my guide staring up intently at the moon, and he expressed great satisfaction at seeing a star quite close to its edge, and exclaimed that our expedition was now sure to succeed, which I am glad to say proved true.

5 Witchcraft.

The Lushais are firm believers in witchcraft. There are several ways of bewitching your enemy. Colonel Lewin has a tale in which the wizard takes up the impression of a person's foot in the mud and puts it to dry over the hearth, thereby causing the owner to waste away. Clay figures into which bamboo spikes are thrust also figure in all cases in which a person is accused of this offence. To cut off a piece of a person's hair and put it in a spring is certain, unless the hair is speedily removed, to cause his death. Several tragedies have occurred on account of the belief in witchcraft. In 1897 three whole families were massacred because it was thought that they were bewitching a very aged chieftainess. The livers of the wizards were cut out and portions carried to the sufferer, but unfortunately she died before being able to taste them and thus prove the efficacy of the remedy. So strong was the feeling about these wizards that four or five households of their relatives had to be given a special and isolated site, as no village would receive them.

The following translation of a Lushai's account of how mankind first learned the black art is specially interesting, as it introduces Lalruanga and Keichalla, who are the heroes of many of the oldest of the Lushai tales. Colonel Lewin gives some excellent stories in his "Progressive Colloquial Exercises." Keichalla is the man who can become a tiger at will, and appears in many tales:—

"Dawi witchcraft was known to Pathian. Vahrika also was something like Pathian. Vahrika had a separate water supply, and Pathian's daughter was always disturbing it. Vahrika said, 'What can it be?' and lay in ambush. Pathian's daughter came, and he caught her and was going to kill her, but she said, 'Don't kill me; I will teach you magic.' So she taught him, and Vahrika taught it all to Keichalla, Lalruanga, and Hrang-sai-puia. Then Lalruanga went to court Zangkāki, and Zangkāki, who was a friend of Pathian's daughter, bewitched Lalruanga, who had forgotten his "dawi bur" (magic gourd), and he said to Chaichim (the mouse), 'Go and fetch my dawi bur which I put in my basket.' So the mouse went to fetch the dawi bur and got it, but the Tuiruang (Barak) river rose very high. The mouse took the dawi bur in his mouth and started to swim over the river. The dawi bur was washed away by the river till it stuck in the fish trap of the Thlangom tribe, who said, 'What is this?' The dawi bur was singing like anything. The Thlangoms broke it open. No sooner had they opened it than they each acquired knowledge of magic. Then the Thlangoms were chanting the magic song. Some Mizo (natives of these Hills) who were passing through the village also heard the song of those who knew magic. The Mizo saw a man eating rice. 'May you be bewitched!' they said. They bewitched him in his rice eating, and for a year after whenever he ate cooked rice it changed into dry uncooked rice, and it swelled inside him till his stomach could not hold it and he died. Thus the Mizo learnt about magic. Nowadays also there is magic, but those who know it won't teach it without payment."

The Lushais maintain that the tribes to the north of them, such as Paihte, Bete, &c., are very proficient at witchcraft, while the Chins consider the Lushais such experts at the craft that when Captain Hall, 2nd Gurkhas, and I forced our way from the west through the then unexplored hills and joined General Symons at Haka in 1890, the chiefs of that village besought the General not to allow any of our Lushai followers to go within sight of it, lest they should, by merely looking at it, cause fearful misfortunes. The belief in the man tiger is common through the Hills and also in Nepal. When a man-eater gave much trouble in Lungleh, our Gurkha Sepoys maintained that it was a man, one of three friends who had assumed this shape and were travelling by different shapes to a previously selected rendezvous, on reaching which they would resume their human forms.

Khuavang zawl.—The Lushais believe that certain persons—both males and females, but more generally females—have the power of putting themselves into a trance and are in a state of communication with Khuavang. This power is called "zawl," and a person who possesses it is called "zawlnei." During their trances they are said to be able to elicit from Khuavang information regarding the particular sacrifice required to cure any sick person, and their information is supposed to be more reliable than the opinion of the puithiam, who bases his state-

Photo by Major Playfair, I.A.

CANE SUSPENSION BRIDGE.

ments solely on the action of the pulse. The method of interrogating a zawlnei is called "thumvor," and is as follows :—

The zawlnei being in a trance is given a shallow basket containing rice, which he or she holds in one hand while an egg is placed in the palm of the other hand. When the zawlnei reverses this hand the egg does not fall. The basket of rice is shaken backwards and forwards, and there appears among the rice the footprint of the animal which it is necessary to sacrifice to ensure the patient's recovery. If it is impossible to trace any resemblance to any animal's footmark the state of the patient is serious and the whole series of sacrifices are needed. Compare the description of the Maibi's method of divination given in McCulloch's account of the Valley of Manipur, page 21. The following two accounts of Khuavang zawl were given me by Lushais :—

Lianthangi was a Khuavang zawl. There was much sickness in the village. One night Khuavang came to her in her dreams and said, "If each house-owner will make a clay metna and place it outside his or her house the sickness will cease." So they did this and the next day they observed as "hrilh," and within 20 days everyone was well again.

Thang-tei-nu was a zawlnei, but concealed the fact; people used to come secretly and make her perform the thumvor, and said she knew everything. She allowed no one to drink zu in her house, and if she drank zu she always got ill and it was "thianglo" for her to perform sacrifice. Khuavang told her this in her dreams.

Khawhring.—In Chapter IV, para. 6, the sacrifice called Khawhring Tir has been described. The belief in Khawhring is universal, and from the following translation it will be seen that the unfortunate women who were accused of being possessed by such a spirit have good reason to be grateful that the control of the country has passed into our hands. The belief is that Khawhring lives in certain women, whence it issues forth from time to time and takes possession of another woman, who, falling into a trance, speaks with the voice of the original hostess of the Khawhring. A missionary described to me a weird scene of excitement which he once saw, the object being to exorcise a Khawhring which had possessed a girl. Amid a turmoil of shouting, drum-beating, and firing of guns the spirit was ordered to quit its temporary abode and return whence it came.

Translation of a Lushai Version of the Origin of Khawhring.

"Wild boars have Khawhring. Once a man shot a wild boar while out hunting. On his return home they cooked the flesh. Some of the fat got on the hand of his sister, who rubbed her head, and the wild boar's Khawhring just passed into her. On the next day, without any provocation, she entered another girl. She took entire possession of her. People said to her, "Where are you going to?" She replied, "It is the wild boar my brother shot." "Well, what do you want?" they said. "If you will give me eggs I will go away," she replied. They gave her eggs and she went. Presently all those who borrowed the "hnam" (a plaited cane band for carrying loads) of the girl with the Khawhring also got possessed. If one with a Khawhring has a daughter the child is always possessed, so no one wants to marry a person with a Khawhring. Even now, we being to some extent Lusheis, we do not like to let a person possessed by a Khawhring enter our houses, and if such a one sits on the bed of a true Lushei she will certainly be fined a metna. Those possessed of Khawhring are most disgusting people, and before the foreigners came they were always killed."

The writer was not a true Lushei, but belonged to one of the clans which are fast being absorbed and are almost indistinguishable from Lusheis.

The Lushais say that sometimes girls walk in their sleep and go and lick up urine, as the metna do, under the zawlbuk, and that when starting forth on these expeditions their feet and hands shine as if they were coated with phosphorus. If a young man wakes a girl up while she is walking thus she is very much ashamed, and generally grants him the favours of her bed to procure his silence.

This state is called "Thlahzung."

CHAPTER VI

LANGUAGE

I PROPOSE, in this chapter, to deal only with Lushai, and to treat of the connection between the different dialects spoken in these Hills at the end of Part II.

Lushai or Dulien, which is the dialect of the Lushei clan, modified, doubtless, by contact with those of other clans, is now the *lingua franca* of the whole Lushai Hills, and is understood in many parts of the adjoining districts. A very complete grammar and vocabulary has been published by Messrs. Savage and Lorrain, now of the London Baptist Mission, and therefore I only propose to give a bare outline of the language here, which is largely borrowed from the above work.

Articles.—The indefinite article can generally be rendered by the numeral one.

The definite article is sometimes represented by demonstrative pronouns or relative particles.

Gender.—Inanimate objects have no gender. In nouns gender may be shown by use of different words, as "tlangval," a young man; "nula," a maiden. This system is only employed when speaking of human beings, by adding suffixes—"pa" and "chal" for males, "nu" and "pui" for females; thus "fa pa," son; "fa nu," daughter; "she chal," bull metna; "she pui," cow metna. "Chal" and "pui" are restricted to full-grown animals. All men's names end in "a," all women's in "i." Some words are the same in both genders—"u," elder brother or sister; "nao shen," a baby; "naupang," child. "I" is the feminine termination in Manipuri also.

Number.—The plural terminations are "te," "ho," and "zong"; sometimes these are combined or duplicated.

Mi zong zong = all mankind.

Lāl te ho = chiefs.

These terminations are omitted when the number can be otherwise inferred.

Sākor paruk = six horses.

Puan tam tak ka pe = I gave many cloths.

When a suffix is added to a noun to denote case, the plural suffix follows the case suffix.

Zawng-a-te an lo changa.
Monkey into s they became changed.

Kan in-a-te an lo-lut-a.
Our house into s they entered.

Case.—Nouns are not inflected. The agent is denoted by the suffix "in."

Lal in a that = The chief killed (him).

The same suffix is used to distinguish the instrument.

Lal in fei in a shun = The chief speared (him) with a spear.

"In" is therefore exactly equivalent to "na" used in Manipuri to distinguish the agent or instrument.

The other cases can only be inferred from the position of the words.

The object immediately precedes the transitive verb governing it.

Lal-in puan a-pe = The chief gave a cloth.

The indirect object precedes the direct.

Suaka puan ka pe = I gave a cloth to Suaka.

Hnena (to) is sometimes used to give greater clearness.

Lal hnena ui pakhat ka pe ang = I will give a dog to the chief.

The thing possessed immediately follows the possessor.

Kawn bawl in a-kāng = The minister's house caught fire.

The following construction is sometimes used:—

Kawn bawl a in a lian e = Minister his house it big is.

The other cases are rendered by suffixes.

Ka in a daraw. Ka in a tang in laraw. Aizawl
My house in put. My house from bring. Aijal
a kalraw
to go.

Adjectives follow the words they qualify, but are not inflected in any way.

Mipa tha = a good man. Hmaichhia thā = a good woman.
Nula-te tha = good girls.

When a noun is used as an adjective it precedes the noun it qualifies, as, "Lung in," stone house.

Adjectives are compared thus

Suaka Nela ai in a chhā k zawk.
Suaka Nela than he stronger.
Suaka is stronger than Nela.

When demonstrative adjectives are compared, "ai-in" is combined with them, thus :—

He sakor he saw ai sawn ashang zawk.
This horse here that than there is taller.
This horse is taller than that.
"Saw saw ai-in" being replaced by "Saw-ai sawn."

When no object of comparison is mentioned "ai-in" is omitted.

Nangma lo azao zawk.
Your jhum extensive more.
Your jhum is more extensive.

The superlative is formed thus :—

Lalzong zinga Khuma a vin ber.
Chiefs among Khuma he bad tempered most.
Khuma is the most bad-tempered of all the chiefs.
Khuma lalzong ai-in a vin ber.
Khuma chiefs than he ill-tempered more.
Khuma lalzong a a vin ber.
Khuma chiefs of he ill-tempered most.
Khuma a vin ber.
Khuma he ill-tempered most.
Khuma is the most ill-tempered.

The numerals are very simple:—

1 = pa khat	4 = pa li	7 = pa sari
2 = pa hnih	5 = pa nga	8 = pa riat
3 = pa thum	6 = pa ruk	9 = pa kua
	10 = shom	

11 = "shom leh pa khat," 12 = "shom leh pa hnih," and so on to 20 = "shom hnih"; then "shom hnih leh pa khat" &c., to "shom thum" = 30, "shom li" = 40, "shom nga" = 50, and so on to "za" = 100, "za leh pa khat" = 101, and so on to "shang" = 1000.

"Shing" = 10,000 and "nuai" for 1,000,000 are hardly ever used; 8,975 = "shang riat, leh za kua leh shom sari leh pa nga."

It will be seen that the real numerals are "khat," "hnih," "thum," &c., pa being equivalent to unit. It is usually omitted when animals or things are mentioned, but retained when speaking of human beings.

Lal pa sari = seven chiefs. Sebong nga = five cows.

With numbers above ten the name of the thing enumerated if a monosyllable, is often repeated. Thus:—

Ni shom hnih leh ni nga.
Days twenty and days five.

Ordinals are formed by adding "na" to the cardinals, thus:—

In shom na lutrawh.
Enter the tenth house.

But—

Ni thum ni a lo-kalraw.
Day three day on come.
Every other day = Ni khat dan a.
Every third day = Ni hnih dan a,
and so on.

Numeral adjectives are formed thus:—

Voi nga, voi shom leh voi khat.
Times five, times ten and times one,
eleven times.

Demonstrative adjectives are:—

He *or* hehi Hei hei hi	This = near the speaker.	Heng, henghi = these.
Saw = that.		Sawng = those.
Khā = that near you.		Khāng = those near you.
Khu = that down there.		Khung = those down there
Khi = that up there.		Khing = those up there.
Chu = that.		Chung = those.

They are generally repeated, thus:—

Khu sava khu kadu e.
That bird down there I want.
Khi zawng khi a liane.
That monkey up there he big is.

When a noun qualified by one of these adjectives is an agent, the agent suffix "in" is combined with the second part of the adjective thus:—

Khu ui khu-an min a sheh = That dog down there bit me instead of Khu ui in khu.

The personal pronouns have several forms, which are the same for both genders.

Nominative	Keima, kei, ka = I. Keimani, keine, kan = we.
Possessive	Keima, keiia, ka = my. Keimani, keini, kan = our. Keimata, keiata, kata = mine. Keimanita, &c. = ours.
Objective	Keimamin, kei min min = me. Keimani min, &c. = us.

The second person is "nangma" and "nangmani"; the third "ama," "anmani."

The possessive of the second person, when used as nominative of verbs, has a curious irregular form "i" in the singular and "in" in the plural.

The pronominal particles "ka" (I), "i" (thou), "a" (he), "kan" (we), "in" (you), "an" (they) must be used with verbs in addition to the pronouns, thus:—

Nangma i kal ang em? = Will you go?
Keimani chaw kan ei mek = We are just eating our rice.

The particle can never be omitted, whereas the true pronoun is generally left out except when required for emphasis.

Reflexive action is denoted in several ways.

The particle "in" is prefixed to the verb in all cases. The following are a few examples:—

Ka in vel
Mani leh mani ka in vel } I hit myself.
Mani in ka in vel
Keimani theoh vin kan in vel = We hit ourselves.

Relative Pronouns are:—

Kha, chu, a piang = who, which, what, that.
A piang, a piang kha, a piang chu = whoever, &c.
Lekha i ziak kha a tha e.
Letter you wrote that it good is.

The pronouns are sometimes omitted, the idea being conveyed by the use of relative participles or verbal nouns.

I lekha ziak a tha e
Your letter written it good is.
The letter you wrote is good.

Interrogative Pronouns are:—

Tu-nge? Tu? Tu-maw? Eng-nge? Zeng-nge? Eng? Eng-maw? = What? Hhoi-i-nge? = Which?

They are used thus:—

Tu-nge a lo kal? = Who has come?
Tu-in-a nge i riak? =
(house in) you stay
Whose =
Tu ar nge i lei? Tu-in-nge vel che?
(fowl) =
Whose you buy? Who hit you?
Tu-nge i vel? =
Whom did you hit?

Tu and Tu-maw are only used thus:—

A lo kal Tu-Maw? *or* Tu? =
He has come Who?
Eng-nge i duh? Khoi-i lekha buh nge i duh? =
What you want? (book) which you want?
Which book do you want?
Eng tui nge i choi?
(water) = What you draw?

The particle "a" preceding an interrogative pronoun has a partitive force.

A tu-nge i ko? = Which of them did you call?

Verbs.

The same form is used for all persons and in singular and plural, the pronominal particles marking person and number.

Shoi = to say

Pres: Ka shoi = I say. Ka shoi mek = I am saying.
Past: Ka shoi *or* Ka shoi *or* tawh } I said. Ka shoi mek a ni = I was saying.
Fut: Ka shoi ang / Ka shoi dawn } I will say. {Ka shoi mek ang = I shall be saying.
Ka shoi tawh ang = I shall have said.

Conditional Mood.

Ka shoi tur = I would say, or, I ought to say.
Ka shoi tawh tur = I would have said, or, ought to have said.

The future terminations are often used in a conditional sense.

Subjunctive Mood.

Ka shoi chuan = If I say, said or had said.

The following forms are peculiar and appear to me of foreign origin. The pronominal prefixes are absent, the person and number being indicated by different forms.

Shoi i la *or* i lang = If I say *or* said.
Shoi la, *or* lang = If thou sayest *or* saidst.
Shoi shela *or* shelang = If he say *or* said.
Shoi i la *or* i lang = If we say *or* said.
Shoi u la *or* lang = If you say *or* said.
Shoi shela *or* shelang = If they say *or* said.

The pluperfect tense is formed by inserting "ta."

Shoi ta i la = If I had said.
Shoi ta u lang = If you had said.

By inserting "ma" the meaning "although" or "even if" is given.

Shoi ma she lang = Even if he says.
Shoi ta ma u la = Although you say.

Imperative Mood.

The imperative has several forms:—

Singular: Shoi rawh, shoi ang che, shoi ta che, shoi te shoi che, all mean "say." The last four forms have a somewhat persuasive meaning.

Plural: I shoi ang, i shoi ang u = Let us say.

The second person plural is formed by adding "u" to the singular form.

Infinitive Mood.

The infinitive or verbal noun is the same as the root shoi = to say.

Ka shoi lai in
I say time at } When I was saying.

A verbal noun can also be formed by the suffix "na."

Ka riak na in
My staying house.

The suffixes "tur," "tur-in," "na-tur," "nan," "an," "in," denotes infinitive of purposes.

Tui in tur ka duh.
Water to drink I want.

Chaw lei tur ka nei lo } I have nothing where-
Rice to buy I have not. } with to buy rice.

The suffix "tu" changes the verb into noun of agency.

Veng-tu = a watchman. Hril-tu = an informant.

Participles: Shoia, shoi-ing = saying.

Negative.

There are two negative particles:—lo and shu.

The first is used except in the conditional and the imperative, when the latter is used.

The particles are placed after the root except in the past tense, when they follow the tense termination.

Ka kal lo = I do not go.
Ka kal ta lo = I did not go.
Ka kal lo vang = I will not go } The "v" is inserted
Ka kal lo ve = I do not go } for sake of euphony.
Kal rawh = Go.
Kal shu = Don't go.
Kal shu se = Do not let him go.
Shoi shu u = Do not say (plural).
Shoi shu i la = If we do not say.

"Nem" and "nāng" are used as negative particles and intensify the meaning.

Ka hre lo = I don't know.
Ka hre nem = I don't know. How should I?
Lal in a¯ka kal nāng = I am not going to the chief's house. Why should I be?

Interrogative Particles.

These are as a rule placed at the end of a sentence. They are "em" and "em ni."

I kal ang em = Will you go?

"Em ni" sometimes implies that the answer is expected in the same form as the question.

I lo-kal em ni = You have come, have you?
A lo-kal lo vem ni = He has come, has not he?

"Maw"—This particle is used when the person asked, instead of replying at once, repeats part of the question—a pernicious and vexatious habit much indulged in by the Lushais.

I dam em? = Are you well?
Keima maw? Ka dam e = Do you mean me? I am well.

The Passive Voice.

The verb when used in the passive voice is pronounced slightly differently. The construction is as follows:—

Lāl in min kāp = The chief shot me.
Lāl kā kā ni = I am shot by the chief.

Verbal Prefixes.

These are a very noticeable peculiarity. They are:—

Zuk = motion downwards. Zuk la ro = Bring it down.
Han = motion upwards. Han en rawh = Come up and see.
Han = motion towards the speaker. A han la ta = He brought it.
Lo = motion towards the speaker = Lāl a lo kāl = The chief arrives.
Ron = motion towards the indirect object.
Lal hnena ron hril rawh = Go and tell the chief.
Min ron pe rawh = Come and give it to me.
Vā = motion from. Vā lā zo = Go and bring.

Adverbs.

There is a peculiar series of adverbs in Lushei, which, besides denoting the manner in which a thing is done, also convey some idea of the appearance of the agent, thus:—

Lal a kāl buk buk = The chief goes.

"Buk buk" shows that the chief is a big, heavy man and is walking slowly.

"Bak bak" similarly used would mean that the chief was medium-sized and walking slowly, whereas "bik bek" could only be used of a small person proceeding slowly.

There are over a hundred such adverbs in Lushei.

Interjections.

The most common are "Ie" = I say! "Khai" = Come! "Ku" = Ho! "Chei chei" denoting disapproval and surprise. There are certain interjections, such as "Karei, Karei!" = Alas! Alas! which are only used by women.

The Lushais are very fond of piling up adverbs to intensify the meaning:—

Ava mak em em mai!
How wonderful very very very!

Ava mak em veleh!
How wonderful very indeed!

Literal Translation of an Account of the Thimzing.

Hmān lai hian thim a lo-zing-a; chutichuan mi
Former time in darkness it collected; then mankind
zawn zawn an in-khawm mur mur
all all they themselves collected (untranslatable adverb)
chutichuan zawng hmul a lo lenga an hgum
then monkey hair it began to grow their spine ends
a thak an hiat thin-a zawng a te
they itched they scratched always monkeys into (plural suffix)
an changa tin lal te chu va-pual a an lo
they changed their chiefs indeed horn-bill into they became
changa mi chhia e-raw chu zawng a te ngau-va
changed people poor on the other hand monkey into grey
te an lo changa. Tin sa lu ro nei
monkeys they became changed. Then flesh head dry had
chuan an tuah a thing ai-in a tha zawh a
those who they put on fire wood than it good more was
chu-te-chuan an dam rei thei zawk an ti. Tin mei-ling
therefore they lived long could more they say. Then embers

tlaivar lem-in puan tial shin in
watched all night more than others cloth striped wearing
sakeia an changa thei tin pitar te hian puanpui
tigers into they changed may be then old women quilts
an sin-a sai a an lo changa.
they were wearing elephants into they became changed.

APPENDIX

Families and Branches of the Lushei Clan.

Family Name.	Branch Name.	Remarks.
Thangur ...	Rokum	All the Lushei chiefs belong to one of these branches.
	Rivung	
	Pallian	
	Zadeng	
	Thangluah	
	Sailo	
	Chenkhual	Descended from Chenkhuala, said to be a brother of Sailova, probably a son of a concubine. The Chenkhual had once independent villages, but are no longer looked on as chiefs.
Pachuao ...	Cherlal	This family is said to be descended from illegitimate sons of Zadenga. Darchaova, Cherlalla, Lianthunga, and Liannghora are heroes of whose prowess many tales are told, and their names appear among the branch names.
	Chhawthliak	
	Chhoalak	
	Chonglal	
	Darchao	
	Lalbawm	
	Lianthung	
	Liannghor ...	
	Vanpuia-hrin	*I.e.*, sprung from Vanpuia.
	Varchuao	
Changte ...	Darchun, Pamte	"Chi" means family, "Kawl" means Burma, and "ngak" is to wait; so perhaps the Kawlchi may be descendants of Changte, who settled temporarily in Burma, and the Ngakchi of some who delayed at some general move of the family.
	Vokngak. Kawlchi ..	
	Padaratu, Tumpha ...	
	Lungte, Ngakchi ...	
	Chonglun	

Chongte ...	Tuichhung, Lungte ... Muchhip-chhuak ... Pamte	*I.e.*, from Muchhip, the name of a hill.
Chuachang ...	Chonchir, Chonchhon ...	"Hang" means black and "ngo" white.
	Lathang	This family and the next are said to be descended from two brothers.
Chuaongo ...	Vanpuia-thla ... ... Hlengel, Hmunpel ... Zongpam, Laller ... ... Chumthluk, Aohmun ...	Descendants of Vanpuia. The Chuaongo are said to have been very powerful, and to have held a position similar to that now held by the Sailo. Their most powerful chief was Vanpuia.
Haonar ...	Haothul, Haobul ... Tuithang, Shenlai ...	
Hrasel... ...	Shelpuia, Sontlunk ... Sumkhum, Sazah ...	
Hualhang ...	Chalbuk, Sialchung ... Bailchi, Chumkal ... Khupao, Fangtet ... Taihlum, Chertluang ...	This family and the next are said to have sprung from two brothers, children of a Lushei woman by a Poi or Chin, and to have originated from a hole in the ground near the Shepui rocks, to the east of the Manipur river. The Hualngo and Hualhang formerly lived together in villages under Hualngo chiefs. On the rise of the Thangur chiefs, a quarrel broke out, and the Hualngo were defeated by a combination of the Sailo, Zadeng, and Pallian, and driven across the Tiao, and took refuge under the protection of the Falam chiefs, where their descendants still are, and are miscalled Whenoh by the officers in charge of the Chin Hills. The Hualhang deserted to the Thangur, and are found scattered in the villages of their conquerors. There are six Hualngo villages in the Lushai Hills containing some 200 houses.
Hualngo ...	Chalthleng, Khupno ... Tuazol, Cherput, Bochung	

Lungkhua ...	Sialchung, Ngalchi ... Ngalchung, Phungchi ... Ngaphawl		
Tochong ...	Topui, Chhakom ... Muchhip-chhuak ... Chemhler, Tobul ...	*Vide* Changte.	
Vanchong ...	Vanlung, Sumkhum ... Chemhler, Chengrel ... Kaithum	The claim of this family to be true Lusheis is sometimes disputed.	

Besides the above families, there is one called Chhak-chhuak, *i.e.*, "Come out of the east." In spite of all enquiries I was unable to find out any reason for the name, which was sometimes said to be the name of a branch of one of the other families and sometimes that of a separate family.

PART II

THE NON-LUSHEI CLANS

INTRODUCTORY

In this part all the clans of the Lushai-Kuki race which are not included by the people themselves among the Lusheis will be briefly dealt with. All these clans practise the jhum methods of cultivation and were originally semi-nomadic, but certain of them, under changed circumstances, have ceased to move their villages and are taking to plough cultivation. There is a varying similarity in the religious beliefs and customs, and it will suffice to point out the principal divergences from those of the Lusheis as already described.

The non-Lushei clans group themselves naturally into five sections:—

1. The clans which live among the Lusheis under the rule of Thangur chiefs and have become practically assimilated by them, and are included in the wider term Lushai, as we use it. Naturally the accounts of these will be brief and will deal principally with the origin of the clans.

2. The clans which, while still retaining a separate corporate existence, have been much influenced by the Lusheis, among or near whom they reside.

3. The Old Kuki clans.

4. The Thado clan with its numerous families and branches, often spoken of as New Kukis.

5. The Lakhers. These are immigrants from the Chin Hills, and would more correctly be dealt with in the Chin Monograph, but a brief sketch of them, though very incomplete, may be useful till a fuller account is written. They call themselves Mara.

CHAPTER I

CLANS INCLUDED IN THE TERM LUSHAI

THESE clans have adopted most of the manners and customs of their conquerors, and to an ordinary observer are indistinguishable from the true Lushei. In many cases the only difference is in the method of performing the Sakhua sacrifice. In few cases some words of the clan dialect are still used, but, generally speaking, there is but little difference noticeable. In cases where the clan had attained considerable strength before its overthrow by the Lusheis the process of assimilation has naturally been slower, and there is more to describe. The following list of clans does not lay claim to being complete, but contains all the best-known names.

Chawte. Members of this clan are found in small numbers scattered among the Lushei villages. They kill a goat as the Sakhua sacrifice, and omit all the Naohri sacrifices except the Zinthiang and Ui-ha-awr. When a mithan is sacrified it is killed in the evening, and the giver of the feast wears some of the tail hairs on a string round his neck.

In the hills between the Manipur valley and Tamu I found two small hamlets of Chawte, who said that their forefather had come from the hills far to the south very long ago. Their language closely resembles Lushei, but they have come much under Manipuri influence. The names of the families in no case agreed with those given me by the Chawte in the Lushai Hills. A detailed account of the Manipur Chawte will be found in (3).

Chongthu. This clan is very widely scattered. The following account of the origin of the clan is given by Suaka, now Sub-Inspector of

Police at Aijal:—"Of all Lushai clans Lershia (Chongthu) celebrated the Chong first of all. Lershia's village was on the hill to the south of the Vanlai-phai. There he celebrated the Chong. He was the richest of all men. Lershia had a younger brother, Singaia. His village was separate at Betlu. He was very rich in mithan, gongs, and necklaces. Once he was moving to another village with all his goods, when a very big snake swallowed him. Even till now Chongthus are always 'upa' to chiefs. It may be they are wiser than the other clans; they are very amiable—maybe they understand how to express matters well. In every village Chongthu are always upa. How many children Lershia had or where they are I do not know. Nevertheless he was the richest of all men. Because he was so rich in mithan, gongs, and necklaces he first celebrated the Chong. His name was also first given to the Chong song. Even till now the Sailo and all Lusheis and all Ralte, if they celebrate the Chong according to their customs, sing Lershia's song—they have not a new song of their own."

From the above it would appear that Chongthu is a nickname given to Lershia on account of his having first celebrated the Chong. Chongthu's name appears in the Thado pedigree as the first of the race to emerge from the earth, and the great-great-grandfather of Thado. The Chiru and Kolhen also claim descent from him, though they cannot give the intermediate names.

Hnamte. This clan lived to the east of the Tyao river. Their most famous chief was Chon-uma, their last village was at Tlāngkua, on the Lentlāng. Bad harvests and general misfortunes brought about their dispersal early in the last century.

Kawlni. A widely-distributed clan sub-divided into at least 12 families said to be connected with the Ralte, *q.v.*

Kawlhring. Kawl = Burma. Hring = Born. This clan had a big village on the Hringfa hill, where the remains of earthworks made by them in their final struggle against the Haka people may still be seen. Messrs. Carey and Tuck in their "Chin Hills Gazetteer," p. 153, say:—"Having settled with their formidable neighbours on the north, the Hakas turned their attention to the Lushais, who at this time occupied the country as far east as the banks of the Lāvār stream, barely 20 miles east of Haka. Their chief centres were Kwe Hring and Vizan, two huge villages on the western slopes of the Rongtlang range, and to this day the sites, fortifications, and roads of the former town may be traced." The Hakas, not feeling equal to attacking their powerful neighbours single-handed, called in the assistance of a Burmese chieftain, Maung Myat San of Tilin, who came with 200 men armed with guns and bringing with them two brass cannons. "The Haka and Burman forces were collected on the spot where Lonzeert now stands, and, marching by night, surprised Kwe Hring in the early dawn by a noisy volley in which the brass cannon played a conspicuous part. The Lushais, who had no firearms, deserted their villages and fled in disorder, and for several months parties of Hakas ravaged the country, eventually driving every Lushai across the Tyao before the rains made that river unfordable."

The people called here Lushais were the Kawlhring. The last Kawlhring chief was Lalmichinga. The clan is now scattered among the villages round Lungleh. There are eight families, but I have not found any branches. The Zinthiang and Zinhnawm are omitted from the Naohri sacrifices.

Kiangte. This clan lived east of the Manipur river, from which place it was driven by the Chins. Kiangte are now found in small numbers in most of the villages in the North Lushai Hills. The clan is divided into seven families, without branches.

Ngente. Although this clan has been practically absorbed its members have retained in an unusual degree their distinctive customs. The Ngente were formerly a somewhat powerful clan living at Chonghoiyi, on the Lungdup hill, where about 1780 A.D. a quarrel broke out between their two chiefs, Lalmanga and Ngaia, and the latter set out with his adherents to form another village, but was pursued and killed by his brother. Shortly after this the clan was attacked by the Lusheis and broken up. The above particulars were given me in 1904, when I was near the Lungdup hill. They seem to account for the Koihrui-an-chhat festival, which is described below from notes supplied to me by Mr. C. B. Drake-Brockman in 1901, embodying information gathered by him from Ngente living at Lungleh, many days' journey from Lungdup. This is an interesting instance of history being embalmed in a custom of which the origin has been forgotten, and I humbly recommend its consideration to those wise men who are ever ready to interpret every custom as affording evidence of their particular theories.

Marriage.—The Ngente young man is no more restricted in the choice of his wife than is the Lushei, but the price is fixed at seven guns, which are taken as equivalent to Rs. 140/-. Of this sum the girl's nearest male relative receives Rs. 120/-. the remainder being distributed as follows:—Rs. 8/- to the "pu," maternal grandfather or uncle, Rs. 6/- to her elder sister, Rs. 4/- to her paternal aunt, Rs. 2/- to the "pālāl," or trustee. Should a woman die before the whole of her price has been paid, her relatives can only claim half the remainder.

Childbirth.—Three months before the birth, the mother prepares zu, which is known as "nao-zu"—*i.e.*, baby's beer, which must on no account be taken outside the house and which is drunk in the child's honour on the day of its birth. Women are delivered at the head of the bedstead, and the afterbirth is placed in a gourd and hung up on the back wall of the house, whence it is not removed. The puithiam sacrifices a cock and hen, which must not be white, outside the village, and, having cooked the flesh there, he takes it to his own house for consumption. On the third day after the birth the child is named by its "pu," who has to give a fowl and a pot of zu. A red cock is killed and some of its feathers are tied round the necks of the infant and other members of the family.

Death Ceremonies.—The Ngente do not attach any importance to burying their dead near their place of abode. They put up no memorials and offer no sacrifices, and make no offerings to the deceased's spirit. The dead are buried wherever it is most convenient. This is a most singular divergence from the general custom.

Festivals.—The Khuangchoi, Chong, Pawl-kut are observed. In place of the Mim-kut they celebrate a feast called Nao-lām-kut, which takes place in the autumn. For two nights all the men and women must keep awake, and they are provided with boiled yams and zu to help them in doing so. On the third day some men dress themselves up as women and others as Chins, colouring their faces with charcoal. They then visit every house in which a child has been born since the last Nao-lām-kut and treat the inmates to a dance, receiving presents of dyed cotton thread, women's cloths, &c., and much zu. Compare the account of the Fanai She-doi, p. 136 *et seq.* below.

Koihrui-an-chhat (*They Break the Koi Creeper*).— A party of young men, being supplied with hard-boiled eggs and fowl's flesh, go off into the jungle equipped with bows and arrows. On the third day they return with the heads of some animals—for choice those of the "tangkawng," a large lizard—and also a long piece of the creeper from which the Koi beans (*v.* Chap. II, para. 18) are obtained. They are received with all the honours paid to warriors returning from a successful raid, and a tug of war with the creeper takes place between the young men and the maidens. The heads of the animals are then placed in the centre of the village, and dancing, singing, and drinking go on round them all night, no young man or girl being allowed to go inside a house till daybreak, when the whole party adjourns to the house of a member of the Chonghoiyi-hring family—*i.e.*, a descendant of one born at Chonghoiyi—and after further libations they disperse.

It is quite clear that this feast commemorates the victory of Lalmanga over Ngaia—compare the account of the reception of a raiding party given in Part I., Chap. III, para. 9. The use of bows and arrows is an interesting survival.

The tug of war with the creeper is found among the Old Kuki clans as one of the incidents of the spring festival, and in the Manipuri chronicle we find references to such amusements being indulged in. The Ngente evidently combined the play, intended to keep green the memories of their ancestor, with the usual ceremonies of the spring festival.[1]

The Ngente do not practise the Khāl sacrifices.

Language.—In the *Linguistic Survey* Dr. Grierson gives a translation of the parable of the Prodigal Son in the Ngente dialect supplied him by Mr. Drake-Brockman, and sums up his description of the dialect as follows:—"But in all essential points both (*i.e.*, Ngente and Lushei) agree, and the difference is much smaller than between dialects in connected languages."

Paotu. A very insignificant clan, of which I have found only one family. The clan formerly lived on a hill north of the Tao

[1] Cf. "Manipur Festival," *Folklore*, Vol. XXI, No. I.

peak, to the east of the Koladyne, and were probably driven out by the Chins at the same time as the Kawlhring.

Rentlei. There are five families in this clan, which has long been absorbed by the Lusheis, but the Rentlei maintain that at one time, when they lived in a big village on the Minpui hill to the east of the Tyao river, they were the more powerful and showed their contempt for the Lusheis by throwing stones at the skulls of the pigs which the latter used to place on posts outside their houses after performing the Sakhua sacrifice, and this led to the Lusheis placing the skulls inside their houses, whereas the Rentlei to this day adhere to the custom of putting them outside. This clan is still looked on with respect, and chiefs frequently take Rentlei brides.

Roite. This clan is divided into seven families, one of which has a branch. There is nothing of interest to be noted about it.

Vangchhia. This clan has only three families and one branch. Its members are said to be generally wealthy, and therefore prudent parents strive to get them as "pu" to their children. Their Sakhua sacrifice is elaborate, a mithan being killed in front of the house, a cock at the head of the parents' bed, and a boar at that of the children. There is a great feast, followed by nine days' "hrilh."

Zawngte. Now an insignificant clan, of which I have not obtained a single family name. Under a chief called Chengtea they lived on a hill north of Thlan-tlang, which is still known by their name. They were ejected by the Chins probably at the same time as the Kawlhring and Paotu. The eldest son inherits. They place their dead in hollowed-out logs in small houses outside the village, and leave them there for three months. In these particulars they resemble the Vuite. As among the Chawte, after killing a mithan the household of the giver of the feast wear some of the hairs of the tail on strings round their necks.

CHAPTER II

CLANS WHICH, THOUGH NOT ABSORBED, HAVE BEEN MUCH INFLUENCED BY THE LUSHEIS

Fanai

A CLAN which was rising into eminence, when our occupation of the country put a stop to its further aggrandisement. The chiefs trace their pedigree back six generations, to a man called Fanai, who lived among the Zahaos, to the east of the Tyao. His great grandson, Roreiluova, was a slave, or at least a dependant, of a Zahao chief, and was sent with 70 households to form a village at Bawlte, near Champhai, in Lushei territory, with the intention, no doubt, of enlarging the Zahao borders, but Roreiluova entered into peaceful relations with the Lushei chiefs, and gradually severed his connection with the Zahaos, and, moving south-west, occupied successively various sites to the west and north-west of Lungleh, between the Lushai and Chin villages, maintaining his position with considerable diplomatic skill, often acting as intermediary between his more powerful neighbours. He died at Konglung early in the nineteenth century, having attained such a position that his sons were at once recognised as chiefs, and on our occupying the country in 1890 we found eight Fanai villages, containing about 700 houses, grouped along the west bank of the Tyao and Koladyne rivers, between Biate on the north and Sangao on the south. Roreiluova's descendants seem to have inherited his skill in diplomacy, for they kept on good terms with their neighbours, and whenever these quarrelled managed to assist the stronger without entirely alienating the weaker.

The clan is subdivided into six families and one branch.

The Fanai now talk Lushai and dress in the same way,

Photo by Major Playfair, I.A.

FANAI.

except as regards the method of dressing the hair, which is parted horizontally across the back of the head at the level of the ears, and the hair above this is gathered into a knot over the forehead, while that below is allowed to hang loose over the shoulders. They generally follow Lushai customs. In the series of feasts which an aspirant for the title of Thangchhuah has to perform, the Chong is replaced by the Buh-za-ai (buh=rice, za=100), performed as among the Lushais. The She-doi feast has to be gone through twice, and is followed by a very similar feast called She-cha-chun (spearing of male mithan), which completes the series. Wealthy persons perform the Khuangchoi, but it is not necessary. The Mi-thi-rawp-lām is prohibited. The following account of the She-doi is taken from my diary of the 14th May, 1890.

"We went up at once to the village, where a peculiar dance was in progress. Lembu's wife was being carried about on a platform, round which a wooden railing had been fixed to enable her to maintain her position. This platform had four long poles passed underneath it, and a number of men and women, holding these, were moving the platform about in a manner which must have been most uncomfortable for her Majesty. They lifted it up and down, then swayed it to one side, then to the other, then ran in one direction and stopped suddenly, then in another, and pulled up with a jerk. During all this time the royal lady maintained a solemn silence, and showed complete indifference to the whole proceeding. Her head-dress consisted of a band round which at intervals coloured bands of straw were plaited. From this chaplet porcupine quills stood up all round, to the ends of which the yellowish-green feathers of parrots were affixed, each terminating in a tuft of red wool. At the back, an iron crossbar, about 6 inches long, was tied horizontally, and from this a number of strings of black and white seeds depended, at the end of which glistening wing-cases of green beetles were attached. Except for this startling head-dress, the Queen was dressed much as usual, except that her waist cloth was longer and more gorgeous. Having been carried about for some time, her Majesty showed her appreciation of the attentions of her subjects by distributing gifts. First she threw a small chicken, which was eagerly scrambled for and torn to pieces by the young men anxious to obtain it, next followed a piece of white cotton wool, which no one would pick up, and then some red thread, which was scrambled for eagerly.

"May 15th.—This morning a mithan was sacrificed. The animal was tied by the head to one of the sacrificial posts, on which his skull was to be placed later on. The chief then came out with a spear in one hand, a gourd of rice beer in the other. The puithiam, or sorcerer, accompanied him, also carrying a gourd of beer. The pair took up their stand just behind the mithan, and the puithiam began mumbling what I was told were prayers for the prosperity of the village. The prayers were interrupted by the chief and the sorcerer taking mouthfuls of beer and blowing them over the mithan. When the prayers were finished, they anointed the animal with the remains of the liquor, and the chief then gave it a slight stab behind the shoulder, and disappeared into his house. The mithan was then thrown on its side and killed by driving a sharp bamboo spear into its heart. The animal was then cut up. Later on another was killed, without any special ceremony, and the flesh of both cooked in the street. Later on there was a dance. Three men arrayed in fine cloths, with smart turbans, came up the main street, crossing from side to side. With bodies bent forward and arms extended, they took two steps forward, then whirled round once, beat time twice with the right foot, two steps, whirled round again, beat time twice with the left foot, and so on, keeping time with the royal band, consisting of a gong, a tom-tom, and a bamboo tube, used as a drum. The dancers, having been well regaled with beer, proceeded to dance each a *pas seul* of a decidedly indecent nature. The chief was prohibited from crossing running water for a month after this sacrifice had been performed." After this feast there is five days' "hrilh" for the whole community, and during this no flesh may be brought into the village. The skull of the mithan is kept on the post in front of the chief's house for a month, during which time he may not cross water or converse with strangers. On the expiry of a month a pig and a fowl are sacrificed and the skull is then removed to the front verandah.

The only difference in the ceremonies connected with childbirth is that the Ui-ha-awr sacrifice is only performed if the child's hair has a reddish tinge and the whites of its eyes turn yellowish.

The Sakhua sacrifices are very elaborate, and consist of a series commencing with the Vok-rial, which is necessary when a new house has been completed. A sow is killed at the head of the parents' sleeping place, and whatever portions of the flesh are not at once consumed are placed beneath it till the next day. The house during this time is "sherh." No one may enter it, and the occupants must not speak to strangers nor enter the forge. Later on a boar is killed in the front verandah, and the heart, liver, and entrails, known as "kawrawl," are placed under the parents' sleeping place for five days, and are eaten by the parents, the father sitting with his back to the partition wall and the mother facing him. During these five days a hrilh as above is observed. This sacrifice is called "Vok-pa"—*i.e.*, "Boar"—and is followed by the "Hnuaipui"—*i.e.*, "Great Beneath"—a full-grown sow being killed under the house, and its head and sherh buried at the foot of one of the main posts. The flesh is cooked beneath the house, but eaten in it. A three days' hrilh follows. The series concludes with "Hnuaite"—*i.e.*, "Lesser Beneath"—which is similar to the former, but a young sow is killed.

These sacrifices are performed as the necessary animals become available.

A dead Fanai is buried in the usual Lushai way, but no rice is placed in the grave. An offering of maize, however, is suspended above it. It may be noted that in the Zahao country rice is not cultivated, the staple crop being maize. The Fanai do not kill tigers, giving as the reason that a former ancestor of theirs lost his way, and was conducted back to his village by a tiger, which kindly allowed him to hold its tail.

The Rālte. This clan is found scattered in the Lushai villages to the north of Aijal, in which neighbourhood there are also one or two villages under Rālte chiefs. I have already—in Part I., Chapter V, para. 1—given the legend regarding the repeopling of the world and the closing of the exit from the Chhinglung owing to the loquacity of the pair of Rālte. The names of these mythical ancestors were Hehua and Leplupi. Their two sons were Kheltea and Siakenga, who quarrelled over the distribution of their father's goods, which Kheltea, the younger, had taken, thus conforming to Lushei custom, and set up separate villages, and from them have sprung the two eponymous families into which the Rālte clan is divided. The Khelte have always occupied a predominant position, and all the chiefs belong to this family. Lutmanga, Kheltea's youngest son, is said to have made the first cloth from the fibre of the Khawpui creeper. He collected a community at Khuazim, a hill north of Champhai, and from him all the Rālte chiefs are descended. In the early years of the nineteenth century the Rālte villages were near Champhai, and Mangkhaia, a Rālte chief of importance, was captured by some Chuango, a family of the Lushei clan, then living at Bualte, above Tuibual (known to the Chin Hills officers as Dipwell). He was ransomed by his relatives, but Vanpuia, the Pachuao chief, not receiving a share, ambushed Mangkhaia on his way home and killed him. According to another account Mangkhaia filed through his fetters with a file given to him in a roll of smoked meat, and was killed as he was escaping. His memorial stone is famous throughout the Hills, and stands at the southern extremity of Champhai. Mangthawnga, father of Mangkhaia, joined Khawzahuala the Zadeng, then living at Tualbung, but, being ill-treated, the Rālte joined Sutmanga, a Thado chief then at Phaileng, who treated them well. Thawnglura, son of Mangthawnga, showed his gratitude to Sutmanga by assisting the Sailo chief Lallianvunga, father of Gnura (Mullah)—whose village Colonel Lister burnt in 1850—to attack him. Sutmanga then fled northwards. It is satisfactory to know that Thawnglura's treachery was rewarded by the enslavement of his clan, who till our occupation of the Hills remained vassals of the Sailos. The Rālte are very quarrelsome, and have to a great extent resisted absorption into the Lushais. In some Sailo chiefs' villages there are so many Rālte that the chief himself speaks their dialect, and though Lushai is understood little else but Rālte is heard in the village.

The Rālte are linguistically connected with the Thado, and, like the Thado, they used not to build zawlbuks, but are now following Lushai custom in this respect.

MEMORIAL STONE IN CHAMPHAI KNOWN AS MANGKHAIA, LUNGDAWR.

The Khelte family has ten and the Siakeng family eleven branches. To the various sums paid to the relatives of the bride among the Lushais, the Ralte add "dawngbul" and "dawngler"—sums of Rs. 3/- paid to her male and female paternal first cousins.

The two families have slightly different customs as regard sacrifices. The Khelte sacrifice to Sakhua is a boar, which is killed at the head of the parents' sleeping place and then cooked on the hearth. The skull is hung on the back wall of the house in a basket with six pieces of the liver and three of the skin. The chant is as follows:—

Ah—h. You whom our grandmothers worshipped!
Ah—h. You whom our grandfathers worshipped!
Ah—h. You of our birthplace!
Ah—h. You of our place of origin!
Ah—h. You who made the Khelte!
Ah—h. You who made the Tuangphei!
Ah—h. In what we have done wrong!
Ah—h. In what we have sung amiss!
Ah—h. Make it right!

The Siakeng, after killing the boar as the Khelte do, entertain those of their own branch, but before the flesh is eaten it is divided into three portions, which are placed for a short time successively on the floor, on the sleeping-place, and on the shelf over the hearth, being thus offered to the spirits of the house, the couch, and the hearth.

Of the Naohri sacrifices the Khelte only perform the Hmarphir, which they call "Thangsang" and the Ui-ha-awr, while the Siakeng perform the Vawkte-luilam, called by them "Chhimhal," and the Ui-ha-awr.

They have adopted most of the Thangchhuah festivals, but not the Mi-thi-rawp-lam. When a mithan is killed it is not speared as among the Lushais, but killed by a blow on the forehead. The skull is placed at the foot of the partition wall for three days, and on the fourth it is taken out and placed at the foot of the memorial post. Some ginger, beans, and salt are placed on a dish and an old man takes the skull, and all dance round the post three times to the beating of drums and gongs. Then ginger is thrown three times on to the skull, after which the house-owner's wife pierces the skull with a spear, but if she be pregnant this must be done by a man. The skull is then placed on one of the posts of the platform in front of the house till the Khuangchoi has been performed.

On the occasion of the first death occurring in a new village a spot is selected beyond the line of houses, and the corpse is buried there, subsequent interments being made close at hand. It is considered "thianglo" to bury in a village. A well-to-do Khelte after death is dressed in his best, and seated with his back to the partition wall while his relatives and friends drink and dance before him. A bier is made by elderly persons, and on this the corpse is placed in a sitting position, with his weapons in his hands, and three times lifted by old men and women up to the rafters, while drums and gongs are beaten, after which the body is carried out to the graveyard.

The birth customs generally resemble those of the Lushais.

The Paihte or Vuite.

This is a clan of some importance still. There are eleven Vuite villages, numbering 877 houses, in the south-west corner of the Manipur State and two in the adjoining portions of the Lushai Hills. When we occupied the Hills we found many of this clan living in a species of slavery in the villages of important Sailo chiefs. They have mostly rejoined their clansmen, from whom they had been carried off as prisoners of war.

The clan is generally known to the Lushais as Paihte, but Vuite is the term more commonly used by its members and in Manipur. Vuitea and Paihtea were the sons of of Lamleia, who was hatched out of an egg. There were two eggs, and Aichhana, a Thado, tasted one, and, finding it bitter, threw it away and put the other among the rice in the bin, and in due time Lamleia was hatched out, and the present Vuite chiefs claim to be his direct descendants, enumerating seventeen generations. The Thado version of this story is that Dongel, Thado's elder brother, had incestuous intercourse with his elder sister, and on a male child being born their mother was so ashamed that she hid the child in a hollow tree, thinking it would die, but when she found it was alive after several days she brought it into the house and concealed it in the paddy bin, and produced it a few days later, saying that she had found two big eggs in a hollow tree and had tasted one and had found it very bitter. The second she had placed in the paddy, where it had been hatched by the sun's rays. Hence the child was called Gwite, from "ni-gwi," the Thado for a ray of sunshine. The Vuite, of course, do not admit this tale to be true, but my informant tells me that in his father's time, when the Dongel and Vuite lived near to each other, the former paid "sathing"—*i.e.*, a portion of each animal killed—to the latter, in recognition that the Vuite were descended from the elder sister of their ancestor. The Vuite, however, always tried to avoid accepting such presents, and when the Dongel moved away the custom died out. The first Vuite village is said to have been at Chimnuai, near to Tiddim. The name of this site comes first in the Vuite Sakhua chant which I obtained in the Lushai Hills. Being attacked by the Sokte and Falam clans, they joined the Thangur chiefs, but were ill-treated and fled to the neighbourhood in which they now live, and waged war with their oppressors till the establishment of our rule. They at one time approached the Manipur plain and in 1870, under Sumkām, they raided a Manipuri village, to avenge a charge of being wizards. They appear to be closely connected with the Malun, Sokte, and Kamhau clans of the adjoining Chin Hills, and Dr. Grierson places them linguistically in the same group as these clans and the Thado. In their dress and habitations they resemble the Lushais, but the place of the zawlbuk is taken by the front verandah of the houses of certain persons of importance, in which are long sleeping bunks in which half a dozen or more young men pass the night. The young fellows help their host in his house-building and cultivation, and once a year he gives them a feast of a pig. This custom prevails in most of the non-Lushei clans, and also among the Kabui Nagas in the Manipur Hills.

The women do not wear the huge ivory earrings of the Lushai but cornelians or short lead bars.

The general constitution of the clan and the village is very similar to that of the Lushais. As regards marriage they are monogamists, in this particular forming a very remarkable exception to all their cognates. The marriages of paternal first cousins are allowed—in fact, among chiefs they are the rule.

The parents of a young man who desires to marry a girl go to her house with an offering of zu, and if this is accepted the girl is at once taken to their house, but the bridegroom continues for two or three months to sleep with his bachelor friends. The marriage is not considered final nor is any payment made till a child is born, and if this does not occur within three years the couple separate, but on the birth of a child the full price agreed on must be paid up and divorce is not countenanced. On my enquiring what would happen in case the lady subsequently proved fickle, my informant smiled in a superior manner and said that such behaviour was unknown among his people. The Vuite object to giving their girls to the Lushais on account of the tendency of Lushai husbands to discard their wives on the slightest excuse.

Although the Vuite do not maintain that before marriage their girls are invariably chaste, yet one who errs is looked down on, and in consequence abortion and infanticide are said to be common. "Sawnman" at Rs. 23/- is demanded from the seducer.

As among most non-Lushei tribes, the eldest son inherits. The punishments for offences are similar to those among the Lushais, but the Vuite assert that the crime of sodomy is unknown among them. Murder can be atoned for by the payment of seven mithan to the heir of the murdered man, and accidental homicide by that of one mithan and a gun. In the days when war was common they used to ambush their enemies more than was usual among the Lushais, but they never went head-hunting simply for honour and glory. As regards "boi," they follow Lushai customs closely.

Pathian is acknowledged, and in general their religious beliefs resemble those of the Lushais, but they have no idea of a separate abode for the spirits of warriors. They believe that departed spirits have two or more lives in the land beyond the grave.

For their Sakhua sacrifice a boar is killed on the front verandah and cooked within the house. The skin of the head, the testicles, heart, snout, and liver are placed on a bamboo over the verandah, which must be freshly thatched.

Immediately after birth the child is washed, and a fowl is

killed, and its feathers are worn round the necks of the mother and infant. The mother may go out of the house, but for four days after the birth both parents abstain from all work. On occasion of the naming two or three pigs if available should be killed and much zu drunk. The Khāl sacrifices, with the exception of Uihring, are not performed, but most of the other sacrifices are made.

The custom of paying "lukawng" on the death of a person is unknown, and the funeral ceremonies generally are very unlike those of the Lushais.

After death the corpse is placed on a platform and fires are lit round it, and young men and maidens sleep near it. The skin is hardened and preserved by being rubbed with some greasy preparation. The body is dressed in the best cloths available, and a chaplet of the tail feathers of the hornbill is placed on its head. During the daytime the corpse is kept in the house, but in the evening it is brought out and seated on the verandah while the villagers dance and sing round it and drink zu, pouring it also into the mouth of the corpse. This disgusting performance goes on for a month or more according to the social position of the deceased. The corpses of those who have attained Thangchhuah honours are kept for a year, at least, in a special shed encased in a tree trunk. Before burial the corpse is carried round the village. In case of a violent death, which does not as among the Lushais include deaths in childbirth, the corpse is placed in the forge and the puithiam sacrifices a fowl, after which the usual ceremonies take place. The Kut festivals are not observed, but after harvest the owners of houses in which young men lodge kill one or two pigs. The honour of Thangchhuah is obtained by giving the following feasts:—(1) Buh ai, one mithan being killed; (2) Sheshun, one mithan being killed; (3) Chawn, three mithan and two pigs being killed. No other feasts are given and windows may be made by anyone. Most of the superstitions common among the Lushais are believed, but gibbons are freely killed. The Vuite are very much afraid of witchcraft, but deny all knowledge of it. When a new site for a house has to be chosen an egg is taken and one end is removed. It is then propped up on three small stones and a fire is lit under it. If the contents boil over towards the person consulting the omen the site is rejected as unlucky.

The Rāngte.

This is a small clan which, after various vicissitudes, has settled down in thirteen hamlets, containing 372 houses, under their own chiefs in the south-western hills of Manipur. They claim connection with the Thados, but resemble the Lushais in many respects, which no doubt is due to their sojourn among them. They also claim relationship with the Vaiphei. They say that their original villages were on two hills called Phaizang and Koku, whence they were ejected by the Chins and took refuge with Poiboi, one of the Sailo chiefs who opposed us in 1871, whence they migrated northwards to their present place of abode. Their language shows that their claim to being allied to the Thado is not without foundation. The clan is divided into eleven eponymous families, named after Thanghlum and his ten sons, Thanghlum being supposed to be the son of Rāngte. The constitution of the villages is practically the same as that of the Lushais, except that there are no zawlbuks. The young unmarried men sleep in the house of the girl they like best. An attractive young lady may have several admirers sleeping in her house, and they will continue to sleep there until she expresses a preference for one of them. Marriage is not very strictly limited, but matches with another member of the clan or with some member of one of the Thado families are most usual. The price of a wife—"manpui"—is one blue cloth, one mattress, and three mithan, which is paid to the nearest male relative to the bride on the father's side, but besides this the bride's paternal uncle receives one mithan, which is termed "mankang." If there be three brothers, A, B, and C, B will take the mankang of A's daughters, C that of B's, and A that of C's. Should a man have no brothers some near relative will take his daughter's mankang. The eldest son inherits everything, and is looked on as the head of the family. He receives the "manpui" of all the females, and in his verandah are hung all the trophies of the chase obtained by his brothers and their children, but on the death of one of these brothers the connection ceases, and the deceased's eldest son inherits his property and is looked on as the head of the family by his

Vuite Memorial.

Rangte Grave.

younger brothers. Like the Vuite, the Rāngte claim that sodomy is unknown among them. In their religious beliefs they employ the nomenclature of the Thados, though there is a little variation. The place of Pupawla on the road to Mi-thi-khua is taken by an old woman, named Kul-lo-nu, who is evidently the same as the Thado Kulsamnu, who troubles all except the Thangchhuah. Thlan-ropa is known as "Dāpā," but the legends regarding him are similar to those told by the Lushais.

On the birth of a female child, zu is drunk, but should the child be a son, a pig and a fowl have to be killed, and three days later the puithiam comes and sprinkles the mother with water, muttering charms as he does so, after which ceremony she can go out. Immediately after a death everyone present seizes the nearest weapon and slashes wildly at the walls, posts, shelves, and partitions, shouting, "You have killed him! We will cut you limb from limb, whoever you may be." The young men then go out in search of wild birds and beasts, the bodies of which are hung on posts round the grave. The corpse is adorned with the head-dress of hornbill's feathers, as among the Vuite and most of the Old Kuki clans. The corpses of ordinary persons are buried without much ceremony close to the house, but the Thangchhuah are carried round the village, as among the Khawtlang, and then enclosed in hollow tree trunks, and kept for periods varying from two months to a year in special sheds, with fires smouldering beneath them, after which the bones are buried. In this it will be noticed that the Rāngte custom is a composite of Lushei, Vuite, and Khawtlang.

Lukawng is only paid if the deceased has been a great hunter or warrior. In their marriage ceremonies the Rāngte differ but little from the Lushais. The "Khāl" sacrifices are omitted, but most of the others are performed.

Thangchhuah honours are attained by giving only two feasts—the "Chong," at which a hen has to be sacrificed and two pigs and a mithan killed, and the "Mai-thuk-kai," at which two mithan, three pigs, and a hen have to be killed. The guests hold hands and form a circle round the house of the giver of the feast, who has to anoint the head of each of them with pig's fat. The Buh-Ai is unknown, but the Ai of wild animals is performed as among the Lushais.

CHAPTER III

THE OLD KUKI CLANS

THE term Old Kukis has long been applied to the clans which suddenly appeared in Cachar about 1800, the cause of which eruption I have explained when dealing with the history of the Lushais, but Dr. Grierson in the *Linguistic Survey* has included in this group a number of clans which had long been settled in Manipur territory, and my enquiries all go to prove the correctness of this classification. It appears practically certain that the ancestors of the Old Kukis and the Lushais were related and lived very close together somewhere in the centre of the hills on the banks of the Tyao and Manipur rivers. The Old Kuki clans of Manipur seem to have been the first to move, as records of their appearance there are found in the Manipur chronicle as early as the sixteenth century, and, though the chronology of the chronicle is not beyond suspicion, I think this may be taken as proof that these clans appeared in Manipur a good deal earlier than their relations the Bete and Rhangkhol entered Cachar. What the cause of this move was it is impossible to say. Probably quarrels with their neighbours, coupled with a desire for better land, combined to cause the exodus, and the movement, once started, had to continue till the clans found a haven of rest in Manipur, as their relatives did centuries later in British territory; for they were small, weak communities, at the mercy of the stronger clans, through whose lands they passed.

All these Old Kuki clans are organised far more democratically than the Lushais or Thados. Lieut. Stewart in his Notes on Northern Cachar says:—" There is no regular system of government among the Old Kukis and they have no hereditary chiefs as among the New ones. A headman called the 'ghalim' is appointed by themselves over each village, but he is much more a priest than a potentate, and his temporal power is much limited. Internal administration among them always takes a provisional form. When any party considers himself aggrieved, he makes an appeal to the elders, or the most powerful householders in the village, by inviting them to dinner and plying them with victuals and wine."

Among the clans which settled early in Manipur, each village has been provided with a number of officials with high-sounding titles and little power, in imitation of the Manipur system. Among those who have settled in British territory the ghalim has been transformed into the "gaonbura"—*i.e.*, head of the village—and has acquired a certain amount of authority, whilst among the Khawtlang and Khawchhak clans, which after various vicissitudes, including a more or less lengthy sojourn among the Lushais, recently entered Manipur territory, the ghalim has become a feeble imitation of a Lushai lal.

The Old Kuki Clans of Manipur.

Under this heading I propose dealing with the Aimol, Anal, Chawte, Chiru, Kolhen, Kom, Lamgang, Purum, Tikhup, and Vaiphei, who are now found in various parts of the hills bordering the Manipur valley, and who resemble each other in very many respects. In spite of this resemblance, the clans, while acknowledging their relationship to one another, keep entirely apart, living in separate villages and never intermarrying.

In the Manipur chronicle the Chiru and Anal are mentioned as early as the middle of the sixteenth century, while the Aimol make their first appearance in 1723. They are said to have come from Tipperah, but at that time the eastern boundary of Tipperah was not determined, and the greater part of the present Lushai Hills district was supposed to be more or less under the control of the Rajah of that State. A short distance to the east of Aijal there is a village site called Vai-tui-chhun—*i.e.*, the watering place of the Vai—which is said to commemorate a former settlement of the Vaiphei. It seems probable, therefore, that the Aimol and Vaiphei left their former homes in consequence of the forward movement of the Lusheis. The remaining tribes all claim to have come from various places to the south of Manipur—the Anal from the Haubi peak, the Chiru from "the Hranglal hill far away in the south," the Kom from the Sakripung hill in the Chin Hills; the other clans can give no nearer definition of the home of their forefathers than far away to the south. Like the Lushais, they all assert that they are descended from couples who issued out of the earth, the Chhinglung of the Lushais being replaced by "Khurpui"—*i.e.*, the great hole.

The Anal assert that two brothers came out of a cave on the Haubi peak, and that the elder was the ancestor of the Anals, while the younger went to the valley of Manipur and became king of the valley. Another tradition says that the Manipuris, Anals, and Thados are the descendants of three men, whose father was the son of Pakhāngba, the mythical snake-man ancestor of the Manipuri royal family, who, taking the form of an attractive youth, overcame the scruples of a maiden engaged in weeding her jhum (compare Hodson's "Meitheis," page 12). These legends were probably invented after the clans had come in contact in order to account for the resemblances between them. The Chiru claim to be descended from Rezar, the son of Chongthu, the ancestor of the clan of that name still found in the Lushai Hills, whose name also appears in the Thado pedigree. The Lamgang tell the following tale:—On the Kangmang hill, away to the south, there is a cave. Out of this came a man and a woman, and were eaten up by a tiger which was watching. A god who had two horns, seeing this horrible sight, came out and drove away the tiger, and so the next couple to emerge escaped and became the ancestors of the Lamgang. The Purum claim to be descended from Tonring and Tonshu, who issued from the earth. It is said that "Pu rum" means "hide from tiger," which connects them closely with the Lamgang legend. The Kolhen's ancestors were a man and woman who sprang out of Khurpui provided with a basket and a spear, and lived at Talching, and had a son and daughter called Nairung and Shaithatpal, the direct descendants of whom are said still to be found among the Kolhen.

The Chawte told me the tale of the peopling of the world out of a hole in the ground, adding the graphic touch that an inquisitive monkey lifted up a stone which lay over the opening, and thus allowed their ancestors to emerge.

It is not quite clear whether these clans are eponymous. The Chiru say that their clan is named after an ancestor, but can give no pedigree. The Aimol say that there is no general name for the various families, and that Aimol is the name of the village site. It is probably Ai-mual. "Ai" is the Lushai name of a berry and also means crab, and appears in Ai-zawl or Aijal. "Mual" is the Lushai for a spur of a hill. It is a very common, in fact almost a universal, custom to call a new village site, if it has no recognised name, after the site of the old village, and probably the original Aimual would be found in the centre of the Lushai Hills.

All these clans have come much under Manipuri influence, and the Chiru, Aimol, Kolhen, Chawte, Purum, and Tikhup have abandoned the ancestral architecture, and now live in houses built on raised earthen plinths like the Manipuris.

The remaining clans still adhere to the ancient style, their houses being raised some four or five feet off the ground on posts. The walls are of planks, and the roofs of thatching grass; they remind one much of the Falam houses. Round each village are clustered the granaries—small houses raised well off the ground and placed sufficiently far from the dwelling houses to make them fairly safe from fire. Where the houses are raised sufficiently pigs and poultry live under them; but cattle sheds are common, most of these clans having learnt the value of cows and buffaloes from the Manipuris. The handsome breed of goats so common in a Lushai village is seldom if ever seen, but animals of an inferior sort are generally kept.

The Chiru, Kom, and Tikhup still build zawlbuks. No woman is allowed to enter these buildings, which, besides being the dormitories of the unmarried men, are used for drinking bouts. They are externally very like those built by the Lushais, but have several fireplaces evidently used for cooking, and the general hearth in the centre is absent. Some of the clans which do not now build zawlbuks say that they believe their forefathers did so. In the absence of the zawlbuk the young men generally sleep in the houses of well-to-do villagers, but among the Purum I am told that "if a man has one unmarried son and one unmarried daughter, the boy goes to sleep at the house of a man who has an unmarried daughter; though they sleep in this way they are very careful about their characters." Have we here stumbled on the real origin of the "young men's house"—a desire to prevent incest? The young women also have houses in which they gather at time of festivals, but they do not sleep there.

The rotchem, the Lushai mouth-organ, is found among all these clans, but rather smaller and ornamented with fowls' feathers. The Anal make a speciality of long bamboo trumpets, on which they perform with considerable skill, producing sounds indistinguishable from those of a bugle. The trumpets are from four to five feet long, and have bell-shaped mouths made of gourds.

Most of these clans have adopted various dances from the Manipuris, their own dancing being of the monotonous nature common to the Lushais and Kukis.

In dress and method of wearing the hair Manipuri influence is also noticeable, the men generally wearing coats and loin-cloths and turbans. The women are more conservative and adhere to the short petticoat. The hair is generally worn very much in the Lushai fashion, but the Chiru men are an exception to this. They part their hair in the middle and brush it down straight, and trim it level with the bottom of the ears. They bind a narrow fillet of cane round the head slightly above the eyes. The Kolhen women gather the hair into two heavy rolls, which hang down in front of each ear. The Tikhup maidens have adopted the Manipuri method of dressing the hair.

The ivory discs worn in the ears by Lushai women are not found, but metal rings are worn in a similar manner by both sexes.

The Manipuris have instituted in each village a number of posts with high-sounding titles, similar to those in use among themselves, but traces of the older organisation are to be found. Thus the Aimol recognise a man called Thompa, of the Chomgom family, as the head of the clan, but he has no power

Photo by M. Little, Esq., Loc. Engineer.

AIMOL NAUTCH PARTY. THE YOUTH IS HOLDING A ROTCHEM.

and receives nothing, while in each village are four officials who receive a portion of every animal killed in the chase. They are called "kamzakhoi," "zakachhunga," "zupalba," and "pakang-lakpa." The last two titles have a distinctly Manipuri sound about them. The usual titles found are "khul-lakpa"—*i.e.*, chief of the village—"lup-lakpa," "zupalba," and "Methei lumbu"—*i.e.* Manipuri interpreter—but there are others. The khul-lakpa and lup-lakpa are hereditary posts. Among the Lamgang there are seven such hereditary posts. Among the Chiru the khul-lakpa, besides receiving a portion of each animal killed, also gets his house built for nothing, which brings him very near to the Lushai "lāl." Among the Kolhen the khul-lakpa's and lup-lakpa's posts are not hereditary, but on the death of either his successor must be chosen out of the same family, but his sons are ineligible. The new official has to give a feast, killing a pig, which is eaten by the whole community, and the young men and maidens make merry with dance and song. It seems probable that in this may be some idea of averting the evil effects of a breach of the generally accepted custom.

The puithiam is known as "thempu," "khulpu," or "bulropa," and both he and the blacksmith are sometimes rewarded, receiving a day's labour from each householder they serve, instead of a donation of rice.

The Lushai system of "boi" is generally unknown, which is only natural in such democratic communities.

The following animals are not generally eaten—tigers, snakes, cats, crows, or kites; and among the Lamgang the rat is also considered unfit for food.

Each clan is divided into eponymous families and generally marriage is restricted to the clan, but alliances within the family are prohibited. The Aimol clan is divided into five families—Chongom, Laita or Mangte, Khoichung or Leivon, Lanu, and Chaita. Marriage is unrestricted, but it is unusual for either sex to marry without the clan. The Kolhen are divided into twelve exogamous families divided into two groups, which are also exogamous (*v.* below, under Festivals, page 167), but marriage outside the clan is prohibited. Among the Anal, Purum, and Lamgang marriages must be made within the clan, but not within the family.

The Tikhup clan, which only numbers some twenty households, is not sub-divided, but marriage is endogamous. The union of first cousins, either paternal or maternal, is prohibited. The elders of the clan attributed the steady decline in their numbers to this custom of endogamy.

The Chiru and Chawte customs are alike; not only is a young man's choice limited to some family in the clan other than his own, but the actual families from which he may choose his bride are strictly fixed.

Among the Chiru—

A Danla lad may marry a Dingthoi or Shangpa girl.
A Dingthoi lad may marry a Chongdur or Danla girl.
A Rezar lad may marry a Danla girl.
A Shangpa lad may marry a Dingthoi or Danla girl.
A Chongdur lad may marry a Danla girl.

Danla is the family from which the khul-lakpa must be taken, and Rezar has already been noticed as the son of Chongthu, from whom the Chiru claim descent.

Among the Chawte—

A Marem lad may only marry a Makhan girl.
A Makhan lad may only marry an Irung girl.
A Kiang lad may only marry a Makhan or Marem girl.
An Irung lad may only marry a Marem, Thao, or Kiang girl.
A Thao lad may only marry a Makhan girl.

Among the Aimol, Anal, Chiru, and Purum, a young man has to serve his future wife's father for three years, during which he works as if he were a son of the house. During this period he has free access to the girl, though among the Chiru he continues to sleep among the bachelors. Should the girl become enceinte the marriage ceremony must be performed, and the price paid. Among the Aimol the bride's eldest brother gets Rs. 6/- and each of the others one rupee less than his immediate senior. The paternal and maternal uncles receive Rs. 2/- each; the aunt and the elder sister also receive Rs. 1/- each as "niman" and "nao-puan-puk-man," as among the Lushais. Among the Anal and the Purum, the price must not be less than a pig and a piece of iron a cubit in length, but the girl's relatives try to get as much more as they can. The bridegroom has also to feast the family of his bride three times on pork, fowls, and rice, washed down, of course, with plenty of zu. The Chiru girls are only valued at one gong.

Among the other clans, marriage is by simple purchase. A Chawte maiden can be obtained for a spear, a dao, and a fowl, the payment being sealed by the consumption of much zu. The price of a Kolhen girl is a gong and Rs. 7/- to her mother, and Rs. 7/- each to the elder and younger brother and the maternal uncle. This is most curious, for the father is entirely omitted. Can it be a survival of mother right? The Kom girls are valued very high, the father receiving one gong, four buffaloes, fifteen cloths, a hoe, and a spear, the aunt taking a black and white cloth. A Lamgamg bridegroom has to pay his father-in-law three pigs or buffaloes or cows, one string of conch shell beads, one lead bracelet, and one black or blue petticoat. A Tikhup father expects a gong, ten hoes, one dao, and one spear; the maternal grandfather also demands Rs. 7/-.

The price of a Vaiphei girl varies between two and ten mithan. To a certain extent the price of the girls may be taken as an indication of the relative importance of the clan. Marriage by servitude is not found among either the Lushai or the Thado clans; its appearance among the Old Kukis is therefore curious, for as a rule the customs of a clan will be found to resemble those of one or the other of these two main divisions of the Kuki-Lushai race.

Polygamy is, as a rule, permitted. Among the Anal and Lamgang, the first wife is entitled to the company of her husband for five nights, the second for four, and the third for three. It is not quite clear how a second marriage by servitude can be carried out, and probably the rules are modified in such cases. Polygamy is but little practised on account of the expense; among the Kolhen it is prohibited.

In most of these clans the Thado rule of inheritance is followed—viz., the eldest son takes all his father's property, the younger sons only getting what the heir chooses to give them. Among the Anal and Purum, and probably also the Lamgang, the sons of the deceased divide the property, but the youngest son takes the house and supports the widow, thus approximating to the Lushai custom.

In most clans the father of an illegitimate child is fined. Among the Chiru the fine is a pig, a mithan, and two gongs.

Divorce is generally easily obtained. Among the Aimol, if either party repents of the bargain, the payment of a cloth and three pots of zu annuls the contract. Among the Tikhup the cost of divorce is a mithan and a gong. The Anal and most of the other clans insist on the question being submitted to the village officials, who receive fees according to their position, and settle what compensation, if any, shall be paid to either party. As a rule it is very difficult for a woman to obtain a divorce unless her husband agrees, even though he may be extremely unfaithful and brutal. Among the Anal she must give a feast to the village or pay her husband Rs. 50/-.

In case of a wife being led astray the injured husband recovers her price or an equivalent amount (among the Tikhup twice the price) from her seducer. In this the Thado custom is followed, which is more just than that of the Lushais, but not so conducive to morality, for among the the Lushais the whole of the woman's family are interested in keeping her from committing herself and are loud in condemnation should she do so, as they have to refund the various sums they have received on her behalf, whereas among the Thado the seducer simply pays up the price and takes the woman, who is thought very little the worse of—in fact, among the clans which follow this apparently more just custom, women hold a far lower position, being traded from one to another, unless they have influential male relatives who take an interest in them.

All these clans have been given definite sites in Manipur and have practically abandoned the migratory habits of their forefathers, and therefore the idea of property in land, which is entirely absent in the case of the Lushais, is fast springing up. Many villages are moving nearer to the plain in order that the people may take leases from the State of land in the valley and carry on plough cultivation, but they also do a certain amount of jhuming, and proprietary rights in jhum lands are recognised.

The punishment for theft is arranged much on the Lushai system of the theft of certain articles having a fixed fine attached to it. This is generally a pig, two jars of zu, and a brass plate. Among the Chiru the whole fine is consumed by the people of the village, the thief also getting his share. The Kolhen punishment is a fine of Rs. 28/-, a pig, and two jars of zu. In case of rice being stolen, the Tikhup custom is that the village officials at once kill and eat the pig of the thief and then make him pay a mithan as compensation to the complainant. Thefts of minor articles are generally punished by the thief providing a pig and zu for the entertainment of his judges. Manslaughter is punished by the payment of compensation, the amount varying considerably. The Anal demand a mithan and a gong, the Chiru a mithan and a cloth, the Kolhen three mithan, a brass pot, a pig, and two pots of zu, the Lamgang four gongs, ten jars of zu, and a big pig. Petty assaults are punished by fines of pigs and zu. A false charge is often punished by a fine of zu. Most of these clans declare that sodomy is unknown among them, the very notion appearing to them highly absurd.

All disputes and accusations are disposed of by the village officials, who meet sometimes in the house of the khul-lakpa and sometimes at a special spot outside the village where stone seats have been prepared.

Since the settlement of these clans in Manipur territory all raiding and fighting has been stopped, so that they have practically forgotten what were the habits of their forefathers in these respects, but the Kom declare that in the good old days the young Kom warriors went off on head-hunting expeditions, and if successful adorned the village gate with the trophies of their prowess; and there is no reason to doubt that, in spite of their present peaceable behaviour, the previous history of these clans was not less full of raids and counter-raids than that of their neighbours.

The general religious beliefs of these clans show a great resemblance to each other and also to that of the Lushais. Pathian is universally recognised as the creator who lives in the sky, though the name is slightly different, appearing as Pathel among the Anal and Kolhen, and Patheng among the Kom. Mi-thi-khua is generally known as the place of departed spirits, but the Chiru and Tikhup have no idea of a place of greater comfort for the spirits of warriors, though the Chiru believe that the spirits of those that die unnatural deaths go to a separate and inferior place, while those of the other dead go westwards into the sky. The Anal, Kolhen, and Lamgang believe that, after hovering around the grave for some time, the spirit is reincarnated in some new-born child, but that an unnatural death prevents this and the spirit passes away skywards and returns no more. The belief in a being or beings which trouble the spirits on their way to Mi-thi-khua, as Pupawla does with his pellet bow, is very general. The Aimol call him Ramcharipu, and say that he makes the spirits of all, except "Thangchhuah," kill a certain number of lice in his head. The Vaiphei say that a male and a female being guard the road and trouble and detain the spirits of those who have not attained the honours of Thangchhuah. With the exception of the Tikhup, all the clans believe in demons, which they call by various names and which correspond exactly with the Huai of the Lushais. The Aimol call these devils Numeinu, Thanglian Borh, Tuikuachoi. "Numeinu" means mother of woman Borh brings to memory the infantile illness called by that name by the Lushais, while "Tuikuachoi" is evidently the Tui-huai. The Aimol and Chiru perform the Daibawl sacrifices in the same manner as the Lushais. The Chawte sacrifice pigs and fowls in case of sickness, but the Khāl sacrifices are quite unknown to any Old Kuki clans. Lāshi is known to the Aimol and Vaiphei. Among the former the Sakhua sacrifices are performed to this deity, and he is capable of giving success in the chase, The Vaiphei place Lāshi almost on a par with Pathian and sacrifice a pig to him every year. Strange to say, he is supposed to have only one leg. The Sakhua chant of the Vuite commences with an invocation to all the wild animals to collect.

In nearly every clan there is an annual festival in honour of the souls of those who have died during the year, but in no case is the Mi-thi-rawp-lām or any similar festival included in the series of Thangchhuah feasts.

The Aimol sacrifice either a pig or a goat to Lāshi as their Sakhua. The Chawte have been much influenced by Manipuris, and I was first told that the names of their gods were

Pakhāngba and Nungchongba, but on a little further enquiry I found that Pakhāngba was always called Pathian when talking among themselves. The other deity is probably the Manipuri god Nungshaba ("The Meitheis," Hodson, page 98).

Above the hamlet was an oval, level space with a low wall round it. At the eastern end was a small house in which were two stones. This was the abode of Pakhāngba, and to one side was Nungchongba's dwelling place, which consisted of three small stones, with a fourth one placed on the top. In front of these a bull is sacrificed once in three years, and dancing and singing take place every year after the harvest. The Chiru believe in "Rampus," which in some respects appear to be the same as the Lushai "Huai," but in others they appear to be local gods. The four chief Rampus live one on Kobru, a high hill overlooking the northern extremity of the Manipur valley and called by the Manipuris the guardian of the north, one in Kangjupkhul, the village site of my informants, one on Makong hill and one in the valley of Manipur. Twice a year the Rampu of Kobra is honoured with the sacrifice of a dog, while pigs, fowls, or goats are offered to the others. In July a dog is killed in honour of the first three and a pig in honour of the last-named. In case of very serious illness, when the Daibawl sacrifices have proved unavailing, special sacrifices are made to the three chief Rampus above mentioned. These four Rampus are evidently nearer to local godlings than the multitudinous and ill-defined Huais of the Lushais. In July Pathian also is honoured, a pig being killed on behalf of the whole village, while each household sacrifices a fowl. The day is held sacred, no work being done. It is known as Chapui-chol-lai—*i.e.*, holiday in the great heat. The four Rampus can only have come into prominence since the settlement of the hamlet at Kangjupkhul, and it is probable that different ones are worshipped by other hamlets. The Chiru also perform Sakhua sacrifices as the Lushais do. The Tikhup denied all knowledge of any devils or semi-divine beings, saying that they worshipped Pathian and him only. Every year in Phalgun they sacrifice a pig and a cock to Pathian, and much zu is drunk. In cases of sickness sacrifices of pigs or fowls and offerings of flowers, eggs, and rice are made to Pathian. Dogs are never sacrificed. I think this is the only clan in which they are not. I failed to find out the cause of this.

In the other clans the sacrifices are combined with festivals either in connection with the crops, the dead, or Thangchhuah, and are not simply in honour of the god.

The puithiam of the Lushais becomes "thempu" and in some clans "khulpu." The last name seems to indicate his responsibility for protecting the village from all ills and misfortunes by performing the necessary sacrifices (khul = village, pu = protector). He appears here as one of the village officials, which is the natural result of the inhabitants of each village being all of the same clan, instead of many clans, as among the Lushais. The functions and methods of the thempu and khulpu appear to be the same as those of his Lushai *confrère*. There are various restrictions imposed on pregnant women. Among the Anal she may not eat chillies or honey, and her husband must not touch a snake or a corpse. The Kolhen prohibit her from killing a snake, attending a funeral ceremony, and eating a crab, eggs, and a certain vegetable called "chak" in its young state. The Lamgang also debar her from touching a corpse, but the prohibited articles of food are a sort of fish called "ngarin" and a small animal which I have not succeeded in identifying. The birth ceremonies are much alike; in every clan there is a period during which the woman, and in some cases the house, is "sherh." During this time the mother's movements are restricted in some way.

Among the Aimol the period is five days in case of a boy, and three in case of a girl; among the Anal and Purum, three days in both cases; among the Chawte, Kom, and Vaiphei, five. Among the Chiru the period is extended to ten days, during which the mother must not go out and no one but near relations may enter the house. Among the Kolhen the period is also ten days, but all women of the village may enter the house; the mother must eat no flesh, and fowls only may be sacrificed. Cohabitation is prohibited for three months. Among the Tikhup the restriction on the mother's movements lasts only till the disposal of the afterbirth by special persons who clean up the house; till this is done no one may take a light from the fire or remove any article from the house. In every case at the conclusion of this period there is a sacrifice. The custom of the Aimol is for the "thempu" to pour out a libation of zu and herbs in front of the house and invoke the child's spirit to take up its residence within the new-born infant. The name is given at the same time, the father's family choosing the name of a son and the mother's of a daughter. On the day of the birth of an Anal child, the "khulpu" is called, and after he has muttered certain incantations, zu and fish are distributed to the whole village. All sacrificing is prohibited for three days, and cohabitation for three months. When distributing the zu and fish, the household gods—*i.e.*, the Sakhua—are invoked and the soul of the child is summoned. Among the Chawte the thempu attends on the day of the birth, and sacrifices a fowl and sips zu. He then mutters incantations over a piece of turmeric which is then thrown out of the house. On the fifth day a fowl is killed, and as the name selected is pronounced three grains of rice are dropped into a cup of water, and if they sink the name is approved, but if they float another one must be selected and tested in the same manner.

The Chiru ceremonies are more elaborate. After ten days the thempu comes to the house, a rakeng tree is planted in front of it, and then the thempu sacrifices a hen on behalf of the mother, and a cock or a hen, according to the sex of the child, on its behalf. The parents eat the flesh of the birds, and the sherh and bones are buried in the house. Two or three pots of zu are consumed by married persons. The thempu, taking some zu in his mouth, goes round inside the house, blowing it out on the walls and muttering charms. The mother can now leave the house, but for three or four days must not leave the village. The "keng-puna" or "ming-puna"—*i.e.*, "name-giving"—takes place almost immediately. Two cocks or hens, according to the sex of the infant, are killed by the thempu, and their blood smeared on the infant's forehead and navel, some of the feathers being tied in its hair. The Kolhen pierce the child's ears and give the name on the tenth day, the ceremony being the same as among the Chiru on that day. The maternal grandfather is expected to give the child a pair of brass earrings,

M

bracelets, leg ornaments, and a string of glass beads, and it is generally named after him—a custom also followed by the Koms, who combine the name-giving and ear-piercing, giving a feast for the purpose, on the expiration of the five days' sherh. The ear-piercing is done by the paternal aunt. The Lamgang ceremonies are the same as those of the Anal, but the father is prohibited from eating the flesh of fowls during the sherh period, while the mother is under no restriction as regards diet. No other animal may be sacrificed during that time, and cohabitation is not allowed for one month. The Purum customs are severely simple. The thempu comes and mutters charms on the day of the birth, and returns on the third day and makes a libation of zu. No sacrifices are allowed. The name is given on the second day by the midwife, and the ears are pierced on the seventh day, but in neither case is there any ceremony. The Tikhup give the name at a feast, to which the elders of the community are invited; a cock is killed and zu dispensed freely. In case of the parents being poor, this feast may be postponed till the child is two years old.

The custom of summoning the child's soul reminds one of the Lushai prohibition of labour on the part of the parents for seven days after the child's birth, lest its soul, which hovers around them during that period, be injured.

Ceremonies connected with marriage.

Where marriage is by service, it is only natural that the actual ceremony should be of little importance, for the couple have been living as man and wife during the whole time; but there are exceptions.

At an Aimol wedding two thempus are necessary—one of the bridegroom's, and one of the bride's family. Each kills a cock, the feathers of which are tied round the necks of the happy pair, after which there is the usual orgy. The Chiru and Tikhup custom is almost identical, but the village thempu officiates alone. Among the Kolhen, the young man's mother makes six visits to the parents of her future daughter-in-law, taking an offering of zu, and being accompanied by her eldest son-in-law or other male relative, and on the last occasion by two or three women. Two days after the last visit, the price is fixed, and the day for the ceremony chosen by the bridegroom's father and the village officials. The bridegroom, on the day before that fixed for the marriage, goes to the girl's house, accompanied by several male friends, and makes a present of three pots of zu to her parents. The next morning the bride, accompanied by the unmarried girls of the village, goes to her future home, taking with her two jars of zu, a hen, a piece of ginger, a dog, a strap for carrying loads, a new cloth, and a bracelet. She parts from her friends, with many tears, on the doorstep of her new home. The khulpu decapitates a fowl and throws it down; if the right leg falls over the left a happy married life is assured. The night is spent in singing and dancing, and the following night in the same way, but in the house of the bride, who on the next morning quits her father's house for good. On the day of the marriage the bride and bridegroom must not leave the village. This taking of omens by killing a cock is practised by the Lamgang and Kom. Where marriage is not by service the preliminaries in all clans resemble much those among the Kolhen. Among the Vaiphei, and, I think, in some other clans, the young man has to give a feast to the young men frequenting the same dormitory. A similar custom is described in Fielding Hall's "The Inward Light," page 104, as existing in Burma. "It is an old custom for the village boys to band themselves together in a company. . . . But when one marries he ceases to belong to the company, for he is about to enter into another and a wider life. He is a deserter and a traitor to his fellows. Therefore they lay in wait for him and caught him as he went home at night, and, taking him without the village gate, they tried him and found him guilty. With mock ceremony he was condemned to be turned out from their ranks, and to pay a fine wherewith his comrades might drown their sorrow at his desertion. Then with laughter and song, to the light of torches, they took him home in long procession."

Widows are allowed to remarry, but as a rule the brothers of the deceased husband have a prior claim, and if the woman marries anyone else before the annual feast in honour of the dead she has to pay a fine, which in some clans is as much as Rs. 120/-, to her brother-in-law. Until this annual feast has come round she must remain in her late husband's house, but when that has been performed she may return to her father's house if she wishes to, but in that case the brother-in-law will take the dead man's property and children.

Ceremonies connected with death.

All these clans bury their dead in special cemeteries outside the village, and unnatural deaths or deaths in childbirth are universally considered signs that the deceased has failed in some way, and the corpses of such unfortunates are buried outside the cemetery and with scant ceremony.

Among the Aimol, the corpse of the khul-lakpa is carried round the village before being taken to the grave. The corpse of one who has gained honours equivalent to Thangchhuah among the Lushais is enclosed in a rough log coffin and kept for two days amid much drinking and feasting, which recalls the funeral ceremonies of a Lushei chief. With a rich man many cloths are buried and with a poor man at least one. In addition some cooked rice, zu, a dao, some meat, and a bow and arrow are deposited in the grave. The bow and arrow are a survival, for such weapons have been long obsolete. Over the grave a small house is built in which some meat and zu are placed to attract the "Khawhring." Spears are then thrust through the house, which is then thrown away. I am not quite clear whether the "Khawhring" in this case is supposed, as among the Lushais, to have inhabited the body of the deceased, or whether it is believed to be a disembodied spirit which is on the lookout for the soul of the deceased.

Three days after the burial a wild animal is killed and zu and rice are offered, and the spirit of the deceased is asked to go away and not to trouble the living who have sacrificed and made an offering of zu and rice. The Anal make a distinction between deaths in childbirth and deaths by accident or in war. In the former case the body is buried in the cemetery, the grave being dug by those of her household, and food and drink and domestic utensils are deposited therein. The husband has to sacrifice a pig and feast the village before the burial, and the village is "sherh" for that day. The first stones and earth are placed in the grave by aged men, and the filling then completed by young men. The thempu having muttered some charms, the young men and women sing and dance for the deliverance of the soul. In cases of ordinary death the grave is dug by men not of the household, but in case of unnatural death only old grey-headed men may perform the task, and the grave is dug in the jungle and no dance or song terminates the funeral, but the village is not "sherh."

The Chawte make their cemetery some distance from the village. The dead are buried on the day of death. Over each grave a mound is raised and fenced round with a bamboo trellis-work. A small post carved faintly to resemble the human form is placed over the grave of a man, while a hoe, axe, and winnowing fan denote the grave of a woman. On each grave rests a flat basket containing some flowers and a small jar of water. Behind each grave is a rough representation of a house raised some four feet from the ground, which is also ornamented with flowers, and some of the deceased's clothes hang from it, while inside are placed a bamboo full of zu and a small cup, which is filled with clean water, and a handful of raw rice. These are changed every third or fourth day till the Thi-duh ceremony comes round in May, when there is a feast, and portions of meat and some zu are placed on each fresh grave.

On the death of a Chiru, guns are fired and gongs beaten, and a fowl, pig, and goat are killed at once. There is the usual funeral feast, and food and personal effects, including his comb, are buried with him. The house is "sherh" for three days, during which rice is placed in a small basket in the house and then thrown on to the grave. On the third day the house is purified by the thempu sacrificing a cock. In nearly every clan the house has to be purified by the thempu besprinkling it with either consecrated water or zu, and in many cases the funeral party are similarly purified. The Kolhen bury the bodies of those who die natural deaths in front of their houses, as do the Lushais, and the funeral feast closely resembles that held by the Lushais. The body of a khul-lakpa is carried three times round his memorial stone, from left to right. A bow and arrow are placed in the grave. The village is "sherh" for three days for any death. The Lamgang follow the same customs as the Anal, but the bodies of women who die in childbirth are not buried in the graveyard. The Kom and the Purum have the curious custom that the duty of digging the grave in case of an unnatural death falls on the son-in-law of the deceased. They say that the spirit of the dead cries out at the place where he met his death until appeased by an offering of tobacco leaves and rice. The Tikhup funeral is exactly the same as that of an ordinary Lushai. The Vaiphei dress up the corpse and strap it on to a bamboo frame, as do the Lushais, and feast around it for three days if food and drink suffice for so long. At the end of the feast the thempu pours some zu down the throat of the corpse and bids the spirit go in peace, and the body is carried to the grave, but if the deceased has attained Thangchhuah honours, it is first carried round the village. The household of the deceased abstain from washing or dressing the hair till some wild animal has been killed. The custom of giving something to the maternal grandfather or uncle on the occasion of a death, known among the Lushais as "lukawng," is found among several clans. Among the Tikhup and Kolhen, for instance, he receives the neck of the animal killed on the occasion of the funeral, and in the last-named clan he also receives a pipe or Rs. 2/-. The custom known among the Kabui and other allied tribes in Manipur as "mandu," which ordains that a widower shall pay his deceased wife's father a certain sum as the price of her bones, is only found among the Kolhen, with whom it is usual to pay Rs. 5/- or 6/-. Among the Kolhen a child dying within ten days of its birth is buried under the eaves of the house, and is called "thichhiat" equivalent to the "hlamzuih" among the Lushais.

Festivals. 1. *Connected with Crops.*—The Tikhup, the only monotheistic clan in the hills, have no ceremonies connected with the crops, but allow no dancing, singing, or music in the village between the sowing and the reaping.

Among the other Old Kuki clans there is a great resemblance between the festivals, and their connection with the Lushai "Kuts" can be easily traced—in some cases, as among the Kom, the name being actually the same.

A festival which is common to several clans and generally takes place in the spring, though sometimes later, and is supposed to ensure good crops and good luck generally, is known by various similar names, all meaning "Pulling the Creeper."

Kolhen "Keidun" Festival.—This occurs in April. The first day, called "Karamindai," or "Changritakhoi," is occupied by the young men going off to bring in two long creepers. A fowl and a pig are sacrificed and the creepers are hung over a post. On the next day the creepers are brought to the khul-lakpa's stone, and he, saying certain charms, pours out a libation of rice beer, and then a tug of war takes place between two parties selected as follows:—On one side are all the young men of the khul-lakpa's family—viz., the Chongthu—and on the other those of the Jete, to which the lup-lakpa belongs. With the Chongthu pull the young men of the following families—viz., Tulthung, Maite, Tiante, Laishel, Songchungnung, while with the Jete are associated the young men of the Lunglai, Rembual, Mirem Tumtin, and Vanbie. The girls of each family pull on the opposite side to the young men of their family. While the pull is in progress the khul-lakpa sings a song, and when he reaches a certain point the rope is cut in two by a man who stands waiting with a dao. The pull is repeated with the second creeper, and each party carries off the ends it has retained. Marriages are only allowed between the young people who pull on the same side, with the exception of the Chongthu, who, being of the chief's family, may marry a girl of any family except their own. During the festival no work of any sort must be done, but otherwise there are no restrictions as regards villagers or strangers, but the khul-lakpa must abstain from work and from cohabitation for two or three days before. Should a death occur a day or two before the date fixed for the festival, the fact will not be recognised till the completion of the feast, when the funeral ceremonies will take place as if the death had occurred on that day, the corpse being kept outside the village during the interval.

The Anal and Lamgang, as usual, observe the festival in a similar manner. The creeper having been brought to the gate of the village, the headmen and the thempu receive it, and the latter, muttering prayers, pours over it a libation of rice beer, and then ties a piece of it to the gate. The remainder is cut up and a piece is tied to each house in the village. The thempu goes round at night throwing a piece of turmeric into each house and calling out as he throws each piece, "From to-day may all evil and misfortune run away from this house."[1]

[1] Compare the Synteng custom of *beh-dieng-khlam.*—P. R. G.

The Purum celebrate the festival in August, and the unmarried girls take a prominent part in the ceremony. A raised platform is made before the house of the eldest unmarried girl in the village. (In a community where there is no dearth of husbands, and every girl is sure of being married in due course, the prominence given to the eldest spinster is not objected to as it might be in an English village.) On this platform the girls assemble, and the creeper after the usual ceremonies is tied to the platform, and there is a great feast with much dancing between the young folk.

The similarity between these festivals and the "Koi-hrui-an-chat," mentioned under the Ngente, bears out the truth of the tradition that these clans long ago were near neighbours.

The Chiru at the time of cutting the jhums go in procession with drums and gongs to the place chosen and on their return drink much rice beer. In March or April, before the sowing, a festival called "Arem" is celebrated. On the first day a dog is killed at a stone to the west of the village, and a pig to the north in the direction of the hill Kobru. All the men attend, but no women. The animals are killed by the thempu. The flesh is eaten there by the whole party, and the "sherh" are left at the place of sacrifice. There is then a drinking party in the house of the thempu. On the second day all the young men go and catch fish, and on their return they are entertained with two pots of rice beer by the unmarried girls. On the third day the lup-lakpa gives a feast of meat and rice, washed down by much rice beer, to the men only, and later all dance in front of the "chhirbuk"—*i.e.*, Lushai zawlbuk.

The fourth day is spent in visiting each other, drinking and singing at each other's houses. As soon as it is dark men and women meet before the chhirbuk and dance round the stone drinking; then they go to the lup-lakpa's house and drink again, and then to a house where all the unmarried girls are collected and drink again, and then bring the girls to the chhirbuk and dance round the stone again, drinking as they go. This is a pretty heavy day's work, and it speaks well for the young folk if many of them have the energy to complete the programme by drinking and dancing together on the fifth day. During the festival the village is "sherh."

The Chawte, before cutting their jhums, sacrifice a pig and go down to the stream and sharpen their daos—" Trust in God, but keep your powder dry." The above festivals correspond to the " Chap-chăr-kut " of the Lushais, and the following resemble the " Mim-kut." The Purum in September observe " Chulkut " for five days, making and exchanging rice cakes and drinking rice beer, but not sacrificing any animals. The Kolhen observe " Chamershi " for two days in the middle of the rains—viz., in July or August. A pig and a cock are sacrificed in the khul-lakpa's house and eaten there by men only. Old men dance, and rice beer is drunk. This feast is supposed to expel evil spirits. The Chiru in July sacrifice a pig on behalf of the village to Pathian, while each household offers him a fowl. This feast is called the " feast of the hot season rest "—*i.e.*, the few days of leisure after the second weeding of the crops.

The Aimol, after burning the jhums, celebrate a feast they call " Lo-an-dai." Three fowls are killed and eaten in the khulpu's house, and rice beer is drunk, but no gong-beating or singing is allowed.

After the harvest, feasts corresponding to the Lushai " Polkut" are held, but among the Purum a feast called " Shanghong " has to be celebrated in October, just when the grain is filling in the ear. Every householder has to bring a small sheaf of the green rice, which is presented to the village god, and feasting and drinking goes on for three days, during which time the village is " sherh." The Kolhen, before reaping the crop, carry the khul-lakpa or lup-lakpa out of the village towards the fields with beating of drums, and later drink at his expense.

The Kom call the harvest festival " Lam-kut." It lasts three days. No sacrifice is performed, but the young men and girls dance and drink together.

Among the Chawte the custom is practically the same as among the Purum, save that the feast only lasts one day.

The Lamgang and Anal harvest festival is practically the same. In each case the best crop in the village is reaped by the whole community going to the field with dance and song, and subsequently the lucky owner of the crop has to entertain the village for three days. It would appear that all good Lamgangs and Anals must pray to have the second best crop. On the second day of the feast the consumption of meat and tobacco, the carrying of water and wood, and working with axes or hoes are tabu. The feast closely resembles the "Buh-Ai" of other clans. The Aimol custom is very different from that of the other clans. All the men go out in search of game, the flesh of which is eaten in the evening, and drums are beaten and songs sung while the rice beer circulates freely, in contrast to the feast at the sowing time. Dancing is, however, tabu. The harvest feast is called "Sherh an long."

The Lamgang have an extra feast, or rather period of rest, when the grain is all garnered, when for ten days no one may enter or leave the village, and no work can be done, the whole energies of the community being concentrated on eating and drinking well.

2. *Feasts Corresponding with the Thangchhuah Feasts of the Lushai.*—The idea of "Thangchhuah" is found in some form or other in all clans. Even in those clans who have no very clear conception of a special abode for the spirits of those who have earned good fortune in the world beyond the grave by feasts and killing men and animals here below, we find feasts the giving of which confers on the giver special consideration among his fellow-villagers and entitles his corpse to special funeral honours. All these feasts seem more or less connected with the erection of some form of memorial—either a post, such as the Lushai "she-lu-pun," which finds its counterpart among several Old Kuki clans, but among them the erection of the memorial is the important part of the ceremony, whereas among the Lushais the killing of the animal is the more important and the feast is named after that, not after the planting of the post; or a stone or a heap of stones, or a paved platform. All these are erected during a man's life and are quite distinct from the memorials erected in memory of the deceased, and thus connect the Lushai-Kuki race with the Nagas, among whom the erection of stones is a very important function.

The "Mi-thi-rawp-lām" is not included in the Thangchhuah series by any of these clans—in fact, it seems to be omitted by all clans not living under Lushei chiefs. These all have a special annual ceremony to lay the ghosts of those who have died during the preceding year. The explanation of this seems to be that among the Lushais the clans have all been broken up and are scattered in different villages, and therefore an annual clan ceremony is not possible, and it has become a virtuous act for some wealthy member of the clan to celebrate the feast in honour of the dead of the clan. Among the clans which have retained their corporate existence the annual ceremony is natural, and therefore it is excluded from the Thangchhuah series.

The Tikhup can earn consideration after death by giving a single feast. The young men and maidens collect a big heap of stones and arrange a seat of honour near it for the giver of the feast, who is carried down on a litter. The young folk dance and sing and drink before him, and then he is carried back to the village and has to present a mithan to the young men, who feast on it for a day and a night at the house of their leader. A song is composed in honour of the giver of the feast, which is sung at all subsequent feasts.

The Lamgang, Kom, Kolhen, and Anal put up wooden posts, the Chawte erect a post and pave a piece of ground in front of it, while the Aimol put up a stone and make a pavement. Mithan and pigs are killed, and a feast given which lasts several days, the cost being met by the person ambitious of fame.

The Chiru alone seem to have no idea of Thangchhuah, and, as noted before, have no idea of a special abode for good spirits.

The Vaiphei have to give two feasts, at the first of which one, and at the second two or more, mithan are killed. The Kolhen, on occasion of putting up the post, sacrifice a mithan thus:—The thempu first throws an egg at the forehead of the mithan, muttering a charm to drive away all evil; the animal is then speared until blood is drawn, after which it may be shot. They also give the following feasts as part of the Thangchhuah ceremonies:—"Khuang-that"—*i.e.*, "making a drum." The first day is occupied in bringing the log which is to be hollowed into the drum; on the second there is a dance outside the house of the giver of the feast; on the third the mithan is killed after a thempu has broken the egg on its forehead, and then another thempu invokes its spirit, blowing rice-beer over the body, as at the Fanai festival, p. 138. The fourth and fifth days are occupied with feasting.

"Lungainai"—*i.e.*, "collection of stones"—this is very similar to the Tikhup festival, with the carrying of the giver omitted; a mithan is killed as above described. The Aimol have also the drum-making feast, and another in which the giver is carried on a litter, but no heap of stones is made. On each occasion much rice-beer and flesh has to be consumed.

3. *Other Feasts.*—Mostly annual, if necessary provisions are forthcoming. Some of these probably have reference to the crops.

The Purum celebrate "Yarr" in February for seven days. Dancing begins each evening at sundown, and is kept up all night with feasting and drinking. In March they keep "Kumyai" for three days, the young men and maidens dancing and drinking together, but no animals are killed. This seems probably equivalent to the "Chap-chār-kut" of the Lushais, but both it and the Yarr are said to be to please the village god, without any special reference to the crops. The Lamgang have a peculiar feast early in May, when the young men plant a very tall bamboo, from the end of which hangs a wooden representation of a bird, at which every man in turn, commencing with the thempu and the khul-lakpa, shoot with bows and arrows. Mithan are killed and eaten. No woman is allowed to join this festival.

The Chiru and Kolhen celebrate a somewhat similar festival called "Ratek" in the middle of August. A pig and a dog are sacrificed by the thempu outside the village, on the side towards Kobru, and then two or three days later an offering of zu is placed in a small bamboo tube beside the water supply, and the drum is beaten for some time; the party then return to the khul-lakpa's house and are treated to a drink. The following day a tall bamboo is planted in the village with a wonderfully ornamented basket hanging from it, and much zu drunk. The following year the bamboo is taken up and thrown away, the festival being named "Ratek poiyi" (*cf.* Lushai "pai," to throw away). Before the feast young men go hunting, and if they are successful good luck is sure to follow. The first day of the feast a pig and a dog are sacrificed, and zu drunk; on the second, the bamboo is thrown away and more zu drunk in the house of the khul-lakpa. On the third day the unmarried girls of the village give a drinking feast to the young men, and both dance together. Should the zu suffice this portion of the festival may be prolonged for several days.

It is believed that unless these two festivals are carried out every year in their proper rotation, there will be serious mortality among the elders of the village.

Since writing the above, I have found two more small clans, which evidently belong to the Old Kuki group—Lonte or Ronte, of whom there are only nine households, living alongside of the Burma road, close to the Chawte hamlet, with whom they are classed by the Manipuris; and Tarau, eighteen households living slightly to the south of the Burma road.

The Ronte clan is divided into two families, called Lanu and Changom. Marriages can only be made with members of the other family of the clan. They say that they came from the Ngente hill far to the south (*v.* Ngente clan), and claim some connection with the Chiru and Aimol.

The Tarau clan is divided into four families, and marriages are restricted as among the Chawte, Chiru, and Kolhen.

A youth of the Pachana family must marry a girl of the Tlangsha family.

A youth of the Tlangsha family must marry a girl of the Thimasha family.

A youth of the Thimasha family must marry a girl of the Khulpu-in family.

A youth of the Khulpu-in family must marry a girl of the Pachana family.

In both clans the young men sleep in any house, except their parents', in which there are unmarried girls. The Ronte say that formerly they built zawlbuks like the Lushais.

The price of a Tarau girl is a gong or Rs. 30/-, or five years service in the girl's father's house. The Ronte maiden's price is two gongs, and her proper husband is her maternal first cousin. In both clans a fowl has to be killed by the khulpu at the time of the marriage, and the Ronte tie some of its feathers round the necks of the couple. Should a Tarau maiden be led astray both parties are fined a pot of rice-beer, which the villagers share, and the seducer pays the girl's father one pig. The child, when old enough to leave the mother, becomes the property of the father. A Ronte mother must not leave her house till five days after the birth of a daughter and seven after that of a son. On the day of the birth there is a feast, and on the fifth or seventh day, according to the sex of the child, a fowl is killed by the khulpu, and the child's hair is cut, its ears pierced, and its name decided on, the choice being made from the names of its forefathers. The house is purified by being sprinkled with zu by the khulpu.

Among the Tarau, the period during which the mother may not leave her house is prolonged to ten days, at the expiry of which the khulpu kills a cock for male child and a hen for girl, and then purifies the house.

In both clans the dead are buried in a cemetery situated to the west of the village, while the corpses of those who have died unnatural deaths are buried elsewhere with no ceremony. Women dying in childbirth among the Tarau are buried by old men, who have no further hope of becoming fathers, far from the village, while persons being killed by wild animals, or by some accident, such as a fall from a tree, are buried where they die. Persons who are drowned are buried on the bank of the river where the body is found, the grave being dug at the spot where some water thrown up by hand from the river happens to fall. This custom also exists among the Shans of the Upper Chindwin, which lends some colour to the tradition that the Tarau sojourned in Burma before entering Manipur. Among the Ronte, women dying in childbirth, and all children dying under a year of age, are buried to the east of the village, while accidental deaths necessitate the burial being made to the south. The funeral takes place on the day of death except in the case of old men, whose corpses are kept for a day while their friends eat, drink, and dance before them. Whatever animals can be spared are killed in the honour of the deceased, and their sherh are buried with him, together with some rice. Every day till the "Papek" feast, in honour of those who have died within the year, rice and zu are placed on the grave. At Papek a platform of bamboo is constructed near the cemetery, and on it are placed such offering of flesh as the family can afford; much zu is drunk and all dance. The Ronte Sakhua sacrifice consists of a goat, dogs and mithan being prohibited.

Although the Tarau, from their language, are evidently closely allied to the Lushais, they are the only Old Kuki clan I have met which does not worship Pathian. They denied all knowledge of that name, affirming the name of their god was "Rāpu," to whom the Manipuri name of "Sankhulairenma" has been given. Rāpu has a shrine just above the Burma road near to Tegnopal, where every year fish, rice, and zu are offered to him. When the rice begins to fill in the ear there is a five days' feast in the village, during which time the young people dance and drink. A pig is killed, and the liver, ears, feet, and snout are offered to Rāpu. These are called "sar" (*cf.* Lushai "sherh"). Before the cutting of jhums commences a small pig or a fowl is sacrificed to Rāpu so that no one may be cut with a dao during the clearing of the jhums. Dogs are not eaten or sacrificed by the Tarau or the Ronte; the latter also consider the mithan unfit for a sacrifice. In these particulars they form an exception to the general custom of Kuki clans.

The Ronte have a feast called "Va-en-la," which is given with the idea of enhancing the giver's importance in this world and assuring him comfort in the next. A pig is killed and thirty pots of zu are prepared, and the whole village makes merry. A long bamboo is planted in front of the house of the giver of the feast. Throughout its length this bamboo is transfixed with crosspieces of bamboo about 18 inches long; from its end depends a bamboo representation of a bird, whence the name of the feast—"va," in Ronte, as in Lushai, meaning "a bird," and "en," "to see."

To show the similarity between the Tarau and the Lushai language I give a few words of each.

English.	Lushai.	Tarau.
One	Pa-khat	Khat.
Two...	Pa-hnih ...	Ni.
Three	Pa-thum ...	Thum.
Four	Pa-li	Ma-li.
Five...	Pa-nga	Ranga.
Six	Pa-ruk	Kuruk.
Seven	Pa-sari	Siri.
Eight	Pa-riat	Tirit.
Nine	Pa-kua	Ku.
Ten	Shom	Shom.
Father	Pa	Pa.
Mother	Nu	Nu.
Son	Fa-pa	Sha-pa. (Thado, "chapa.")
Daughter ...	Fa-nu	Sha-nu.
House	In	Im.
Sun	Ni	Ni.
Moon	Thla	Thla.
Water	Tui	Tui. To carry water, "tui choi," in both dialects.
Dog...	Ui	Uh.
Mithan	Shial	Shil.
Tree	Thing ...	Thing.
Jhum	Lo	Lou.

The east and west in Tarau are called "ni-chhuak-lam" and "ni-thlak-lam," which are pure Lushai for "the direction of sun rising and sun setting."

FOLKLORE.

1. *Legends.*—A large number of tales have been collected by Babu Nithor Nath Banerji, of the Manipur State Office, from which I select the following. They have all to a certain extent suffered by being told to the Babu in Manipuri instead of in the vernacular of the relaters. This accounts for Manipuri names being used in some cases.

The following is a tale told by the Anals:—"Once upon a time the whole world was flooded. All were drowned except one man and one woman, who ran to the highest peak of the Leng hill [this is interesting, as Leng is the name of one of the highest hills in the present Lushai Hills], where they climbed up a high tree and hid themselves among its branches. The tree grew near a large pond, which was as clear as the eye of a crow. They made themselves as comfortable as they could, being determined to spend the night there. They passed the night, sometimes exchanging whispers, and in the morning they were astonished to find that they had become a tiger and a tigress. [This changing of human beings into animals reminds one of the Lushai Thimzing legend.] Pathian, seeing the sad state of the world, sent a man and a woman from a cave, which was on the hill, to re-people it. The man and the woman emerging from the cave were terrified at seeing the two huge animals, and addressed Pathian thus: 'O Father, you have sent us to re-people the world, but we do not think that we shall be able to carry out your intention, as the whole world is under water, and the only spot on which we could make a resting place is occupied by two ferocious beasts which are waiting to devour us; give us strength to slay these animals.' After which they killed the tigers and lived happily and begat many sons and daughters, and from them the world was re-populated."

The following tale told by the Kolhen resembles in many particulars the story of Kungori told by Colonel Lewin, which is given below:—

The Story of Fachirang and Rangchar.

"Once upon a time there lived a widow; she had a daughter whose beauty attracted many young men of the village. One day a tiger came in the shape of a man and asked to marry the girl. She was much frightened and kept silence. The tiger-man was angry at her behaviour, and recited a charm which made her ugly. Her mother said, 'Look! my daughter who was the most beautiful girl in the village has become ugly; if a man can restore her beauty he may marry her, and if a woman can do it she shall be my friend.' On hearing this, the tiger-man came to the old woman and said, 'Oh! Granny, I am a stranger, and have come from a distant village; let me put up in your house. The old lady agreed, and after a few days he said, 'Oh! Granny, why are you so sad? Tell me the cause of your sorrow. Perhaps I can remove it.' 'Alas, my boy, it is beyond your power to do so,' she replied. The tiger-man, however, pressed her to tell him, and at last she did so, whereupon he replied, 'All right, if I cure her you will give her to me,' and in a few days he had restored her beauty, and they were married and lived together in her mother's house for many years. At length he asked permission to take his wife to his own home, and they started, but no sooner had they passed the village gate than he was changed into the shape of a tiger, and his wife wept much at seeing him thus. An old woman of the village saw them and came and told the people that a tiger was carrying off the girl, so the villagers assembled to consult, but no one would volunteer for the task of rescuing the girl. At last Fachirang and Rangchar, two brothers, set off with a dao and a spear to kill the animal, but after going a very little way Fachirang, the elder brother, said, 'Oh! Rangchar, I don't know what is the matter, but my heart beats so fast that I must remain here; you go and see if you can kill the beast alone.' So the younger brother went on alone till he came to the place where the tiger and the girl were living happily. Rangchar thrust his spear into the breast of the tiger, and it died at once, and Rangchar carried off the girl and returned to where his brother was waiting, and they all three set out for home together. The elder brother married the girl, and they all lived happily together."

The Story of Kúngóri.

(From "Progressive Colloquial Exercises in the Lushai Dialect" by Captain H. Lewin, 1874.)

Her father, who was unmarried, was splitting cane to make a winnowing basket when he ran a splinter into his hand: the splinter grew into a little child; (after a time) the child was brought forth motherless and they called her Kúngóri. They fed her with single grains of millet and rice, and so little by little she grew big. Two or three years passed by and she attained puberty; she was very pretty, and all the young-men of the village wanted to marry her, but her father refused them all. Then the young tiger-man, Keimi, took up the impression of her foot and wrapped it up and placed it on the bamboo grating over the house fire to dry. Then Kúngóri became ill.

Kúngóri's father said, "If there be anyone that can cure her, he shall have my daughter." All the villagers tried, but not one of them could do any good. Then the young tiger-man came. "I will cure her, and I will marry her afterwards," said he. Her father said, "Cure the girl first and you may then have her."

So he cured her; the footprint which he had placed to dry on the fire-shelf he opened out and threw away. Kúngóri became well and Keimi married her. "Come, Kúngóri," said he, "will you go to my house?" So they went; on the road Keimi turned himself into a tiger, Kúngóri caught hold of his tail, and they ran like the wind. Some women of the village were gathering wood and they saw this, so they went back home and said to Kúngóri's father, "Your daughter has got a tiger for a husband." Kúngóri's father said, "Whoever can go and take Kúngóri may have her," but no one dared to take her. However, Hpohtir and Hrangchal, two friends, said, "We will take her." Kúngóri's father said, "If you are able to take her you may have her," so Hpohtir and Hrangchal set off. Going on they came to Keimi's village. The young tiger-man, Keimi, had gone out hunting; before he reached his house Hpohtir and Hrangchal went to Kúngóri. "Kúngóri," said they, "where is your husband?" "He is gone out hunting," she said, "but will be home directly." On this they became afraid, and Hpohtir and Hrangchal climbed up on to the top of the high fire-shelf. Kúngóri's husband arrived. "There is the smell of a human being," said he. "It must be my smell," said Kúngóri. Night fell; everyone ate their dinners and lay down to rest. In the morning Kúngóri's husband again went out to hunt. A widow said (to the two friends), "If you are going to run away with Kúngóri take fire-seed, thorn-seed, and water-seed (with you)." So they took fire-seed, thorn-seed, and water-seed, and they took Kúngóri also and carried her off.

Kúngóri's husband returned home. He looked and found Kúngóri was gone, so he followed after them in hot haste. A little bird called to Hrangchal. "Run! run! Kúngóri's husband will catch you," said the bird. So (the friends) scattered the fire-seed, and the jungle and undergrowth burnt furiously, so that Kúngóri's husband could not come any further. When the fire subsided he again resumed the pursuit.

N 2

The little bird cried to Hrangchal, "He is catching you up." So they scattered the water-seed, and a great river rose. However, Kúngóri's husband waited for the water to go down, and when the water went down he followed after them as before.

The bird said to Hrangchal, "He is after you again—he is fast gaining on you; sprinkle the thorn-seed," and thorns sprouted in thickets, so that Kúngóri's husband could not get on. By biting and tearing the thorns he at length made a way. and again he followed after them. Hrangchal's[1] party became bewildered and hid in a clump of reeds. Hpohtir cut the tiger down dead with a blow of his dao. "I am Hpohtir,"[1] said he. So the tiger died.

Hrangchal and the others went on again until they came to the three cross-roads of Khuavang, and there they stopped. Hpohtir and Hrangchal were to keep guard turn about. Hrangchala went to sleep first while Hpohtir kept watch.

At night Khuavang came. "Who is staying at my cross-roads?" he said. Hpohtira (spoke out boldly). "Hpohtira and Hrangchala (are here)," said he, "crouching under the reeds. We cut off the tiger's head without much ado." Khuavang, hearing and becoming afraid, ran off. So Hpohtira (woke up Hrangchal, saying), "Hrangchal, get up; you stay awake now. I am very sleepy; I will lie down. If Khuavang comes you must not be afraid." Having said this he slept. Hrangchala watched; presently Khuavang returned. "Who is this staying at my cross-roads?" he said. Hrangchala was frightened; (however), he replied, "Hpohtira and Hrangchala (are here); they killed the tiger that followed them among the reed-roots." But Khuavang was not to be frightened by this, so he took Kúngóri. Kúngóri marked the road, trailing behind her a line of cotton thread. They entered into a hole in the earth, and so arrived at Khuavang's village. The hole in the earth was stopped up by a great stone. In the morning Hpohtir and Hrangchala began to abuse each other. Said Hpohtira to Hrangchal, "Fool man!" said he, "where has Kúngóri gone to? On account of your faintheartedness Khuavang has carried her

[1] *a* is merely the masculine termination. Hrangchal-a is a man's name, Hrangchal-i a woman's. The terminations are often omitted when it is known who is meant.

off. Away! you will have to go to Khuavang's village." So they followed Kúngóri's line of white thread and found that the thread entered (the earth) under a big rock. They moved away the rock and saw Khuavang's village below them. Hpohtira called out, "Hoy! give me back my Kúngóri!" Khuavang replied, "We know nothing about your Kúngóri, whom you were taking away." "If you do not (immediately) give me Kúngóri I will use my dao," said Hpohtir. "Hit away," answered Khuavang. With one cut of the dao a quarter of the village died right off. Again Hpohtir cried, "Give me my Kúngóri," Khuavang said, "Your Kúngóri is not here." On this Hpohtir and Hrangchal said, "We will come in." "Come along," said Khuavang, so they went in and came to Khuavang's house. Khuavang's daughter was a very pretty girl. "Here is Kúngóri," said they. "This is not she," said Hpohtir; "give me Kúngóri herself." So (at last) they gave her to him.

They took her away. Kúngóri said, "I have forgotten my comb." "Go, Hrangchal, and fetch it," said Hpohtir; but Hrangchala—"I dare not. I am afraid," said he. So Hpohtir went (himself) to fetch (the comb). While he was gone Hrangchal took Kúngóri out and closed the hole with the great stone. After this they arrived at the house of Kúngóri's father. "You have been able to release my daughter," said he, "so take her." Kúngóri, however, did not agree. Said Kúngóri's father, "Hrangchal is here, but where is Hpohtira?" "We do not know Hpohtira's dwelling-place," he said. So Hrangchala and Kúngóri were united. Though Kúngóri did not wish it, he just married her.

Hpohtira was married to Khuavang's daughter. Beside the house he sowed a koi-seed. It sprouted and a creeper sprang (upwards like a ladder). Hpohtira, when he was at Khuavang's, had a child (born to him), and he cooked some small stones, and when his wife was absent he gave the stones which he had cooked to the child, saying, "Eat." While it was eating Hpohtir climbed up the stalks of the koi creeper and got out. He went on and arrived at the house of Kúngóri's father. They had killed a mithan, and were celebrating the Khuangchoi and dancing. With one blow Hpohtira cut off the head of Hrangchal!

Kúngóri's father cried, "Why, Hpohtira, do you cut off Hrangchala's head?" "I was obliged to decapitate him," said Hpohtir. "It was I who released Kúngóri from Keimi's village—Hrangchala dared not do it. When Khuavang carried off Kúngóri also Hrangchala dared not say him nay—he was afraid. Afterwards we followed Kúngóri's line of cotton thread, which led us to Khuavang's village. Kúngóri (after we had released her from there) forgot her comb; we told Hrangchal to go and fetch it, but he dared not. 'I am afraid,' said he, so I went to get it. He then took Kúngóri and left me behind, shutting the hole in the earth with a great stone. They went away. I married Khuavang's daughter, and while she was absent I climbed up the stalks of the creeper and came here." On this, "Is it so?" said they. "Then you shall be united." So Hrangchala died, and Hpohtira and Kúngóri were married. They were very comfortable together, and killed many mithan; they possessed many villages, and lived happy ever after. Thus the story is concluded.

I condense the following tale told by the Kolhen from the obviously embellished version supplied to the Babu :—

A widow had seven sons and one daughter, called Ringchanghoi, who was very beautiful, and much beloved by her brothers. To prove the truth of their professions of love she sent them off to catch the sun and the moon, that she might wear them as her necklace. Before their departure they built her a fortified house, and told her to remain within it until their return. They also left with her some unhusked rice, which had magical properties, turning red whenever the brothers were in danger. Ringchanghoi one day was sitting in the verandah cleaning her hair when she was seen by the king, who quickly added her to the number of his wives. The youngest brother, returning alone, found the house empty, and at once rejoining the others in the sky, where they were still hunting the sun and moon, told them of the disappearance of their sister. They all returned home, and on entering the house the youngest brother was changed into a parrot, while the others fell down dead. The youngest brother finds his sister and is captured and presented to her, and tells her what has happened, whereupon she sends off her husband, who by a powerful charm restores the dead to life and the youngest brother to his original form, and all ends happily.

In this tale there is some slight resemblance to the Lushai tale of Rimenhoi, as also there is to the tales told by many clans to account for eclipses of the sun and moon. The Kom, for instance, say that the god Awk-pa was drying his rice when the sun and the moon came riding by and scattered it; this vexed Awk-pa, who lay in ambush in a cave, and the next time they came he swallowed them. The resemblance between this tale and the Lushai explanation of an eclipse is very marked. The name "Awk" is the same, and the idea of swallowing is preserved. The Purum, while using the same word for an eclipse, have quite a different story:—"Once upon a time there were seven brothers who went into the forest to cut wood, and shot a deer, and ordered the youngest brother to cook it while they went on with their work. The youngest brother, having cooked the meat, put it on some leaves till his brothers should return. Some leaves from a tree fell on the meat, whereupon the deer came to life again and ran away. The brothers returning got angry and, not believing the tale told by the youngest, killed him and put his body under the tree. Some leaves falling on the corpse, it came to life, and the brothers were much astonished and went home, taking some of the leaves, roots, and bark of the tree with them." On their way they saw the body of a dog floating in a river which they had to cross, and put some bark on it and the animal revived. When they reached home they put the bark, leaves, and pieces of root to dry in the sunshine, leaving their dog to watch them. The sun and the moon, perceiving the usefulness of the things, stole them all and were chased by the dog. When the dog gets too near, the sun and the moon hide, thus causing eclipses. The Kolhen have the same name for an eclipse. and their explanation of the phenomenon is much the same. The god Rikumpu left his dog to watch his garden, and the sun and the moon came to steal, and are still being chased by the faithful hound. The Lamgang say that eclipses are caused by their god catching the sun and the moon, who once stole his tobacco as it was drying. The Anal have much the same idea. The story is worthy of being given at length:—"Once upon a time a very pious man who devoted much time to worshipping God had a pet bitch. The sun and the moon, being envious, tried to take his virtue from the man. To accomplish their wicked purpose they promised to give him their virtue if only he would first entrust them with his. The saint fell into the trap and the celestial rascals ran off with his virtue. The holy man, finding himself defrauded, ordered his dog to catch the thieves. The dog brought a long pole and climbed up it to reach the fugitives, being followed by her master. She reached the sky and still chases the sun and moon, and sometimes catches them. Therefore, when an eclipse occurs the Anal call out, 'Release! Release!' The poor pious man took so long ascending the pole that before he accomplished the journey the white ants had eaten up the lower end and the saint fell to the earth and was killed." Thunder and lightning are accounted for by some clans thus:—Wulai the lizard climbs a tall tree and shouts defiance, whereupon God from the sky hurls his axe at him and he runs down, but the tree is burnt up. The Anal and Kom have also a more poetic explanation of lightning—viz., that it is the glitter of God's sword as he plays with it in heaven, while the Purum also say that it is the glitter of his robes.

Earthquakes are accounted for by assuming the existence of another world below the surface of the earth. The Purum and Kom say that Yangmal the earth worm took a present of a piece of earth to the king of these lower regions. On the way the earth was changed into gold and silver, much to the delight of the monarch, who sent Yangmal back to fetch more, but the worm made excuse that the upper world had been destroyed. To test the truth of this statement the king shakes the world. The Anal and Lamgang say that the people of the lower world shake the upper one to find out if anyone is still alive up there, and so on, an earthquake occurring the Anal and Lamgang villages resound with shouts of "Alive! Alive!" Rainbows are accounted for as the lips of God spread in the act of drinking, or simply his glory.

NOTE.—I must acknowledge the assistance I have received in preparing the account of these Old Kuki tribes from Babu Nithor Nath Banerji, head clerk of the Manipur State Hill Office. My information regarding the Anal, Kom, Purum, and Lamgang was chiefly from his notes, and in a lesser degree I am indebted to him for details regarding the Kolhen and Chiru.

Purum.

Purum.

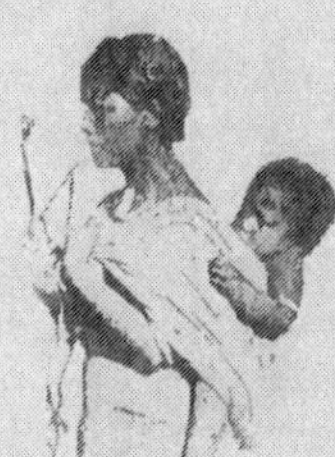

Khawtlang.

Lamgang Man and Woman.

Aimol.

Chiru. Nautch Helmet of Hide.

Chiru.

Chiru.

Rangte.

Anal.

Anal.

Heads of Kuki Clans.

Old Kuki Clans—Khawtlang and Khawchhak

The Old Kukis who appeared in Cachar about 1780 are described by Lieutenant Stewart as being divided into three clans called Rhangkol, Khelma, and Beteh. The first and last are known in the Lushai Hills as Hrangchal and Biate respectively, but the Khelma, whom Dr. Grierson identifies as the Hallam, seem to have emigrated entirely. The Hrangchal and Biate are two of many clans collectively known to the Lushais as Hmar—*i.e.*, North—from the position of their villages with reference to those of the Lushais, and among themselves as Khawtlang and Khawchhak—*i.e.*, Western and Eastern Villages I have found representatives of 16 clans in the Lushai Hills and adjoining portions of Manipur. The most important are Loitlang, subdivided into six families; Hrangchal, with four families; Thiak, with five families; and Biate, with the same number. The old village sites of many of these clans are still called by their names. The Hrangchal are said to have had a large village at Vanlaiphai, in the centre of which valley is a large memorial stone with many carvings on it, which is said to have been erected in memory of Chonluma, a famous Hrangchal chief of bygone days. The Biate assert that when they lived on the hill of that name they were attacked by huge eagles, and had to build stone shelters in which to hide their small children. These erections are still to be seen, and consist of three rough slabs of stone with a fourth as a roof, the whole structure being only about 2 to 3 feet high. It was the Biate, also, who fed Rulpui, as has been described in Part I., Chapter V, 3. The Lungthau, a minor family, attribute their downfall to an attack by Chuckmahs, which led to their seeking refuge with the Sailo chief Lalsavunga, and forming a village at Kelsi, near Aijal, where they were under his protection.

When the aggressions of the Thangur chiefs disturbed the Khawtlang and Khawchhak one section fled through the country of the Thados into Cachar, another took refuge among the Chhinchhuan, a Thado family in the southern portion of the Manipur Hills, to whom they paid tribute. and a certain number joined the Thangur villages. Between those who fled to the Chhinchhuan and the Lushais hostilities were carried on until our arrival in 1890, and, as in the case of the Vuite, we found many of them living in a state of semi-slavery in the Sailo villages, whence they have mostly rejoined their relatives, and there are now 296 households of these people in the south-west of the Manipur Hills and more in the adjoining parts of the Lushai Hills. Lieutenant Stewart, in his description of the "Old Kukis," states that ordinarily the dead are cremated, warriors only being buried. I have never heard of any clan in these hills which cremates its dead. The custom may well have died out owing to the natural wish of the relatives to do honour to the deceased by according him the honours of a warrior. Lieutenant Stewart describes a regular marriage ceremony conducted by the headman of the village, at the foot of a large stone erected in the middle of the village. As far as my enquiries go, the marriage ceremonies differ very little from those of the Lushais.

The dress of the men is the same as among the Lushais, but the women wear a petticoat with a broad white line between two narrower blue ones, and dress their hair in a long plait wound round the head. Zawlbuks are not maintained, but in other respects their villages resemble those of the Lushais. The village organisation is more democratic, the chief being replaced by a headman. The honours of "Thangchhuah" and admission to Pial-ral are obtained by three times celebrating the Buh-ai festival. There is no restriction as to having windows.

When a young man wishes to marry he sends messengers bearing a blue and a white cloth, a hoe, and a pot of liquor to the girls' parents. This is called "In hawn." If the articles are accepted the marriage takes place as soon as the necessary amount of zu can be prepared. The bride's parents kill a pig and the two families feast together. The girl is conveyed to her husband's house by the men who arranged the marriage, the party being pelted with dirt as among the Lushais.

In case of adultery, it is the seducer, not the woman's relatives, who have to compensate the injured husband. This is the common rule among non-Lushei clans.

A boy is named seven days and a girl five days after birth, a red cock being killed and zu drunk. The maternal uncle gives the name.

In common with many Old Kuki clans, the dead are buried in a special cemetery outside the village. The corpse of a "Thangchhuah," dressed in fine cloths and the head adorned with a chaplet of the tail feathers of the hornbill, is carried round the village on a bier by all the old people of both sexes, encircled by a ring of dancers singing a dirge to the accompaniment of drums, and followed by the widow dressed in the scantiest rags and raising loud lamentations. A halt is called opposite the house of every person of importance, and the inmate is expected to regale the party with zu. The circuit of the village completed, the corpse is carried to the grave and buried with rice and other eatables and a flagon of zu. A rough representation of a house is built over the grave and food and drink are placed in it for a year. The grave is fenced round and the heads of any animals which have been killed in the deceased's honour are placed on posts. At the close of a year a cane is stretched between poles over the grave, and from it are suspended pieces of cloth, small baskets containing tobacco and linseed, and the bodies of small animals and birds. This is the final ceremony, and the spirit is supposed to have no further concern with this world.

The Biate in the Lushai Hills worship the images in the Bhuban caves, but I am told that those in the North Cachar Hills differ in this respect. The three images are called Bolawng Raia, Chhinga Raia, and Maituki Raia, Raia being a corruption of Rajah. A fowl, a pig, two eggs, and two kinds of jungle vegetable called "chinghrut" and "hruitung" are offered to these deities outside the village once a year. The following tale is told to account for this worship of images, which is so opposed to general custom:—Long ago Zatea stole a mithan belonging to two Biate chiefs, Chonlut and Manlal, and on their trying to recover their property they were severely wounded. On their way home they noticed that the leaves of the "bung" tree, a species of *Ficus*, attached themselves to their clothes, and at night they dreamt that the leaves spoke, saying, "Do not throw us away; we are sent by the gods of the Bhuban caves to heal you." They applied the leaves to their wounds and were soon healed, and then set off in search of these new gods.[1] It

[1] *Cf.* the Purum tale of the eclipse given on p. 183.

is probable that in the course of their wanderings the Biate at one time lived near the Bhuban, and in that case their adopting the figures as local deities is quite in keeping with what has happened in other clans. Thus the Chiru worship the god of Kobru, though their settlement near that hill is of recent date. The Zote, a clan very closely allied to the Biate, after sacrificing a mithan, place bung leaves in a basket at the foot of the memorial post and throw them away with the "sherh" after three days. This clan pays special honour to Chhura, and after a mithan sacrifice a knotched pole called Chhura's ladder is placed against the gable of the house, and the skull, tail, and entrails are placed over it for three days. The jawbones are hung on a branch specially left for this purpose when the memorial post is being trimmed; a rough fence is made round the posts, on which matting representations of pythons and a bow with an arrow adjusted are hung. The latter is said to drive off the Huai, and reminds one of the similar custom of the Manipuris on the occasion of erecting the first post of a house.

CHAPTER IV

THE THADO CLAN

THE term New Kukis, which appears so often in the records of Cachar and Sylhet in the middle of the last century, and which has been adopted by Dr. Grierson in the "Linguistic Survey of India," may be taken as synonymous with the Thado clan. The clan is a very large one; Dr. Grierson in the "Linguistic Survey" estimates the numbers as follows:—

In Manipur...	20,000.
In Naga Hills	5,500.
In Cachar Plains	5,403.
In Sylhet	534.
Total	31,437.

This estimate omits the members of the clan in North Cachar Hills and in the unadministered tracts between the Naga Hills and Manipur on the west and the Upper Chindwin district of Burma on the east. Allowing for these, we may safely conclude that the clan now numbers about 37,000 souls.

The clan is divided in a manner exactly similar to the Lushei. There are four main families, all named after their progenitors, and these are further sub-divided into many eponymous branches. The whole clan traces its genealogy back to Thado and his elder brother Dongel, and beyond them to mythical heroes who lived below the surface of the ground. The late Colonel McCulloch, in his most interesting "Account of the Valley of Manipur," says, "About the names of those previous to Thado there may be some doubt, but from this great chief, from whom the whole race takes the appellation of Thado, I don't think that there is any." After many enquiries I am quite of the same opinion and have found pedigrees collected from various sources differ but slightly from that recorded by Colonel McCulloch fifty years ago. The original habitation of this clan is said to have been Kochuk, situated very far to the south of Manipur. Here I must differ from Colonel McCulloch, who says the traditional home of the Thados was in the north. There are other reasons besides tradition for believing that the Thados have come from the south, the many resemblances between them and other clans, which either still live in the centre of the Hills or did so till quite recently, and the connection between their language and those of the Sokte, Siyin, Vuite, and Ralte, so clearly established by Dr. Grierson, amply proves the southern origin of this clan. It appears almost certain that the Kamhaus, Soktes, and Siyins were the first to disturb the Thados, many of whom entered Manipur territory to escape from these active foes, while others probably moved westward and settled in the hills to the south of the Cachar district, whence in 1848–50 they were driven into Cachar by the triumphant Lushais, as described in Part I., Chapter I, para. 3. In the Manipuri chronicle there is mention of an expedition against the Khongjais, as the Manipuris call the Thados, as early as 1787, and though the chronicle cannot be accepted as infallible, I think we may conclude that the Thados entered the Manipur Hills about the middle of the 18th century. The different families seem very soon to have separated and, just as among the Lusheis, to have fought among themselves, for tradition speaks of a great battle between the Shit-hloh and the Chhinchhuan, on the Sawnchal hill, some 60 miles in an air-line south-east of Imphal, the capital of Manipur.

The four main families are the Dongel, Shit-hloh, Haukip, and Kipgen. The Dongel are descended from Thado's elder brother, and therefore are considered as rather superior to the rest of the families. The reason why the clan has not been known by the name of Dongel is said to be that Thado was a far greater warrior and killed more men. His name is derived, by the people themselves, from "thāt," "to kill," and "doh," "to war." It is curious that the direct descendants of Thado are known as Shit-hloh. This Shit-hloh was the seventh in the direct line from Thado, and it is said that up till his time the followers of the direct line had been fewer than those of the Kipgen and Haukip, but Shit-hloh was great in council and war, and retrieved the fortunes of his family, and hence his name has been adopted by them. Thus Thado remains as the true clan name, while Shit-hloh, Kipgen, and Haukip are the names of the families, which are further subdivided, as among the Lushais, into many branches, mostly named eponymously. The Kipgen and Haukip have always differed slightly from the Shit-hloh. The reason given for this is that Thalun, the son of Thado, was one day sitting outside his house with his wife, and, being alone together, the lady was somewhat careless as to her garments. Hearing some people approaching, Thalun told her to adjust her dress, and as she did not at once comply he threw a piece of wood at her and killed her on the spot. Being overcome with grief and shame, he fled to another part of the country and married again, the second wife being the mother of Kipgen and Haukip, whereas Elmun, from whom the Shit-hloh claim descent, was the son of the ill-fated first wife.

The number of branches into which these three families have divided is very great, and the connection of all of them with the parent stem is not very well established. Most of them are now of but little importance, the members being much scattered, but the Chhinchhuan, a branch of the Shit-hloh, and Chongput and Hawlthang, both branches of the Haukip family, still are of some importance. The Chhinchhuan chiefs rule over eleven villages, containing 952 houses, in the southern portion of the Manipur Hills, where they have been established certainly over 150 years. The Chongput and Hawlthang chiefs occupy sites in the hills to the west of the Manipur valley, which were assigned to them by Colonel McCulloch about 1850, and rule over some 190 houses.

With the exception of the three branches just mentioned, the Thados have broken up very much, and are found in small hamlets scattered about the territory of totally different clans, without any reference to locality or ethnographical considerations.

All members of these families, however, admit the claims of the head chief to their allegiance, and in token thereof give him, or his nearest representative, a hind leg of every wild animal killed.

The Thados generally are very truculent; in Manipur they have settled themselves among the more peaceable Nagas, and until the British Government assumed control of the State they lived largely on the labour of these unfortunate people, whom they had virtually reduced to slaves. The Manipuris found it easier to acquiesce in this oppression by the Thados than to coerce them, and the Thados were used on many occasions to punish Naga tribes whom the Manipuris were unable to reduce to submission. The superior cunning of the Manipuris enabled them to maintain their influence over the Thados by skilfully playing off one family against another. On one occasion three of the most powerful chiefs were enticed inside the royal enclosure in Imphal and treacherously murdered. At present large numbers of Thados are moving eastward in unadministered country, carrying on the same bullying tactics, reducing the inhabitants, who as yet have no firearms, to the condition of slaves.

Among the Thados are found the remnants of many other clans, which have been practically absorbed, having adopted Thado customs and language. It is asserted that at the time of the Thimzing (*v.* Part I., Chap. V, para. 1) Lianthang and his brother Thlangom, and Lunkim and his brother Changsan, had such large supplies of skulls of animals killed by them that they were enabled to live through that trying time by using the trophies of their skill in the chase as fuel, and from them the present Lianthang, Thlangom, Lunkim, and Changsan clans claim descent. The Changsan are sub-divided into eight families and are considered a clan of some standing, as is shown by the fact that the Shit-hloh will only take wives from Shit-hloh, Changsan, and Mangyel households.

The following clans are said not to be descended from Thado, but to have emerged from the earth after the Thimzing:—Kulho, Shongte, Kullon, Thāngneo, Hānngeng, Henngār, and Thanchhing. They are now to all intents and purposes Thados, most of them having even adopted the Sakhua, or domestic sacrificial rites, of whichever family of the Thado clan they have attached themselves to. Shongte and his younger brother Kullon emerged from the Khulpi, which is the Thado equivalent of the Lushai Chhinglung. Kulho, Thāngneo, and Hānngeng were sons of Shongte, the two latter being by a different mother to the first. Henngār was Kulho's son. Kulho celebrated the Chong festival, and invited his half-brothers, but Thāngneo refused to come, so Kulho disowned him, which angered Thāngneo, so that he proposed to Hānngeng that they should kill Kulho, but Hānngeng refused, saying that the removal of Kulho would make Thāngneo head of the family, but would in no way benefit him. This ancient quarrel is sometimes revived even now, and blows are exchanged when representatives of Kulho and Thāngneo meet round the zu-pot.

The houses of the Thados generally resemble those of the Lushais, but are less regular in their interior arrangements, a big house sometimes having two or three hearths irregularly placed. Zawlbuks are not built, the young men sleeping in the houses of well-to-do people. The houses of the chiefs are surrounded by palisading enclosing a courtyard, along one side of which there is often a platform, which reminds one very much of the Chin houses, and is one of the many trifles tending to confirm the tradition of the southern origin of the clan. The following extracts from Lieut. Stewart's notes on Northern Cachar, written in 1855, show us the Thados as he knew them:—

"Each of the four clans is divided into separate and independent Rajahlics, of greater or less power and numbers, consisting of one or more villages, each of which is presided over by a hereditary chief or Rajah, whose power is supreme, and who has a civil list as long, in proportion to the means of his subjects, as that possessed by any other despot in the world. All these Rajahs are supposed to have sprung from the same stock, which it is believed originally had connection with the gods themselves. Their persons are, therefore, looked upon with the greatest respect and almost superstitious veneration, and their commands are in every case law.

"The revenue exacted by these chieftains is paid in kind and labour. In the former each able-bodied man pays annually a basket of rice containing about two maunds; out of each brood of pigs or fowls reared in the village, one of the young becomes the property of the Rajah, and he is further entitled to one quarter of every animal killed in the chase, and, in addition, to one of the tusks of each elephant so slain. In labour his entire population are bound to devote four days in each year, in a body, for the purpose of cultivating his private fields. On the first day they cut down the jungle, on the second day, the fuel being dry, they fire it and prepare the ground, on the third they sow and harrow, and on the fourth cut and bring in the harvest. Besides the labour of these four days in which the entire effective population, men, women, and children, work for him, small parties are told off during the whole season to assist his own domestic slaves in tending the crop, repairing his house (which edifice is always built afresh by the subjects when a new site is repaired to), and in supplying wood and water for the family. On the occasion of the days of general labour, a great feast is given by the Rajah to all his people; so also, on the occasion of an elephant being killed, to the successful hunters, but this is the only remuneration ever received by them, and calls can be made on them for further supplies and labour, whenever it may be required.

"The Rajah is the sole and supreme authority in the village or villages under him, no one else being competent to give orders or inflict punishment except through him.

"To assist him in carrying on the affairs of government the Rajah has a minister, and more frequently several, called 'thūshois' or 'muntries,' who have the privilege of being exempt from labour and taxation at his hands. This office is not, strictly speaking, hereditary—although in most cases, except when thoroughly incompetent, the son succeeds the father—but is given to those qualified for it, as being men of property and influence as well as of ability, and good spokesmen. The Rajah himself is, on the contrary, invariably succeeded by his eldest son, for whom, should he be a minor, the kingdom is managed by a council of muntries. In default of sons, the Rajah's brother succeeds, and failing him the nearest male relative takes the guddee, the Salique law being in full force.

"Should the Rajah die without any heir to the throne, the

chief muntry, if he be an influential man, takes his place, or some neighbouring Rajah of the same clan is called upon to take the government or usurps it. Each of the clans have one great Rajah, supposed to be the main branch of the original stock, to whom, although those immediately beyond his own villages owe him no allegiance, great respect is shown by all, and acknowledgment of the superior title given, although in power and wealth he may be much poorer than others of the tribe.

"No regular courts are held among the Kookis, but complaints are always heard before the Rajah, assisted by his muntries, whenever they may be made. Heinous crimes are very infrequent among these people. Theft is almost unknown, and they chiefly offend in slight quarrels and disputes among themselves, which are settled by their Rajah, a fine being exacted from the guilty party, according to his means and the extent of his guilt, either in wine, fowls, pigs, goats, cows, or methins. When cases of theft, burglary, or arson occur, the criminal loses his independence and becomes a bondman to the Rajah for the term of his life. Cases of murder and manslaughter are of course taken up by our authorities and punished by our laws. But the punishment awarded for murder among the Kookis was confiscation of all goods and property and perpetual bondage for the murderer, his wife, and family, who thenceforth became slaves of the Rajah and did his work. The only crime punishable by death among the Kookis was high treason, or an attempt at violence on the person of the king, and treacherous commerce with an enemy of the clan: the victim in these cases was cut to pieces with dhaos, but of course no such extreme measures can be resorted to by them in the present day. In cases of adultery and seduction the punishment is left in the hands of the aggrieved husband or father. In the former case, death might be inflicted on the adulterer by any means with impunity, but more generally it was, and now invariably is, the custom to compound with him for a large sum of money, something over and above the original price of the wife. The adulteress then becomes the property of her lover.

"In cases of seduction every effort is made, and in most cases

O 2

successfully, to have the guilty couple married forthwith, a penal price being put upon the bride. All the women in the village, married or single, are perfectly at the pleasure of the Rajah, and no voice would be lifted against him for cohabiting with any of them, the only prevention being a sense of immorality and an understanding among the royal families of the whole tribe generally that such conduct is *infra dig.*; indeed, there is little temptation, for the Rajah may have as many wives as he likes or can keep, both polygamy and concubinage being in common practice, female slaves living generally in the latter condition with respect to their masters."—Stewart's "Notes on Northern Cachar," pp. 45–48.

This description is still fairly accurate, but the gradual breaking up of villages, coupled with the increased control by Government and State officers, has lessened the power of the chiefs and modified custom to a considerable extent. Lieutenant Stewart gives the following account of how the people hunted before guns were common among them:—

"The Kookis are great hunters, and are passionately fond of the sport, looking upon it, next to war, as the noblest exercise for man. They kill tigers, deer, and smaller game by means of poisoned arrows. The bow is a small one made of bamboo, and very slightly bent, the string being manufactured of bark. The arrow, the head of which has a barbed iron point, is about 18 inches long, being drawn to the chest and not the ear, and therefore delivered with no great force, the destructive effect lying chiefly in the poison. With such an instrument the great art in hunting lies in stealthily approaching the animal near enough to deliver the arrow with effect, and in following it up after being wounded to the spot where it is found lying dead. In this the Kookis excel, being able to prowl about the jungle as noiselessly as tiger-cats, and being equal to North American Indians in distinguishing tracks. Tigers are also killed by spring bows with poisoned arrows set in the jungles and by poisoned panjies planted in their paths.

"Elephants are slain in great numbers by the Kookis wherever they are to be had, not only the tusks but the flesh being highly prized. Parties of 20 and upwards go out in pursuit of them at a time When some recent elephant track is discovered in the forest, two or three of the party ascend some convenient tree, whose branches overhang the track, the remainder follow it up, and having got on the other side of the herd scare it towards the ambush by shouting, beating gongs, and discharging firearms. Here, while passing, the animals are assailed from above with long spears having huge iron barbs covered with deadly poison; every wound inflicted results in the death of the animal at not more than half a mile from the spot on which he was hit. So wary are the elephants, however, that it is seldom that more than two out of a herd are killed. At the place where their game is found dead, they commence cutting him up, and extract his tusks; laden with these and as much of the flesh as they can carry, they return home, and other parties go out and encamp in the neighbourhood of the carcase until they have entirely consumed it, or are driven away by the effluvia of decomposition. Portions of the flesh that they cannot immediately eat are dried and smoked to be kept for future consumption. The Kookis also hunt the methin or wild cow, which they have likewise succeeded in domesticating, having introduced the breed to Northern Cachar.

"The deadly poison used by the Kookis is, they say, extracted from a tree which does not grow in these parts, but the article is brought to them for sale by tribes inhabiting the borders of Manipur. The substance is of a dark blue or black colour and of about the consistency of common resin. To make it serviceable it is ground down with capsicum seeds and tobacco juice, so as to form a pulp, with which the weapons are smeared, cotton soaked in the mixture being also tied to the iron under the barb. I had once the cruelty to try the effect of this poison on two domestic fowls. To one I administered internally a dose equal to about two common-sized pills, and I punctured one of the legs of the other, so as merely to draw blood, with the pointed bamboo about the size of a toothpick which had been dipped into the mixture. The latter died in twenty minutes without much apparent pain, and in the former no effects whatever could be perceived, and it may be crowing to the present day. Another poison, called 'deo-bi,' is used by the Kookis to kill fish, and has an intoxicating effect upon them forcing them to the surface, when it is thrown into the water. The Kookis also spear fish, but have not much idea of catching them by the hook or net."—Stewart's "Notes on Northern Cachar," pp. 62, 63.

When the track of a tiger is found the "thempu" lifts the earth on which the footprint is and lays it on a leaf of the "ai" plant. He pours some zu on it and then, muttering charms, he wraps it up in the leaf and drops it into a pot, which he places to his ear and professes to be able to hear whether the pursuit of the animal will be crowned with success. The customs as regards "boi" approximate to those of the Lushais, and where they differ it is always to the disadvantage of the boi; thus a criminal seeking refuge in the chief's house has to pay a mithan before he can be accepted. On a chief's death each boi has to kill a pig at his funeral. Slavery by purchase is recognised and is not restricted to the chiefs—another point of resemblance between the Thados and the Chins.

The village organisation is much the same as among the Lushais, but the minor chiefs, while collecting all dues from the people of their villages, pay certain dues to the head of their family. The crier is known as "tlāngsam," but he receives no remuneration. The "thirdeng," or blacksmith, is known as "thirshu," and receives a day's labour from every householder in the village as his pay.

The thempu only receives zu, and this only from those he cures—a system tending to increase the skill of the practitioners.

As regards marriage the rules are not very clearly defined, but young men of the families which sacrifice a sow to their Sakhua will not generally take girls from the families which sacrifice a mithan. Strange to say, the sow-sacrificers have no objection to providing brides for the mithan-slayers, the cause probably being that in certain cases the wife's Sakhua has to be propitiated and the cautious sons of sow-killing families object to the extra expense involved by marrying a wife whose Sakhua demands a mithan. Lieutenant Stewart states that strict rules existed prohibiting the intermarriage of cousins, however remote, but my enquiries tend to show that at present the prohibition only extends to paternal cousins to the third generation.

Marriage is by purchase, the sums to be paid being:—

"Manpi" (Lushai "manpui")—three to 30 mithan, according to the family of the bride, to the father of the girl or his representative.

"Golha" (Lushai "palal")—Rs. 4/- or 5/-.

The bride's elder sister, one cloth of dark blue.

The father's younger brother, one mithan, called "mankang," but if he is living in the same house as the father then the nearest male relative who is living separately receives this.

Although a man has paid the full price for his wife, yet he has, on her death and the death of each of her sons, to pay a further sum called "longman" to her nearest male relative. Supposing Pathong marries Thonghlu's daughter and has by her two sons, one of whom dies, it is Thonghlu's duty to kill a pig in honour of the deceased and to take the skull and all the flesh except that of the head and the entrails to Pathong. The skull is placed over the grave and the flesh eaten by the family. Pathong now has to pay Thonghlu the price of the pig and Rs. 9/-, but if he prefers he may, instead of these two sums, give one mithan, however small, Rs. 1/-, and a hoe. It is often found cheaper to give the mithan. Suppose Thonghlu is now gathered to his fathers, leaving a son, Kanpu, and Pathong's wife also dies, then Kanpu must kill the pig and will receive the mithan. Pathong departs this life and his son marries and begets a son, Komyang, and Kanpu also dies leaving a son, Nelet. Now on the death of Pathong's remaining son, Nelet must kill the pig and will receive the mithan from the dead man's son, Komyang, and as this extinguishes the liability on account of Thonghlu's daughter, Komyang, in token thereof, will also give to Nelet one spear and one tinder-box. These payments, unfortunately, are seldom made on the spot, and claims on account of great-aunts or even more distant female relatives are frequently brought up for decision. In case of women who die in childbed or in any unnatural manner her "longman," as this payment is called, has not to be paid. "Longman" reminds one of the Lushai "lukawng," and very similar customs are found among the Old Kuki and some Naga clans.

In common with nearly all non-Lushei clans, a Thado co-respondent, and not his victim's relatives, has to pay the injured husband all the expenses he had incurred in the marriage and also a fine of one mithan. The same rule applies to the seducer of a widow living in her late husband's house. On a man's death his eldest brother can insist on marrying the widow and taking all the children. "Sawnman" is enforced as among the Lushais, but should the father refuse to take the child when it is old enough to leave its mother, he is called on to pay a second mithan, and he forfeits the right to receive the marriage price in case of a girl. The eldest son inherits and, failing a son, the nearest male relative. Adoption is practised as among the Lushais, the ceremony being known as "Phunkai" (Lushai "Sā-phun").

In case of accidental homicide the offender has to kill a pig at his victim's funeral and provide a blue cloth to wrap the body in. Should the death have been caused by a gunshot wound the gun is forfeited to the heir of the deceased. The Thados claim that rape and sodomy are unknown among them.

There is no doubt that head-hunting was indulged in in olden days, and on the death of a powerful chief at least one freshly taken head had to adorn his grave.

Lieutenant Stewart, in the book already quoted from, gives a good deal of information about the religious beliefs of the Thados. He says they recognise one all-powerful god, whom they call Pathen (Lushai Pathian), who has a wife, Nongjai. I have enquired about Pathen's wife, but though all my informants say that it is usual to speak of Pathen Nongjai together, none could say whether Nongjai was Pathen's wife—an equally powerful being, sharing power with Pathen—or simply another name for Pathen. Stewart also provides Pathen with a son, Thihla, but my informants all agree that the Thihla are demons of the hills, rivers, and forests—in other words exactly the same as the Huais of the Lushais. Ghumoishe, mentioned by Stewart, is the king of all these Thihla, and he has a wife, Imungshe. They are supposed to inhabit the densest forests on the highest mountain tops, and when passing through such their dread names are never mentioned. About this demon Stewart says: "By some he is said to be the illegitimate son of Pathen, but others deny the relationship, and say that he has no connection with the god whatever. The idea of making the origin of evil proceed thus from an illegitimate source is exceedingly clever." None of my informants would venture a guess even at Ghumoishe's parentage. Kuchom, whom Stewart gives as Ghumoishe's wife, is nowadays, as far as I can find out, unknown, as also is Hilo, said by Stewart to be the daughter of the last-named couple and to be the goddess of poisons. The Thihla are divided into Thingbulnga, the Thihla of the big trees; Shongbulnga, of the rocks and stones; Tuikhumnga, the demons of the water, of whom Tuikhumlen is the king. These water spirits are said to be far more powerful than those of the woods or rocks, and therefore are often spoken of as Tui-pathen. They also receive a fourfold sacrifice, of a white fowl or an egg, a pig, a dog, which must not be entirely black, and a he-goat, whereas cocks or hens are considered quite good enough for the Thingbulgna or Shongbulgna.

Zomi is a female spectre, a sight of which is a sure forerunner of some dire misfortune, which can only be averted by the immediate sacrifice of a dog. Pheizam correspond to the Lāshi. Nuaijingmang is an evil spirit which lives underground.

After death the spirits of men and women, great and small, all go to Mi-thi-khua. The only advantage which the spirits of those who have slain men and beasts and given feasts obtain is that Kulsamnu does not dare to detain them, whereas she, sitting by the roadside, seizes all other poor wandering souls, and troubles them sorely unless their relatives who have gone on before come to their rescue.

I have been unable to find any traces of ancestor worship, nor is it mentioned either by Stewart or McCulloch. This is extremely curious, as the Thados attach the highest possible importance to a long pedigree and, as has been seen, nearly every other clan practise some rites to appease the dead.

Religious Rites and Sacrifices.—The Daibawl sacrifices are made as among the Lushais, but not the Khāl. The Dongel and Shit-hloh families sacrifice a sow to Sakhua, but the Haukip and Kipgen kill a mithan. This difference is said to date back to the time when the Haukip lived on the banks of the Run or Manipur river, near to Tiddim, and sacrificed a mithan to Rulpui.

or the great snake. The Chhinchhuan are said to have recently adopted the Vaiphei method of propitiating Sakhua, and in consequence the Shit-hloh have ceased intermarrying with them.

Besides the sacrifice to Sakhua the Thado have a special sacrifice known as "Pathen biak na" ("speaking to Pathen"). This consists of killing a small pig in the closet at the end of the house and a white cock in front of the house. The crop, entrails, and bones are "sherh" and are placed on an oaken post in front of the house, and a thirty days' "hrilh" is observed.

The Ai ceremonies are much the same as among the Lushais, but in that of the tiger the carrying of the porcupine is unknown. Directly a tiger is shot a bamboo skewer is hammered into its ear hole, to make sure that it is dead, and when the body is brought up to the village an egg is placed in the mouth by some female relative of the lucky hunter, who addresses the dead animal thus: "Oh! Ho! You stole that, did you? And so a peg has been driven into your ear." She then jumps across the body from side to side and from head to tail. After this the skin may be removed. In connection with cultivation, a ceremony called "Daibun" is performed after the burning of the jhums. Seven bamboos adorned with cotton wool are placed round the jhum as an offering to the "Thihla" of the locality, who are further propitiated later on by an offering of an egg and some leaves placed on a bamboo in the middle of the jhum. This is called "Daikam." Wanolnaunu died because she was so lazy that it was too much trouble to live, so if any of her signs are found in a new jhum, a sacrifice has to be performed to avoid a failure of the crops. A tree which has two trunks which unite some feet above the ground is said to represent her fingers, and a red fowl must be sacrificed and the tree dug up by the roots. A spring is said to be her tears, and a goat must be sacrificed. If a wallow is found a pig must be offered. If a woman is not blessed with offspring within the usual time of the marriage there are three methods of procedure:—The woman may go to her father's house, and he will kill a cock and they will drink zu together, after which he ties a string round her neck. If this is not successful she may go to her husband's eldest brother or cousin, and he will repeat the performance. If there is still no result the thempu is called in and kills a black hen inside the house, and its flesh, mixed with stones and other ingredients, is compounded by him into a medicine which the poor woman desirous of offspring has to eat. On the occasion of the birth of a child the mother may not leave her house for five days in case of a son and three in case of a daughter. When these periods have expired she goes to her father's house and takes a fowl or a pig, according to her means. This is called "Nau-bil-vu." The mother also gives her father or sometimes her mother a cloth on the occasion of the birth of a child, and the recipient kills a pig in honour of the occasion. In case of a child getting sick the thempu sacrifices a fowl, called "Ar-kang-tha."

The marriage ceremonies of the Thados are described by both McCulloch and Stewart, and do not seem to have changed at all during the 55 years that have elapsed since their accounts were written. Neither account, however, is quite complete. The bridegroom, accompanied by his friends, taking with them at any rate a portion of the sum to be paid for the bride, go to the village where the girl lives, and for three days the young men of the village wrestle with them. On arrival they are met with showers of filth from the children of the village. The girl's parents have to give a pig or a mithan and much zu to celebrate the occasion. At the conclusion of the feast the bride sets out for her future home dressed in her best and wearing a gong on her head. The actual marriage ceremony takes place in the house of the father of the bridegroom and consists of the thempu killing a fowl, feathers from the right wing being placed in the hair of the young couple. They then drink out of the same cup of zu, and the thempu, muttering charms, binds a cotton thread round their necks, which must be worn till it falls off from old age.

The thempu then presents each with a comb. Only very near relatives may use the same comb. Stewart says husband and wife may share a comb, but my information is that uterine brothers and sisters may do so. A Lushai correspondent writes that among them the use of another man's comb may cause a headache, and that a person of a higher clan would be contaminated if he used the comb of a member of a lower one. To see whether the union will prove harmonious the thempu takes a hair from the head of each and moistens them in zu and then twists them together. If the hairs remain twisted all will go smoothly, but should they fly apart many bickerings and disputes are to be expected. The parents of the bridegroom give a feast to all concerned, and this completes the ceremony, but the young couple do not at once commence sleeping together. If they have not been previously acquainted they often sleep apart for a month, and for lesser periods according to the degree of their acquaintance.

Eligible brides are even now carried off and married against the wishes of their parents, by ardent lovers belonging to powerful families.

Immediately a death occurs guns are fired and a special funeral chant called "Lā pi" (Lushai "Hlā") is sung three times. The funeral ceremonies of ordinary people are practically the same as among the Lushais, but in the case of those who have performed the "Chong" the ceremonies last seven days, and each day the corpse is carried in and out of the house seven times with much shouting, and a mithan has to be killed on each day. Every relative and slave has to attend and bring some animal to be killed. The skulls of all these adorn the great man's grave, and, in former days, at least one fresh human skull taken specially for the occasion from some other clan had to be added to the other trophies over a chief's grave. Sometimes the body of a great chief may be placed in a small house at a short distance from the village and partially dried over a slow fire; and a curious survival of the times of war is found in the practice, now dying out, of severing the head and burying it in an earthen pot in a separate place. This was done to prevent the heads being found and removed as trophies, should the village be raided. The entrails of the first animal killed in honour of the deceased are placed on leaves at the foot of the post against which the corpse rested during the funeral feast, and are left there for several days, even up to one month, and at every meal a handful of rice is taken out of the pot and placed on the leaves, before anyone is allowed to eat. This portion for the dead is called "thi an chhe." As among the Rangte, efforts are made to obtain some wild animal or bird, and if the hunters are successful the entrails of the animal, or the whole animal if it be not edible, are buried with the " thi an chhe " in the grave, without waiting for the expiry of the month.

Unnatural deaths (" thichhia") are considered unlucky, and the custom regarding the disposal of the corpse in such cases is the same as among the Lushais. Memorial stones are not generally put up by the Thados, but are occasionally found among the Chhinchhuan, perhaps from their proximity to the Lushais.

A man who has performed the Ai of a tiger is honoured with a special memorial. Two posts, one some four feet long and the other about three, carefully squared and with the four sides ornamented with transverse notches, are placed in the ground some five or six feet apart. The longer post terminates in a spike, on which are impaled several oval-shaped pieces of wood, which indicate the number of animals killed by the deceased. Between the posts and to one side a long pole is planted leaning over between the posts, and from this hangs half a dried gourd shell, convex side uppermost, from the rim of which hang tassels of rough wooden beads, and from the centre hangs a piece of wood 7 or 8 inches long, of which one end is forked and the other a knob. This represents " thotche," a sort of rat found in the jungle and said to be the master of the jungle. If this animal is burnt in the jungle the " Thihla " of the place will be angry and punish the persons responsible. Children eat the flesh of the thotche. The posts are called " thingel " and remind one of the memorial posts of the Chins, and the be-tasselled gourd is a sign among those people that the owner of the house before which it is displayed has killed a man.

A woman who has performed the Buh Ai is also honoured with a special memorial, consisting of an upright stone some three feet high, in front of which are placed three others supporting a flat stone. A space of about four square yards in front is enclosed by a line of stones set on edge, the whole of the interior being planted with small stones, which are supposed to show the number of baskets of rice reaped on the occasion of the Ai. The feasts connected with the cultivation known by the Lushais as " Kut " are not practised, but when the rice is

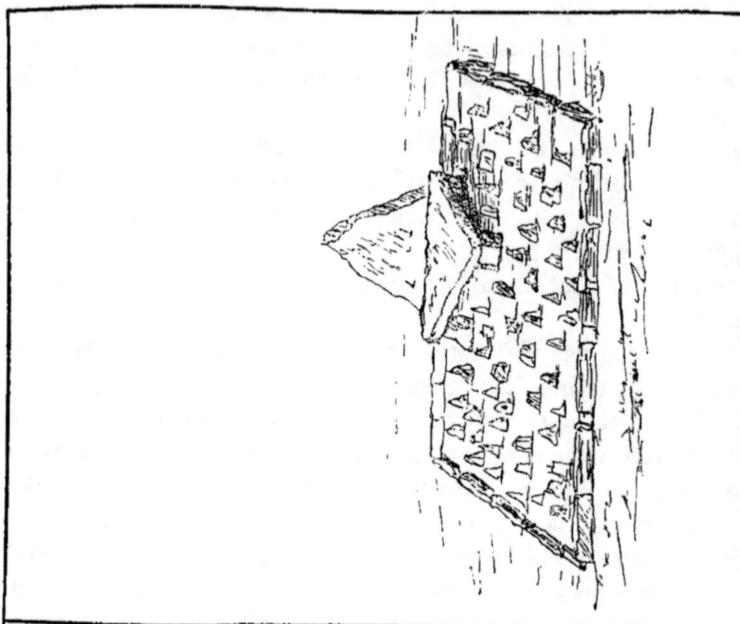

Memorial to a Woman who has performed the Buh Ai.

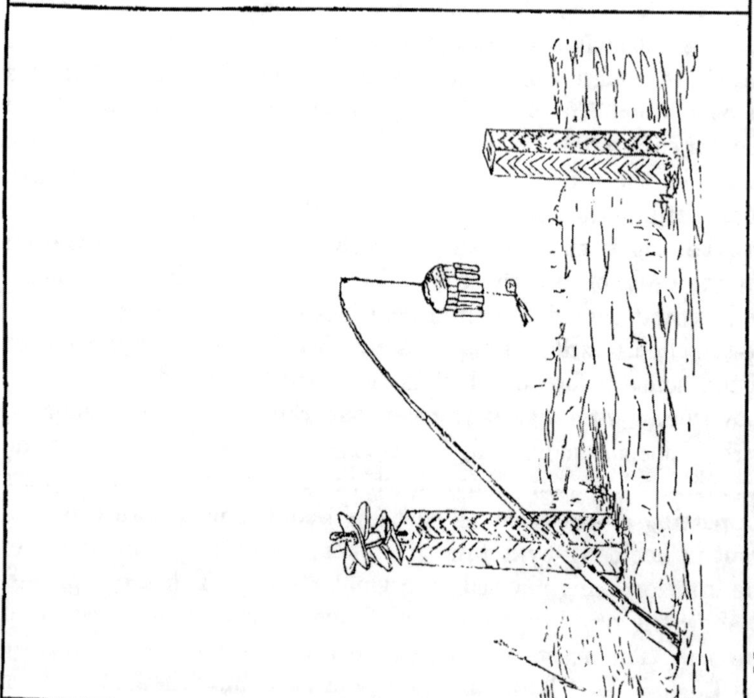

Memorial to a Man who has performed the Ai of a Tiger.

well up the whole community goes to the jhums, dancing and singing, and beating drums and gongs. In the jhums they work vigorously in perfect silence for a considerable time and then burst forth into song and dance, and eat their fill of rice washed down with zu. There is another feast connected with the crops called "Hun," which takes place when the rice is about a foot high. Each household prepares two pots of zu, one for the husband and one for the wife, and a post called "shekhon" is planted before each house. This post has two horizontal arms projecting, one near the top and one near the ground, the upper one being the longer. These are perforated, and three reeds are passed through the holes. Each household kills a white cock at the foot of the shekhon. The flesh is cooked in the house and eaten by the householder alone. The "sherh" and bones are hung on the shekhon. The zu in the householder's pot may only be drunk by other householders, but that in the wife's pot is dispensed to all comers. For five days after this feast no one but members of the household may enter the house. Nothing out of the house may be given away, and the householder must do no work, nor may he attend a funeral.

The series of feasts performed by the Lushais to attain the honours of "Thangchhuah" is not customary among the Thados, though some informants say that in olden days some such custom prevailed, and the "Chong" feast, at which seven mithan and two of every other sort of domestic animal had to be killed, is not performed now only because none can afford the expense. It will be remembered that "Chong" is the name of the first feast in the Thangchhuah series. Among the Haukip I am told that a position equivalent to Thangchhuah is attained by thrice celebrating the Ai of one of the following—tiger, bear, elephant, or hornbill.

Thado Folk Tales.

Benglama is the equivalent of the Lushai Chhura, and there are many tales about him which are common to both clans and in fact seem to be known to almost all representatives of the Kuki-Lushai race. The following is a translation of a portion of a tale written down in Lushai for me, but told by a

Thado. Benglama had visited a village and got himself much disliked, and everyone was trying to catch him :—"Once they made a ladder and cut the lower side partly through and made a great quagmire underneath. Benglama climbed up it, it broke, and he fell down into the mud. Then a tiger came up. 'My friend, if you help me out you may eat me,' said Benglama. Then the tiger pulled him out. Then the tiger—'I will eat you up,' he said. Benglama—'I will just go and wash myself clean,' he said. 'Presently I will eat you up,' he said again. Benglama—'I will go and ease myself,' he said, 'otherwise you will dislike my dung,' he said. Where he went to ease himself he cut a cane. The tiger—'Why do you do that?' he asked. Then Benglama—'It is going to blow and rain like anything, therefore I am going to tie myself to the stump of a tree,' he said. Then the tiger—'If that is so, tie me up first,' he said. He tied him up. Then he (Benglama) also put a mallet, that all who passed by might beat the tiger. Benglama went away. Then the wild-cat came along. The tiger—'My friend, you and I are just alike; we two are friends, we are brothers—undo me,' he said. He undid him. Then the wild-cat left him, going into a pangolin's hole. Then just as he was going in, the tiger caught him by the foot. 'What you have got hold of, that is not me, it is a tree root,' he said. The tiger let him go, but remained watching for him, but the wild-cat always slipped out at the other side, and was always eating fowls by Benglama's house. The tiger—'My friend, what is it you are eating?' he said. Then the wild-cat—'Oh, I am only just eating the bones of my hand,' he said. The tiger was always eating his paw, and it hurt very, very much indeed. Presently the wild-cat went to the tiger and said to him, 'If you were to take a torch and go near to Benglama's house you would be able to catch some fowls,' he said. So the tiger went up, but Benglama saw him, and heated some water. When it was very hot indeed, he poured it into a tui-um (bamboo tube for holding water) and threw it over the tiger. The tiger said, 'My friend! My friend! I am dying, I am all burnt up,' he said. The wild-cat—'There is a waterfall some way down stream; if you roll down that you will be well,' he said. He rolled down and so he died."

How Benglama Tried to Climb to the Top of the Big "Bung" Tree.

"This Benglama—his wife was going to start for the jhum, and she spoke thus to him. To her husband his wife said, 'Benglam, when the sun shines through our doorway, cook the rice, do,' she said. 'When the sun shines on the top of the bung tree in front of our house, then clean the rice and tie up the goat,' she said, and she also left her child with him. His wife then left him to go to the jhum. Then he, according to his wife's orders, when the sun shone in the doorway prepared to cook the rice. As often as he put the pot on the fire it fell off again. Presently the sun shone on the top of the bung tree. 'Did my wife say cook the food on the top of the bung tree?' he said. Then saying, 'I will clean the rice,' he prepared to climb to the top of the bung tree with the rice, mortar, and pounder, with the goat and the basket of fowls; but he could not climb up, he kept on falling down again. Just then his child, being hungry, began to cry and cry. Then Benglama, saying, 'Is his frontanel hurting?' pricked it with his hairpin. Then the child died. Benglama, saying, 'Has it gone to sleep?' laid it down on the sleeping machan; he did not know that it was dead. Then his wife came back from the jhum, and Benglama just before had fallen from the bung tree and was nearly dead, and lay on the sleeping platform groaning terribly. His wife said, 'Are you ill?' and he—'Speak! Why, I can hardly speak, I have fallen from the top of the bung tree and am nearly dead, don't you know?' he said to her. Then she looked at her child; and his wife—'Our child here is dead; how has it happened?' she said. The Benglama—'Go on! it's not dead, its head was hurting and I pricked it; it is just asleep,' he said to her. Then his wife—'It is dead indeed; go and bury it,' she said. Then Benglama wrapped it up in a mat and carried it over his shoulder, and the body dropped out behind him, and he placed the mat only in a cave, and on his way back he saw his child's body. 'Whose child is this?' he said, and kicked it about with his feet."

The Story of Ngamboma and Khuptingi.

"Formerly Ngamboma and Khuptingi, before they were

born, while in their mothers' wombs, they loved each other. When the time for them to be born came near their mothers' bellies pained them. Then if their mothers put their bellies near to each other they got well. Then the children were born. In the jhums when they were placed apart in the jhum house while their mothers were at work they always got together. When they grew bigger they loved each other, and Ngamboma wanted to marry Khuptingi, but their fathers and mothers did not think it wise. Then Ngamboma made an image of Khuptingi in beeswax and tied it to a stump of a tree on the bank of the stream, and whenever the water rose Kḫuptingi got ill and when it went down she got better. Thus it went on for one year. One day the stream rose and carried away Khuptingi's image, then Khuptingi died. They placed her body in a dead-house. From the decaying matter which fell from her body flowers sprang up, and Ngamboma watched them always. One day a wild cat was going to take away those flowers, but Ngamboma caught it and said, 'Why did you think to steal my flowers—I'll just kill you?' he said. Then the wild cat—'Protector! Do not kill me; I am sent by Khuptingi,' he said. Then Ngamboma—'Where is Khuptingi, then?' he said. Then the wild cat—'If you catch hold of my tail we will both go (to her),' he said. Then the wild cat towed him to the village in which Khuptingi was in the sky, in Mi-thi-kḫua (the dead-people's-village), and they arrived at Khuptingi's house and they slept there, and they ate rice also together. When they slept together Khuptingi was only bare bones, and Ngamboma said, 'What bones are these?' and he threw them to the top of the wall and to the bottom of the wall (*i.e.*, all about the room). Then the next day Khuptingi—'I am not well,' she said. Ngamboma—'What is the reason?' he said. The Khuptingi—'Last night when I was sleeping near you you threw me to the top of the wall and to the bottom of the wall; for that reason I am in pain,' she said. Then their villagers said, 'Let us go and fish,' they said. They went. The place where they caught fish—indeed it was not a stream, it was a patch of bamboo. The dead called the bamboo leaves fish, and they filled their baskets cram-full, but Ngamboma said to himself, 'They will stop the holes in the baskets with the leaves when they come to the stream so that the fish may not fall out by accident,' he said, and he stopped the holes (in his basket) with leaves. Then they all returned to the village. Ngamboma, by diverting a stream, caught a few fish and returned. When they reached their houses the dead roasted the leaves which they called fish, but when Ngamboma tried to roast them the leaves all burnt up. Then Khuptingi said to Ngamboma, 'The others have caught so many fish; why have you caught so few?' Ngamboma roasted the real fish which he had caught, but they burnt up just like the bamboo leaves. Then one day the people again went out to hunt. In the place where they went hunting they saw a huge black caterpillar; the dead called it a bear. Ngamboma did not see it, and by accident trod on it and killed it. Then the dead said to Ngamboma, 'That bear which ran towards you, have you seen it?' they said. Ngamboma—'I have not seen it,' he said. Presently they saw the caterpillar which he had trodden on, 'Hei-le! Why, you have shot it!' they said. They carried it up to the village and all the dead ate up its flesh entirely. Ngamboma, however, did not care to eat any of it. Then Khuptingi said to Ngamboma, 'Living people and dead people, we shall not be able to live together comfortably; therefore, if you now build yourself a house here and then return to your home, when you die you will be able to live in it?'—thus Khuptingi said. So he set to work to build a house. The dead called the arum trees, and they split them with axes and built (with them), but Ngamboma just split those arums with his nail very quickly. 'Can one build houses with such stuff?' he said. Then, splitting real trees into planks, he built his house. Then Khuptingi said to Ngamboma, 'If you go to your house and call all the villagers together and sacrifice a mithan, and when you have finished eating its flesh you put on very good cloths and wear round your neck the sacrificial rope (the rope the mithan was bound with), and call on my name, then you will die and will be able to come to our village,' she said. Just as Khuptingi said it came to pass; he died as he was lying on his bed, then they were able to live together with comfort. When he saw the house that he had built in Mi-thi-khua, he said, 'Who built that house?' The dead said to him, 'You built it while you were alive.' Then they married in Mi-thi-khua, it is said.

"It is because of this story of Ngamboma and Khuptingi that we say nowadays people are in Mi-thi-khua."

CHAPTER V

THE LAKHER OR MARA CLAN

THIS clan emigrated from the neighbourhood of Thlan-tlang (called by the Chin Hills officers Klang-klang) in comparatively recent times. They are closely allied to the Southern Chins, and a description of them belongs more properly to the Chin Monograph. Much of the information in Messrs Carey and Tuck's Gazetteer regarding the Southern Chins applies to the Lakhers. I therefore propose to give only a brief description here.

The clan calls itself Mara, Lakher being the name used by the Lushais. The Chins, I believe, call them Zo, and the Arracan name for them is Klongshai. The following extract from my diary, dated 10th February, 1891, gives a brief account of the advent of this clan:—"In the evening I had a long talk with the chiefs and found out the origin, according to them, of the feud with the Mrungs (in the Chittagong Hill tracts). In the lifetime of Thonglien's father, the Bohmong of that time sent to ask the Mara clan to come and make friends. A deputation went, taking with them two large elephant tusks as a peace offering. The Bohmong had two of the party treacherously killed, and hence the feud which has led to so much bloodshed. I am told that the first Mara to come here (Saiha) were a colony under one of Thonglien's ancestors. They came from Thlan-tlang to where Vongthu now is, and then moved further east till they settled somewhere on the Blue Mountain. Finding themselves too small a colony to hold their own, they sent for the rest of the clan, who, under Lianchi, Hmunklinga's great-grandfather, came and settled where Ramri now is. After a few years a few of the Chinja tribe arrived and were received into the village. These were followed by more and more until eventually the Mara left the Chinja in possession of Ramri and moved across the Blue Mountain, where they have remained ever since." There are other Lakher villages besides those referred to in the above extract, and the clan is found in considerable strength to the south of the Lushai Hills boundary, in territory which is at present unadministered. Members of the clan are also found in the Lushai and Chin villages adjoining the real Lakher country, which lies in the loop of the Koladyne or Kaladan river, south of latitude 22°3′.

Their villages are more permanent than those of the Lushais though the houses are built of the same materials, the proximity of large supplies of bamboos having led the immigrants to abandon the substantial timber buildings of the land of their origin for more flimsy structures. The sites are, however, levelled and the villages are seldom moved. Before the reign of peace which has followed our occupation of the Hills, each village was surrounded by a triple line of stockading or by an impenetrable belt of thorny jungle, through which a narrow pathway, defended by three gates, led to the village. Inside the houses the sleeping platforms of the Lushais are absent and the hearth is in the middle of the floor. If the owner has slaves or a married son, the interior is divided into compartments by partitions which extend three-quarters of the way across the house.

The men smoke but little, but much relish the nicotine water from the women's pipes, which differ slightly in shape from those used by their Lushai cousins.

Dress.—I have been unable to detect any difference in dress between the Lakhers and the Southern Chins. The men wear a narrow loin-cloth twisted round the waist, one end being passed between the legs and slipped under the waist-band, the only other garment being a cloth about 7 feet by 5, worn as the Lushais wear theirs, and made either of cotton or silk. Blue and white check cloths are very much fancied, but are imported from Burma, whence also comes a very rough cotton

LAKHER CHIEF AND FAMILY

cloth with large brown checks. The silk cloths are made by the women and are fine pieces of work, taking an industrious woman as much as a year to weave.

The dress of the women is more elaborate—several petticoats reaching almost to the ground and held up by a massive brass girdle, made after the pattern of the chain of a cog-wheel. These petticoats are generally of dark blue cotton, but sometimes the outer one is a very elaborately worked piece of silk, similar in pattern to the man's cloth. Each petticoat is merely a strip of cloth wide enough to go one and a half times or even twice round the body.

While clothing her nether extremities thus decently, the Lakher woman wears a jacket which consists really of little more than two very short sleeves joined at the back and tied loosely together in front. This absurd little garment does not by several inches reach to her petticoat. The jacket is generally of home-made cloth or silk of a pattern similar to the men's cloths. A loose cloth of the favourite blue and white check is wrapped round the body for warmth, but discarded when any work is being done.

The men wear the hair tied in a knot above the forehead. A very narrow turban is often worn, being passed round the back of the head low down and the ends twisted round the knot of hair. Chiefs affect the high turban of the Thlantlangs.

Women wear nothing on their heads, except in wet weather, when both sexes wear hats like the Lushais. The raincoat of the Chins is also used. Special cloths and plumes are worn by those who have killed men or given certain feasts, as among the Lushais.

Ornaments.—The amber necklaces so dear to the Lushais do not find much favour with this clan, who value especially necklaces of a stuff known as "pumtek," but as this is very rare, necklaces of glass-beads, cornelians, buttons, coins, etc., are generally all that commoners can obtain. The women are particularly fond of necklaces; the men wear but few, which is in marked contrast to the custom of the Lushais.

The men ornament their top-knots with combs, the backs

of which are sometimes of ivory, sometimes of wood lacquered in various patterns. A long pin of iron or bone is always worn in the top-knot, and is used for scratching the head as well as for cleaning out the pipe.

The women wear their hair rolled round a very heavy two-pronged brass skewer, the weight of which, sometimes as much as 3 lbs., keeps the hair low down on the nape of the neck.

Constitution of Society.

The Lakhers, in common with the Chins, are less democratic than the Lushais and their cognates. The power of the chiefs is greater, and the chiefs' relatives and other wealthy people form a kind of peerage and lord it over the lesser fry, being seldom interfered with unless their doings endanger the interests of the chief. Slaves with the Lakhers are real slaves, not merely unpaid servants as among the Lushais. A slave is the absolute property of his master, and may be sold like any other possession. Female slaves are not allowed to marry, but are encouraged to become mothers, as their children are the property of their owners. Male slaves who win their master's favour are sometimes married at their owner's expense, but they and their children remain slaves. Parents and other relations sell children when they are in pecuniary difficulties, and captives taken in war are naturally the slaves of their captors.

In the matter of marriage the Lakher's choice is as little limited as that of the Lushai, but, owing to the power of the upper class, there is great competition to secure a bride of good birth, and this leads to girls being married before they attain puberty. After her marriage such a child-wife helps in the household of her husband's mother, but sleeps with her own parents. The following extract from a report on the Lakhers sent me by Mr. Whalley, of the E. Bengal and Assam Police, cannot be improved on:—"The advanced age, as regards males, at which marriage takes place is due to the recognised obligation on the part of every male to marry the daughter of a house of higher standing than his own, with the consequently disproportionate advance in the amount of the marriage price. Too frequently a male on coming into his inheritance is occupied during his years of vigour in paying off the debt of his mother's marriage price, and can only afford to take a wife of a higher station than his own when he is no longer capable of becoming a father. In the interval he takes a concubine, generally of a lower class than his own. On the other hand, the marriage or betrothal of children by their parents is common. Such marriages are on two scales. In both from the date of betrothal the bridegroom commences to pay the marriage price in irregular instalments; in one, however, he contracts, if he becomes a father by his bride, to pay the whole marriage price, and can claim the return of all payments made if the decease of his bride precedes such an event; in the other he pays only a proportion of the whole fixed beforehand, which is not recoverable, even if marriage is never consummated. The first is in more general favour with parents, as even in the case of the death of the prospective bride it is by no means certain that, in view of the disparity in position of the families, the bridegroom will be able to compel disgorgement of the instalments paid."

"The above description of customs refers *mutatis mutandis* to all classes of society except slaves. The desirability of an unmarried girl varies directly with the social position of the parents; appearance, industry, and chastity are entirely subordinate factors, and exercise very little influence on the marriage price demanded. There is a strange custom by which a husband who finds his wife incompatible may exchange her for any of her sisters still unmarried. A younger brother, again, whose parents are dead, even though already married, takes over as a rule the wife as well as the liability of an elder brother who has predeceased him. The precedence of such wives should be regulated solely by the position of their parents, and breaches of this rule, owing to the partiality of the husband, lead frequently to bitter feuds."

The following valuable note on the marriage price of a Lakher girl, and on the dues payable at death, by Mr. R. A. Lorrain, is inserted just as received:—

The important position occupied by the bride's eldest brother and her maternal uncle are noticeable.

PARTICULARS OF MARRIAGE PRICE PAID BY A MARA FOR HIS BRIDE.[1]

NAME OF PRICE.	AMOUNT OF PRICE.[2]		No.	TO WHOM PRICE IS PAID AND OTHER PARTICULARS IN REGARD TO THE MARRIAGE CUSTOMS OF THE MARA TRIBES.
	Common People.	Ruling Clan.		
O-Kia	Rs. 20/- Gong (7 spans). Gun.	Rs. 150/- One slave. Two Mithan.	1	*When the whole family live in the same house*, none of the sons having their own houses, then the Prices Nos. 1, 2, 3, 4, 5, 6, and Nos. 9, 10, 11, have all to be paid to the father of the bride.
Sei-pi-hra	Rs. 20/- Gong (7 spans). Gun.	Rs. 50/- One Mithan (female).	2	*If the family is divided* and the eldest son has a house of his own, then the father has price No. 11 and the eldest son must have price No. 1, while the prices Nos. 2, 3, 4, 5, 6, and Nos. 9, 10, are at the eldest son's disposal and he may or may not share with the youngest son as he pleases.
Chaw chyu	Rs. 20/- Gong (7 spans). Gun.	Rs. 50/- One Mithan. Gun (syulô).	3	
Sei-chei-hra	Rs. 20/- Gong (7 spans). Gun.	Rs. 50/- One Mithan. Gun (syulô).	4	
Nô-hla	Rs. 2/- Brass pot (4 spans).	Rs. 10/- Beer pot (Ra-cha).	5	
Saw-hla	Rs. 1/- Full grown hen	Rs. 2/- Brass pot (4 spans).	6	
Kei-ma...	Rs. 2/- Brass pot (4 spans).	Rs. 5/- Beer pot (Ra-cha).	7	No. 7 has to be paid to the friend of the father of the bride if the sons and father live in the same house. But if the family is divided, the eldest son having his own house, then this must be paid to his friend instead of the father's.
Lao-khyu	Rs. 2/- Brass pot (4 spans).	Rs. 5/. Beer pot (Ra-cha).	8	No. 8 has to be paid to the bride's mother's brother (bride's uncle).
Rai-pi-hra	Rs. 2/- Brass pot (4 spans).	Rs. 10/- Beer pot (Rai-pi).	9	
Aw-rua-haw-na	Rs. 5/- Beer pot (Ra-cha).	Rs. 50/- One Mithan. Gun.	10	

[1] At the wedding the bridegroom has to kill half the number of pigs that are killed by the bride's family, thus:—

Bride's family, 5 pigs killed; the bridegroom kills 3 pigs=8 pigs.
,, 10 ,, ,, ,, ,, 5 =15 pigs.

[2] The amount of price in these columns are all equal to one another in value and the bridegroom chooses only one out of each price according to what he has.

Name of Price.	Amount of Price.		No.	To whom price is paid and other particulars in regard to the Marriage Customs of the Mara Tribes.
	Common Psople.	Ruling Clan.		
Si-sa-zi or chhi-sa-zi. { s U-thei-ps... ...	Rs. 10/- A "Sisa" bead.	Rs. 20/- A "Sisa" bead.		*Note.*—No. 11, divided into thres sums, hss to be givsn on engsgement before the marrisge, and is kept by the father of the bride.
a Lia-pa	Rs. 5/- Brsss pot (5 spans).	Rs. 10/. A "Sisa" bead	11	
s Ssi-hnai-pa ...	Rs. 2/- Brass pot (4 spsns).	Rs. 5/. Besr pot (Ra-cha).		

PU-MA.[1]

Name of Price.	Common People.	Ruling Clan.	No.	To whom price is paid, &c.
A-ma-pi	Rs. 20/- Gong (7 spsns). Gun.	Rs. 150/- One slave. Two Mithan.	12	Pu-ma hss to be paid by the bridegroom to the brids's "Pu-pa," that is, tbs bride's mother's brother (uncle). He therefore recsives the prices Nos. 12, 13, 14, 15 and 18.
Aw-rua-baw-na	Rs. 5/- Bser pot (Ra-cha).	Rs. 50/. Ons Mithan. Gun.	13	
Nô-hla	Rs. 2/- Brass pot (4 spsns).	Rs. 10/- Beer pot (Ra-cha).	14	
Saw-hla	Rs. 1/. Full grown hen.	Rs. 2/- Brass pot (4 spsns).	15	
Kei-ma...	Rs. 2/- Brass pot (4 spsns).	Rs. 5/- Bssr pot (Ra-cha).	16	No. 16 has to be paid to the friend of the "Pu-pa" (bride's uncle).
Lao-khyu	Rs. 2/- Brass pot (4 spans).	Rs. 5/- Beer pot. (Ra-cha).	17	No. 17 hss to be paid to the brids's grandmother's brother on her mother's side (bride's great uncle), or it is sometimes paid to the "Pu-pa's" (bride's uncles) wife's fsther (father of sunt by marriage on the mother's side).
Pha-vaw. { s U-thei-pa	Rs. 7/- A "Siss" besd.	Rs. 20/- A "Siss" besd.		
a Lia-pa	Rs. 2/- Brsss pot (4 spsns).	Rs. 10/- A "Siss" besd.	18	
s Sei-hnai-pa ...	Rs. 1/- A large fowl.	Rs. 2/- Brass pot (4 spans).		

1 If the "Pupa" wishes for these prices to be paid he has to go to the bridegroom's house after the marriage (some other day) and kill a big pig. Then the prices have to be met quickly, or at least some of them, and the bridegroom also has to go to the "Pupa's" house and kill a pig in exchange for the pig that was killed for him. If the "Pupa" is dead (or when dead) his children can claim the prices in his stead

DEATH DUE.[1]

Name of Price.	Amount of Price.		No.	To whom Price is paid and other particulars in regard to the Marriage Customs of the Mara Tribes.
	Common People.	Ruling Clan.		
Ru	Rs. 10/- or more. Gong. This price is often nearly as heavy as the "O-kia."	Rs. 80/- or more. One Mithan (large). This price is often nearly as heavy as the "O-kia.'	19	At the *death of a wife* this price has to be paid as a death due by the husband to the dead wife's father or eldest brother as the case may be. At the *death of a husband* the eldest son of the dead man has to pay the price to his father's mother's brother (the dead man's uncle). If there is no son, the dead man's brother will pay, and then the dead man's daughters, when they marry, their marriage prices will go to this brother of the dead man (his nieces' marriage prices). If there are no daughters then he has his dead brother's possessions as a recompense, and he will also care for the widow unless she prefers to go to her own family once again.

[1] The death-due upon a woman is heavier than that upon a man. The death-due upon a prosperous man is more than that upon a poor man.

One out of each of the above prices has to be paid by the bridegroom before he is out of debt for his bride, and it will be found that:—

(1) An *ordinary person* has to give for his bride about Rs. 153/-, or £10 4s.

(2) One of the *ruling clan* has to give for his bride about Rs. 671/-, or £44 14s. 8d.

Then at death the death-due must be met, for No. 1, from Rs. 10/- to 20/-, or 13/4 to £1 6s. 8d.
for No. 2, from Rs. 80/- to 150/-, or £5 6s. 8d. to £10.

Needless to say, many of these prices are kept on credit, and often have to be met after death by the son or the son's son, making it a terribly complicated matter on the whole.

Reginald A. Lorrain,
May 4th, 1911. *Pioneer Missionary to the Lakhers' or Maras'.*

Offences against property and person can generally be settled by payment of a fine, but the Lakhers have no fixed custom in such matters, and a person of quality generally takes the law into his own hands if he considers himself aggrieved.

Head-hunting used to be indulged in and is still practised by the Lakhers in unadministered tracks. In case of a chief's death it was proper to kill someone of a distant village before drums or gongs were beaten, but it was thought "thianglo" to bring back the head on such an occasion. As regards their religious beliefs, the Lakher equivalent of Pathian is Khazang. Mr. Whalley writes:—"All spirits, with one doubtful exception to be noted later, whether malignant or benign, are slaves of the great spirit Khazang or Loitha. Whereas the attributes and the names of the lesser spirits vary from village to village and individual to individual, this great spirit has a firmer outline and permits of some attempt at description. The picture they draw is primitive, almost touching in its childishness. The Khazang or Loitha is small and brown and almost hairless. He is capable of sexual love and has children. He is material in his essence, but superior to natural laws such as those of time, space, and gravity. He is immortal, and has an immaterial wife and immaterial children. For his continuance the world exists with its revenue. In their own phrase he 'eats' the domains of the lesser spirits through all nature as a chief 'eats' villages (*i.e.*, receives tribute in supplies from villages). He regards individual men much as these same men regard individual ants. Nearer to the heart and farther from the intelligence of the Lakhers is the mysterious Pi-leh-pu, the all-mother and all-father (strictly translated 'grandmother' and 'grandfather,' the term is generally used for ancestors)—a being not anthropomorphised or materialised, partaking in some shadowy way of the functions both of guardian angel and of originator of the human race."

In the course of my enquiries I did not come across any references to Pi-leh-pu, but there seems good reason to think that the term is applied to the mythical ancestor of the clan. In the Lushai Mi-thi-rawp-lam, it will be remembered that in the centre of the frame round which the effigies of the ancestors of the celebrants are fastened there is a white effigy to represent the mythical ancestor of the whole clan. In some respects Pi-leh-pu seems to resemble the Lushai Sakhua.

The Ram-huai of the Lushais are known as "Hri-pa" and the Lāshi as "Sakhia." After death the spirits pass to Mi-thi-khua, the road to which is by the village of Lunchoi and passes up a precipice. It is so narrow that women with child have to widen it as they go, for which purpose a hoe is buried with them, or at least laid beside the corpse during the funeral feast. Pial-ral is called "Pe-ra'," and to reach it all sorts of animals must be killed and the Ai ceremony performed for each. The Khuangchoi feast is also considered, if not absolutely necessary, at least very useful. Triumphs in the courts of Venus will not help the spirit to pass to Pe-ra'. Women can only reach that happy place if their husbands take them. A series of feasts or sacrifices closely resembling the Thangchhuah feast of the Lushais is performed, but I was assured that the performer's state in the next world was not in any way affected thereby, the feasts being equivalent to the Lushai Sakhua sacrifice. The series consists of—

Vok-rial.—A very small pig which has been brought up in the house is killed and eaten.

Vok-pa.—A boar of five fists' height which has been brought up in the house is killed, a black hen being also sacrificed at the same time.

The "sherh" are kept inside the house for three days, during which time none of the household may do any work, but the house is not closed and anyone may share in the feast. The Vok-rial is performed three times and the Vok-pa twice, and then a mithan is killed and all share in the feast. The performer of the She-shun may not cross a big stream or enter another village till he has sacrificed a hen. Subsequently he again performs Vok-rial, which is said to conclude the sacrifices to Sakhua. A feast in which two mithan are killed is called "Bawi." It is followed by Khuangchoi, in which at least five mithan must be slain.

The spirits of the dead are supposed to become mist after having lived two or three lives in the other world.

Ten days after the birth of a child the mother goes to the water supply and washes herself. She then takes the child to her father's house, where she receives some rice and a fowl, which she takes home and eats. Sacrifices are not done at this time. Children's heads are shaved at three months, and the hair is allowed to grow at nine years with girls and at eleven with boys. The bodies of stillborn children are buried outside the village without any ceremony, but no purification, either of the house or village, is considered necessary.

Death. The usual funeral feast, which in the case of wealthy persons may last three to five days, precedes the burial. Some time afterwards a second feast is given and a portion is put aside for the spirit of the deceased. At the funeral feast the corpse is laid out with fine cloths and ornaments and a dance is performed by two women and one man. In other respects the Lakher

LAKHER BASKETS.

and Lushai customs are very much alike. There is an annual feast in honour of those who have died during the year. It is called "Lachhia." A pig is killed and the young men and maidens dance attired in their best clothes, and the usual large quantities of zu are consumed.

In cases of unnatural death no one may leave the village till the sixth day. On the fourth day a hen is sacrificed outside the village. The corpse is buried beyond the village boundary fence. Deaths in childbirth are considered unnatural deaths. If the firstborn in a family dies within a few days of its birth the corpse is buried anywhere, without ceremony, and the household abstain from work for one day. Such a death is called "naw-dawng" (Lushai "hlamzuih").

Many of the Lushai sacrifices are performed. The Khāl takes the following form:—A fowl is killed at the head of the bed in the name of the father, a month later one is killed in the name of the mother, and in successive months one is killed for each child. The flesh of these fowls can only be eaten by the parents. The Uihring sacrifice is known as "An-hmu"; a dog is killed outside the house, the hills inhabited by their ancestors being named. The "sherh" are hung on a tree or a bamboo. The husbands of women who are enceinte may not enter the house on such occasions. The following sacrifices of the Lushais are not performed—Hring-ai-tan, Khuavanghring, Tui-leh-ram, Bawlpui. In the Thla-ko a cock is killed outside the village and the spirit is summoned. Khawhring is unknown, and they maintain that there are no wizards or witches among them.

There are three festivals connected with the crops—(1) "Kicheo" or "Kutsa-zawng," which takes place in January; feasting and drinking are the main features of this festival, which is preceded by a general hunt, as the flesh of wild animals, birds, or land crabs is absolutely necessary. (2) "Paku," which comes just before the sowing of the rice, closely resembles the Lushai Chap-chār-kut. (3) "Lalia"—this corresponds to the Lushai Mimkut; the children are fed with maize cakes, and if any member of the family has died within the previous year some cakes are put aside for his spirit.

The superstitions of the Lakhers resemble those of the

Lushais. To kill a python is sure to result in the death of the killer. Even to see a loris is unlucky and to kill one is fatal. The sight of two snakes copulating will also be followed by serious illness, if not by death. The Lushai Chawifa is known as " Thla-shi-pu," and if it falls in the jungle that is the place to cut your jhum, for then you are sure of a good crop. It seems that Thla-shi-pu is merely a meteor; the Lakhers have not surrounded this natural phenomenon with the myths which the more imaginative Lushais delight in. In choosing the site for a village a cock is taken, and if it does not crow the site will not be selected, but if one of the party dream of dead persons or bad things this is also sufficient cause for rejecting the site.

Among the Lakhers there are no priests of any sort; every man is his own priest. At the marriage ceremony the fowl is killed by the man who has arranged the match.

CHAPTER VI

LANGUAGE

THE languages of all the clans dealt with in this monograph, except the Lakher, are very similar, and also bear a strong resemblance to those of their neighbours.

Dr. Grierson, in the "Linguistic Survey of India," uses the term "Kuki-Chin" to describe all the languages spoken by the clans I have dealt with and their cognates, but he adds:—"Meithei-Chin would be a better appellation, as the whole group can be subdivided into two sub-groups, the Meitheis (Manipuris) and the various tribes which are known to us under the names of Kuki and Chin." Dr. Grierson considers that all the Kuki-Chin languages belong to the Burmese branch of the Tibeto-Burman family, and he subdivides them as follows:—

I. Meithei,* or Manipuri.

II. Chin languages—

1. Northern group: Thado, Sokte,* Siyin,* Ralte, and Paite or Vuite.
2. Central group: Tashon,* Lai,* Lakher, Lushai, Banjogi,* and Pankhu.*
3. Old Kuki group: Rhangkhol, Bete (Biate), Hallam, Langrong, Aimol, Anal, Chiru, Lamgang, Kolren (Kolhen), Kom, Purum, Mhar (Hmar or Khawtlang), and Cha.*
4. Southern group: Chinme,* Welaung,* Chinbok,* Yindu,* Chinbon,* Khyang or Sho,* Khami.*

With reference to the connection between the different clans, Dr. Grierson writes:—"The terms Old Kuki and New Kuki are apt to convey the idea that the tribes so denoted are closely

[1] Clans marked * are not dealt with in this monograph.

related to each other. But that is not the case. Not only do their customs and institutions differ considerably, but their languages are separated by a large group of dialects in the Lushai and Chin Hills, and the so-called New Kukis (Thados) are, so far as we can see, a Chin tribe, most closely connected to the inhabitants of the northern Chin Hills, while the Old Kukis are related to tribes more to the south."

The account of the causes of the Old and New Kuki incursions into Cachar, given in Part I, Chap. I, Section 3, which was written before I had read Dr. Grierson's book, agrees entirely with his conclusions.

A detailed account has been given in Part I of the Lushai language, and, considering the full manner in which the dialects of all these tribes have been dealt with by Dr. Grierson in the "Linguistic Survey of India," it seems superfluous to attempt to give outlines of them, and therefore I propose only to draw attention to the many points of similarity between them. The works I have consulted are:—"The Linguistic Survey of India," Vol. II, Part III, Lorrain and Savidge's "Grammar and Dictionary of the Lushai Language," Mr. T. C. Hodson's "Grammar and Small Vocabulary of Thado," and the appendix to Lieutenant Stewart's "Notes on Northern Cachar," 1855.

In going through Mr. Hodson's vocabulary of the Thado language, the first thing that struck me was the absence of the letter R. Further examination showed that where R is used in Lushai and certain other languages G or Gh is substituted in Thado. Many instances of this will be found in the following comparative vocabulary.

In many cases F in Lushai, Rhangkhol, and Langrong is replaced by Ch, sometimes softened into S in Thado, Manipuri, and some Old Kuki dialects. I have so far only found the following examples, but the material at my disposal is very insufficient, and I have no doubt that, given complete vocabularies, many more would be found:—

"Fa" in Lushai, "cha" in Manipuri and Thado, meaning "child."

"Fār-nu" in Lushai and Langrong, "chār-nu" in Aimol, Kolhen and Lamgang, "sār-nu" in Chiru, Kom, and Hallam, meaning "sister."

"Fāk" in Langrong, "chāk" in Manipuri, "cha" in Aimol, Anal, Kolhen, Lamgang, "shāk" in Chiru, meaning "to eat." In Lushai we have "chaw-fāk-hun," "rice-eat-time." Until I found that "fāk" meant "to eat" in Langrong, the Lushai equivalent for dinner-time had always puzzled me, as the Lushai word for "to eat" is "ei."

"Fawp" in Lushai, "chop" in Thado, "chup" in Purum, meaning "to kiss."

"Fāng" in Bete, "chāng" in Thado, meaning "paddy," while "fāng" in Lushai means "a grain."

"Fep" in Lushai, "chep" in Thado, meaning "to suck," as sugar-cane.

"Feh" in Lushai, "to go to the jhums," "feh" in Rhangkhol, "to go"; "che" in Thado, Aimol, and Anal, and "chatpa" in Manipuri have the same meaning.

"Fing" in Lushai, "ching" in Thado, "singba" in Manipuri, mean "wise."

"Fu" in Lushai, "chu" in Thado mean "sugar-cane."

"Fang-hma" in Lushai, "fung-mat" in Bete, "chung-mai" in Thado, mean "a pumpkin."

N in Lushai sometimes becomes "shi" in Lai or Haka dialect, as "ni" in Lushai and "shi" in Lai, meaning both "to be" and "aunt."

G and K are often interchanged and also R, L, and N.

In Lushai we have "lung" meaning both "stone" and "heart," while in Manipuri we have "nung" meaning "stone," and though "heart" is translated by "puk," we have "nung-siba" "to be sad," evidently composed of "nung" and "siba," "to die," and also "nung-ngaiba," meaning "happy," showing that "nung" once meant heart.

In many of these languages, similar words are used but have slightly different meanings. For instance, "shang" in Lushai means "tall," while in Thado and Manipuri we have "sang" meaning "long."

"Leng" in Lushai means "to stroll," and "lengba" in Manipuri means "to walk," but is only used of important personages who would be likely to move slowly and in a dignified manner.

In Lushai "shāt" means "to cut," but as a Lushai's house

consists of timber and bamboos, he always uses "shāt" when he speaks of building a house, and we find "sha" in Thado and "sāba" in Manipuri mean "to make," "to build."

In Lushai the verb "ni," "to be," is conjugated completely, but in Manipuri "ni" means "is" and has no other tenses.

Manipuri:	Ma	ai-gi	i nau	ni.	
Lushai:	Ama	ka	nau	a ni.	
English:	He	my	younger	brother	he is.

The following comparative vocabulary gives in the first two columns the Thado and English words as given by Mr. Hodson. The first word in the column of remarks is always Lushai, and where it has not exactly the same meaning as the Thado word the correct meaning is given; then follow, where necessary, the equivalents in other dialects.

About one word in every three given in Mr. Hodson's vocabulary has been found to resemble closely the Lushai word having the same or a similar meaning. Mr. Hodson's vocabulary has no pretensions to be a complete dictionary of the Thado language. Were such available I believe the number of similar words in the two dialects would be found to be even greater. As regards the Old Kuki dialects the information available is not sufficient to make a thorough comparison. It is clear that they are very closely allied to Lushai and Thado and to each other. The connection between Manipuri and what Dr. Grierson calls the Chin languages will, I believe, be found on further enquiry to be closer than at first appears.

COMPARATIVE VOCABULARY OF THADO AND LUSHAI LANGUAGES, WITH NOTES ON THE OTHER CHIN LANGUAGES AND MANIPURI OR MEITHEI.

Thado.	English.	Lushai and Remarks.
Ā	Fowl	Ar. Old Kuki dialects, Ar.
Ā-eng or A-yeng	Turmeric	Ai-eng. Beteh, Aishel.
Āi	Crab	Ai. Beteh, Iae.
Ā-le	True, right	Awle, all right.
Ashi	Star	Arshi. Old Kuki dialects the same.
Bān	Arm	Bān.
Bat	To owe	Bat.
Be	To beat a drum ...	Beng.
Be	Pulse	Be, all sorts of peas and beans.
Bon	To wrestle	Buan.
Bong	Cow	Se-bong.
Bong-hlo	Mud	Bol-hlawh.
Bu	Paddy	Buh.
Chem	Dao	Chem. Same in Old Kuki dialect.
Chep	To suck	Fep.
Chi	Salt	Chi; and in Old Kuki dialects also.
Chok	To buy	Chawk. In most Old Kuki dialects, Chok or Chak, and Purum has Lei, which is the commoner word in Lushai.
Da	To spread	Da, to pnt.
Chol	Tired	Chawl, to rest when tired.
Cham	Level	Cham.
Dang	Other	Dang.
Dai-tui	Dew	Dai.
Dāngka	Silver	Tāngka.
Deng	To beat	Deng, to pound, to hammer.
Ding	To stand	Ding.
Di	Correct	Dik.
Doi	Magic	Doi; and in Old Kuki dialects.
Doi	Weak	Doih, cowardly.
Dui	To love	Duh, to like, to desire.
Dum	Tobacco	Dum-ei, Dum-bawm, tobacco box; but the usual word is Vai-hlo.
Eng	Yellow	Eng.
Ga	Fruit	Ra; also Beteh.
Gam-la	Distant	Rām, country; Hla, distant. In Old Kuki dialects, La, Hla, and Lak.

Thado.	English.	Lushai and Remarks.
Gam-mang	Forest	Rām. The Lushai Hills being covered with forest, Ram means both country and forest. Mang appears in the Manipuri, U-Mang.
Ge	To pass the night ...	Ria(k). *Cf.* Manipuri. Lek.
Gel	Hail	Rial. Manipuri, Lel.
Ghai	Pregnant	Rai.
Ghāl	Enemy	Rāl. Manipuri, Lāl; Beteh, Rāl.
Ghi	Heavy	Rit. Beteh, Rik.
Ghin	Sound	Ring, loud.
Ghop	Lean	Rawp, to become thin, to waste away.
Ghu	A bone	Ru; also in Manipuri and Old Kuki dialects.
Ghu	A thief, to steal ...	Ru; also in Beteh.
Ghul	A snake	Rul; also in Old Kuki dialects. Manipuri, Lil.
Gim	To worry	Rim, tired, toilworn.
Go	A bamboo	Ro, a particular sort of bamboo.
Go	To cremate	Rawh, to heat, to roast.
Ha	Tooth	Ha, and in all Old Kuki dialects.
Hāl	To set fire to... ...	Hāl; also in Beteh.
Hām	Blow through ...	Hām, to play a wind instrument.
Hao	Rich	Hao-sak; the k is nearly silent.
He	To know...	Thei, to be able; Hre or Hriat, to know. Manipuri, Heiba, to know how to do.
Hem	Sharp	Hriam.
Hem	To soothe ...	Thlem, to pacify.
Hla	Month, the moon ...	Thla; and Manipuri and Old Kuki dialects, Tha or Thla.
Hla	Wing	Thla.
Hla	Song	Hla.
Hling	To suffice	Tling-tlak, to complete.
Hlut	To enter...	Lut,
Hon	Garden	Huan.
Hot	To shake	Hot, to stir with spoon.
Hui	A dog	Ui. Hui or Ui in Manipuri and all Old Kuki dialects.
In	House	In; and in all Old Kuki dialects.
Kāl	To climb	Kāl, to go; also in Langrong.
Kalson	To walk	
Kan	Dry...	Kang, to dry up. Manipuri, Kangba.
Kāp	To shoot...	Kāp.
Kel	Goat	Kel; and in all Old Kuki dialects.
Ket	To be broken... ...	Keh.
Kha	Bitter	Kha.
Kha	Chin	Kha, the lower jaw.
Khel buk	Thigh	Khel, side of upper part of thigh.
Khoi	Bee	Khoi.
Khom	To collect	Khon. Manipuri, Khom-silba.
Khong	Drum	Khuang.
Kho-shi	To feel cold	Khua a shik.
Khu	Cough	Khuh.
Khubu	Knee	Khup. Manipuri, Khuk-u; Beteh, Rakhuk,
Khut	Hand	Kut. Rhangkhol, Gut; all other Old Kuki dialects and Manipuri, either Khut or Kut.

Thado.	English.	Lushai and Remarks.
Keng	Leg	Ke.
Keng bai	Lame	Ke bai.
Ki	Horn	Ki. Manipuri, Chi or Ji; Beteh, Raki.
Ko	To call	Ko; and the same in Manipuri. In most Old Kuki dialects, Ko, Koi, or Kai.
Kol a phe	To lighten	Kawl a phe; and the same in Beteh.
Kong	The waist	Kawng, the loins.
Korka	A door	Kongkhar.
Ku	Village	Khua. Manipuri, Khul. Variations of this are found in all dialects.
Ku	To cover...	Khum. Manipuri, Khumba.
Khul	A hole	Khur; and in Old Kuki dialects.
Kum	Year	Kum. Manipuri, Kumsi, this year. All Old Kuki dialects have Kum.
La	To take	Lak, with almost silent k. In all Old Kuki dialects the word is very nearly the same. It also has the meaning to bring, and so may be compared with the Manipuri Lak pa, to come.
Lai	Middle, navel ...	Lai; and in Beteh also.
Lai	To dig	Lai, to dig, to hoe.
Laili	Writing, the art of reading and writing	Lai-shuih, paper, reading and writing. *Cf.* Manipuri, Lairik laishuih, writing materials, and Kachcha Naga, Laishi.
Lam	Direction	Lam. *Cf.* Manipuri, Lom or Rom.
Lambi...	Road	Lam-lian, though Kong, or Kāl-kong is the general word, Lam-lian being generally used for a made road as compared with a path. In Manipuri, Lambi; and in most Chin and Old Kuki dialects, either Lam or Lampi.
Le	Tongue	Lei. This word with very slight variations is found in Manipuri, Old Kuki, and all Chin dialects.
Le	Earth	Lei. *Cf.* Manipuri, Leipak, earth, country.
Lei-chung	Bridge	Lei, Lei-lawn.
Lei-ka	White ant	Lei-kha. Manipuri, Leisau.
Len	Net	Len.
Len	Big	Lian, contracted into Len. Beteh, Lien. *Cf.* Manipuri, Turel or Turen—*i.e.*, Tui, water, and Len, big, though water in Manipuri is Ising.
Leng	To fly	Leng, to stroll or float in the air. In Manipuri the word means to walk, but is only used of the Rajah or very important persons.
Lim	Form, shape	Hlim, shadow, shape, picture.
Lo	Jhum, cultivation .	Lo. This is another word which is found in nearly every dialect.
Lo	Medicine, drug ...	Hlo.
Lo	Suffix of negation...	Lo, not.
oi	Buffalo	Loi. *Cf.* Manipuri, Iroi; Beteh, Siloi.

Thado.	English.	Lushai and Remarks.
Lu	Head	Lu. Common to all Chin and Old Kuki dialects. *Cf.* Manipuri, Luchingba, principal.
Lui	Old	Hlui; also in Beteh.
Lum	Hot, as water ...	Lum.
Lung	Heart disposition ..	Lung; also in most Old Kuki dialects.
Mai	Face	Hmai. Manipuri, Mai, and Beteh, Hmai.
Maiche	Vegetables	Mai, a pumpkin.
Man	Price	Man. Common to Manipuri, Chin, and Old Kuki dialects.
Māng	Dream	Māng; also in Manipuri.
Māng	To lose, to be spoilt	Māng, to die out; Maug ang, to be upset in mind. Manipuri, Mangba, to lose; Manghālba, to spoil.
Mao	Woman	Mo, a bride, daughter-in-law.
Me	Fire...	Mei, another universal word.
Me	Tail...	Mei; also in Manipuri.
Me	Cloud	Ro-mei, haze.
Me-hol	Charcoal...	Mei-hol.
Me-khu	Smoke	Me-khu.
Me-tai...	Widow	Hmei-thai.
Mel	Appearance	Hmel, face, appearance.
Miu	Name	Hming. Manipuri, Ming.
Min	Ripe	Hmin.
Mi	Person	Mi. This word is found in all the dialects under consideration.
Mit	Eye	Mit, which with very slight variations is found in all dialects.
Mol	Hill	Mual, a hill, a spur of a hill.
Mom	To chew	Hmom, to put into the mouth whole.
Mu	Hawk	Mu.
Mu	Beak	Hmui, beak, upper lip. In most Old Kuki dialects, Mur.
Mu	To see	Hmu. Similar word used in all Old Kuki dialects except Anal, Purum, and Lamgang.
Mul	Feather, hair, fur...	Hmul.
Mu mul	Moustache	Hmui hmul.
Mut	To sleep	Mut, lie down, sleep.
Na	Leaf...	Hna. In Manipuri and Beteh, Na.
Na	Nose	Hnar. Manipuri, Chin, and Old Kuki very similar.
Na	Ill	Na, pain. Manipuri, Na.
Nai	Near	Hnai. Manipuri, Nakpa; Chin and Old Kuki dialects, Nai or similar words.
Nāl	Slippery	Nāl. Manipuri, Nālba, slippery, smooth.
Nam	To smell...	Nam. Manipuri, Namba; Beteh, Num.
Nām	A strap for carrying loads	Hnām.
Nau	Younger brother or sister	Nau. Found in Manipuri and in many Old Kuki dialects, sometimes Nai.
Nem	Soft	Nem; also in Beteh.
Nga	Five and Fish ...	In all Chin, Old Kuki dialects, and Manipuri.

Thado.	English.	Lushai and Remarks.
Ngai	To be customary	Ngai ; has many meanings.
Ngoi	Fishing weir	Ngoi.
Ngol	Mad, foolish	Ngol-tawt, obstinate, uncontrollable. Manipuri, Ngaoba.
Ni	Sun, day	Ni. In all Chin and Old Kuki dialects and in Manipuri, we have.
Ni	Aunt	Ni ; also in most Old Kuki dialects.
Noi	To laugh	Nui. Manipuri, Nokpa ; Beteh, Inui.
Nom	To wish	Nuam, contracted into Nom.
Nau-shen	Baby	Nau-shen.
Nu	Mother, female suffix.	Nu, in nearly all these dialects. Appears in Manipuri in Nupi, woman, and "I cha nupi," my child female—*i.e.*, daughter. Nupi is especially interesting because it combines both the Lushai female suffixes Nu and Pui.
Nunga	After, behind	Nunga. Most dialects very similar. *Cf.* Manipuri, Back, Namgan.
Nunga	Girl	Nula.
Ole	Alligator	Awle. Beteh, Ove.
Pa	Father, and male suffix	Pa, in all these dialects and Manipuri.
Pa-gong	A widower	Parol ; note the change of g into r.
Pasal	A male	Pasal, a husband ; Pasal-tha (man good), a brave man, hero. The word is used for man in several Old Kuki dialects.
Paten	The creator	Pathian. With very slight variations common to all these clans except Manipuris.
Pe	To give	Pe. Very similar terms in all these dialects. Manipuri, Piba.
Pengpulep	Butterfly	Phengphehlep ; Beteh Phelep. The Lushai may be Pheng, flat ; Phephe, to move ; Hlep, a slice.
Phai	Level	Phei.
Pho	To dry in the sun	Pho. In Manipuri the word has the same meaning and also means paddy.
Phung	Clan	Phung-chang, fellow-clansman.
Phut	To place upright in the ground	Phun.
Pi	Grandmother	Pi.
Pi	Feminine suffix for animals.	Pui. Found in many Old Kuki dialects. In Manipuri, "bi" is the feminine termination of adjectives.
Pi	Suffix denoting great.	Pui. Common in one form or other to nearly all these dialects.
Po	To carry	Paw, to carry on the back.
Pol	Straw	Pawl.
Pon	Cloth	Puan. The word in Chin and nearly all Old Kuki dialects is either the same or very similar.
Pu	Grandfather	Pu ; and in Manipuri and all Chin and Old Kuki dialects. The word has also other meanings, such as maternal uncle.

Thado.	English.	Lushai and Remarks.
Pu	To carry on the shoulder.	Puak, to carry on the back. Manipuri, Puba, to carry.
Pum	Body	Pum, belly. Manipuri, Puk. There is a curious dissimilarity here in most Old Kuki dialects, in which Won or some such word is used for belly.
Pum	Raft...	Pum.
Sa	Animal	Sa. The word is used generally for wild animals. In Lushai it is prefixed to the names of wild animals and to those of such domestic animals as are not indigenous. Thus, Sa-kor, a horse; Sa-kei, a tiger; while Kel, a goat, Shial, a mithan, Ui, a dog, have no prefix. Sa is used in the same manner in Manipuri—Sagol, a horse; Sangamba, an otter; Saji, a barking deer, &c. The word is found in Old Kuki dialects.
Sam	Hair	Sam. In Manipuri, Chin, and Old Kuki.
Sāng	Tall...	Shāng. Manipuri, Sangba, long.
Sāng	Thousand	Shāng. Beteh, Shang.
Sa-ku	Porcupine	Sā-kuh. Manipuri, Sa-bu.
Sanga	Wild cat...	Sa-nghar.
Sāt	To cut	Shāt, to chop.
Sāt	Hot, of weather ...	Sha. Manipuri, Saba.
Sha	To build...	Shāt, to cut. As all buildings and bridges were originally of timber, building meant cutting, and a Lushai always says, "In ka shàt," "I build a house." In Manipuri, Sāba means to make or build.
Shai	Elephant	Sai.
She	To say	Shoi.
Shelda	Mithan	Shiel, but in conjunction She; She-pui, full-grown cow, mithan.
Shem	To make...	Shiam. Manipuri, Semba.
Shi	To be cold	Shik.
Shil	To wash the body..	Sil, to wash.
Soi, with "tu"...	To converse	Thu, word; Shoi, to say.
Shok	A slave	Sal is the Lushai for a slave; but Suak, found in so many names, evidently means slave (*v.* Part I, Ch. IV, p. 6). All Old Kuki dialects have very similar words for slave or servant.
Sum	Goods	Sum. This word seems only to be found in Langrong among Old Kuki dialects. In the other dialects we find Nenun, Nei, Neina, which correspond to the Lushai Nei, to own; or Lal or Ral. Lal in Lushai means chief—*i.e.*, the rich man; *Cf.* Hausa—in Lushai, rich, and in Thado, a chief.
Sunga	Within	Chhunga.

Thado.	English.	Lushai and Remarks.
Tam	Many	Tam. In Aimol, Chiru, Kolhen, Kom, and Purum, Tam is a plural suffix.
Tangka	Rupee, silver ...	Tangka.
Tangval	A young man ...	Tlāngval.
Tāt	To kill	Thāt. Manipuri, Hatpa.
Te	To be permitted; to be able	Thei, to be able.
Tha	New	Thār. Beteh, Thur.
Thal	Arrow	Thal. Manipuri, Tel; Beteh, Thul.
The	Edible fruit	Thei. Manipuri, Hei.
Thi	Blood	Thi. Beteh, Thi; Manipuri, I.
Thi	Iron...	Thir.
Thing	Tree...	Thing. *Cf.* Manipuri, Sing, firewood.
Thou	Fat	Thao. *Cf.* Manipuri, Mahau, fat, grease, and Thau, oil.
Ti...	To die	Thi. *Cf.* Manipuri, Si-ba.
Ti	To say	Ti. In most Old Kuki dialects, The.
Tin	Finger nail, claw ...	Tin.
Tou	A fly	Tho-shi, a mosquito.
Tui	Water	Tui. Ti, Tui, or Dui in all Chin and Old Kuki dialects. *Cf.* Manipuri, Tu-ren (Tui-len), a river.
Tunge...	Nowadays	Tuna, now.
Tu	Grandchild	Tu. Is found in this sense through all these dialects.
Ve	Left (direction) ...	Vei. Manipuri, Woi.
Vo	To beat	Vuak, or Vel. Aimol, Ve; Kolhen, Wel; Kom, Wuk; Purum, Wel; Lai (Haka), Vel; Siyin, Vat.
Vok	Pig	Vok. Manipuri, Ok. Vok or Wok are found in all Chin and Old Kuki dialects.
Wān	The sky	Vān.
Wa-phol	The pied hornbill...	Va-pual. Va is a prefix denoting bird, employed as Sa is with animals. Wa is used in the same way in Thado.
Wat	Leech	Vang-vat.
Wompi	Bear	Sa-vom. Manipuri, Sa-wom.
Wu	To stink	Uih.
Wun	Skin	Vun. Manipuri, Un.
Wut	Ashes	Vut. Manipuri, Ut.
Ya-cha	To be ashamed ...	Zah-thlak, shameful.
Yan	Night	Zan.
Yeng	Yellow	Eng.
Ying	Dense, as jungle ...	Zim.
Yao	To complete	Zaw.
Yu	To sell	Zuar.
Yu	Rice beer	Zu, a word found in one form or other throughout the Hills.

SKETCH MAP SHOWING THE LOCALITIES INHABITED BY THE DIFFERENT CLANS

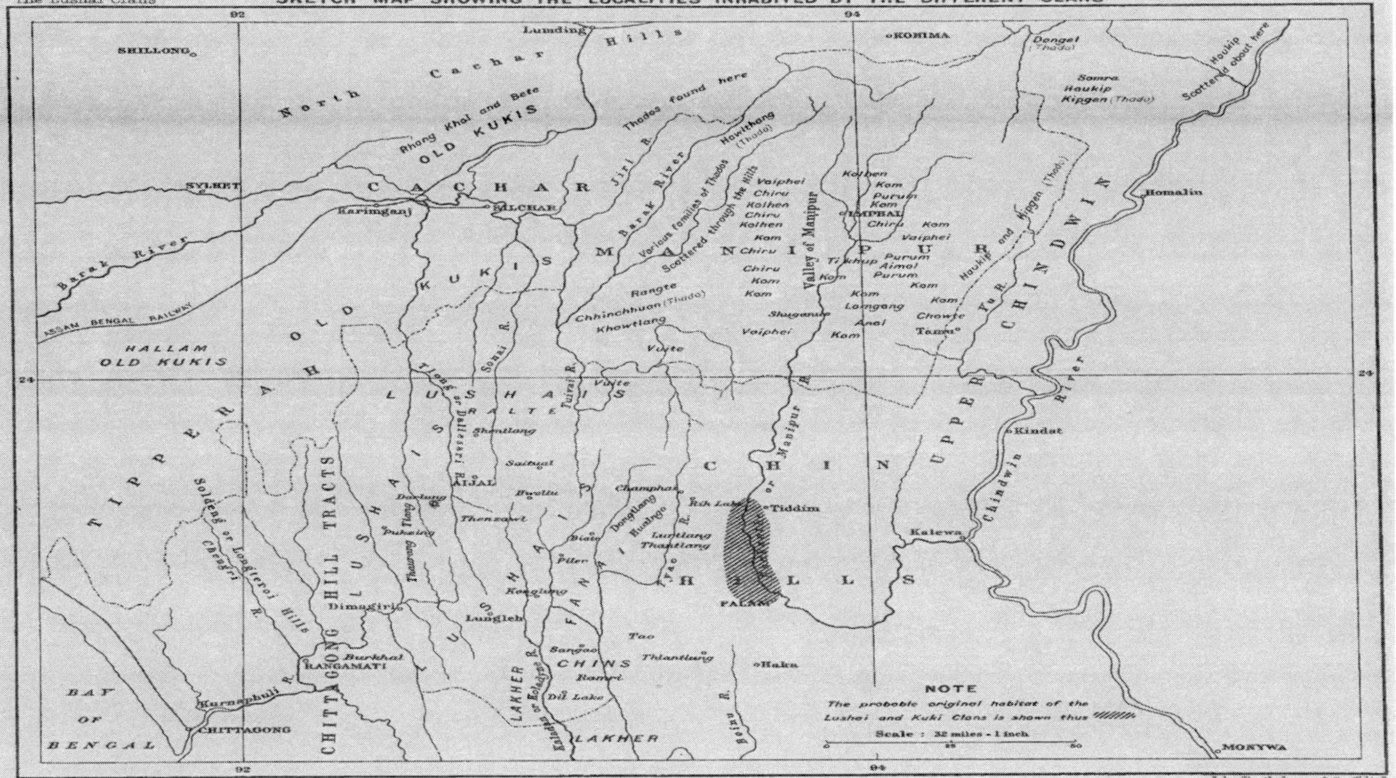

INDEX

For words not explained, but having Roman numerals set against them, see GLOSSARY.

WORKS ON ANTHROPOLOGY.

THE KACHARIS.

By the Rev. SIDNEY ENDLE. With an Introduction by J. D. ANDERSON, I.C.S. Illustrated. 8vo. 8*s*. 6*d*. net.

THE NĀGA TRIBES OF MANIPUR.

By T. C. HODSON. Illustrated. 8vo. 8*s*. 6*d*. net.

THE TODAS.

By W. H. R. RIVERS. Illustrated. 8vo. **21s.** net.

ANCIENT HUNTERS AND THEIR MODERN REPRESENTATIVES.

By Prof. W. J. SOLLAS, D.Sc., F.R.S. Illustrated. 8vo. **12s.** net.

THE MAFULU MOUNTAIN PEOPLE OF BRITISH NEW GUINEA.

By ROBERT W. WILLIAMSON. With an Introduction by A. C. HADDON, F.R.S. Illustrated. 8vo. **14s.** net.

MELANESIANS AND POLYNESIANS. Their Life-Histories Described and Compared.

By GEORGE BROWN, D.D. Illustrated. 8vo. **12s.** net.

NATIVE TRIBES OF SOUTH-EAST AUSTRALIA.

By A. W. HOWITT, D.Sc. Illustrated. 8vo. **21s.** net.

THE NORTHERN TRIBES OF CENTRAL AUSTRALIA.

By Prof. BALDWIN SPENCER and F. J. GILLEN. Illustrated. 8vo. **21s.** net.

THE OLD NORTH TRAIL: or, Life, Legends, and Religion of the Blackfeet Indians.

By WALTER MCCLINTOCK. Illustrated. 8vo. **15s.** net.

LONDON: MACMILLAN & CO., LTD.

WORKS ON ANTHROPOLOGY.

THE BAGANDA. An Account of their Native Customs and Beliefs.

By Rev. JOHN ROSCOE, M.A. Illustrated. 8vo. **15s.** net.

MAN AND BEAST IN EASTERN ETHIOPIA.

By J. BLAND-SUTTON, F.R.C.S. Illustrated. 8vo. **12s.** net.

AT THE BACK OF THE BLACK MAN'S MIND; or, Notes on the Kingly Office in West Africa.

By R. E. DENNETT. Illustrated. 8vo. **10s.** net.

NIGERIAN STUDIES; or, the Religious and Political System of the Yoruba.

By R. E. DENNETT. Illustrated. 8vo. **8s. 6d.** net.

NOTES ON WEST AFRICAN CATEGORIES.

By R. E. DENNETT. 8vo. Sewed. **1s.** net.

THE LOWER NIGER AND ITS TRIBES.

By Major ARTHUR GLYN LEONARD. With Map. 8vo. **12s. 6d.** net.

TRAVELS IN WEST AFRICA.

By MARY H. KINGSLEY. Abridged Edition. Extra Crown 8vo. **7s. 6d.**

WEST AFRICAN STUDIES.

By MARY H. KINGSLEY. With an Appendix on the Niger Delta by the VICOMTE DE CARDI. Illustrated. 8vo. **21s.** net. Cheaper Edition with additional chapters, but excluding de Cardi's appendix. Extra Crown 8vo. **7s. 6d.**

LONDON: MACMILLAN & CO., LTD.